W9-AZI-444

Sherman's March

By Richard Wheeler

VOICES OF 1776

VOICES OF THE CIVIL WAR

WE KNEW STONEWALL JACKSON

WE KNEW WILLIAM TECUMSEH SHERMAN

THE SIEGE OF VICKSBURG

SHERMAN'S MARCH

WILLIAM T. SHERMAN.

SHERMAN'S MARCH

RICHARD WHEELER

THOMAS Y. CROWELL, PUBLISHERS
NEW YORK / *Established 1834*

 For information address Thomas Y. Crowell, Publishers, 10 East 53rd Street, New York, N.Y. 10022. Published simultaneously in Canada by Fitzhenry & Whiteside Limited, Toronto.

FIRST EDITION

Designed by Sidney Feinberg

Library of Congress Cataloging in Publication Data

Wheeler, Richard.
Sherman's march.
Bibliography: p.
Includes index.
1. Sherman's March to the Sea. 2. Sherman, William Tecumseh, 1820–1891. 3. Sherman's March through the Carolinas. 4. Generals—United States—Biography. I. Title.
E476.69.W47 1978 973.7 78-3321
ISBN 0-690-01746-4

---

78 79 80 81 82 10 9 8 7 6 5 4 3 2 1

To Leonard O'Leary and to the memory
of his wife Kathryn, with thanks
for their steadfast encouragement

CONTENTS

PREFACE

Sherman's March continues a series of eyewitness histories and biographies I began with *Voices of 1776* in 1972. Though much has been written about Sherman's march, this seems to be the first time the story has been told chiefly in the words of those who lived it. Sherman himself has been given special attention. A feature I have found of particular satisfaction is that, as with my previous book, *The Siege of Vicksburg,* I have been able to include numerous accounts by women.

The book attempts to be more than a loose compilation of eyewitness material in which errors and false impressions have been allowed to stand as "part of the times." The quotes have been selected, researched, and linked together in such a way as to present a narrative that stresses historical veracity. At the same time, however, the book is aimed at the general reader rather than at the student of history.

Being unwilling to clutter the narrative with numbers, I have not specified the sources of the individual quotes. Most, however, can be traced through the bibliography. In transposition, some alterations have been made in paragraphing, capitalization, punctuation, and, occasionally, in spelling. Any other tampering that has been done—for the sake of clarity and conciseness, and also to rid certain passages of faulty information—is indicated by brackets and ellipses.

The book's illustrations are from the war years and the period immediately after, many having been done by artists who were on the spot. Chief sources represented are *Harper's History of the Great Rebellion, Frank Leslie's Illustrated History of the Civil War, The Soldier in Our Civil War,* and *Battles and Leaders of the Civil War.*

Sherman's March

1

THE MAN BEHIND THE IMAGE

IT WAS ON THE MORNING *of September 3, 1864, that Union General William Tecumseh Sherman telegraphed from Georgia to Washington, D.C.: "Atlanta is ours, and fairly won." The campaign southward from Chattanooga, Tennessee, had been long, arduous, and bloody, but now the Confederate army was beaten and in flight. Sherman's satisfaction was enhanced by a prompt congratulatory message from President Abraham Lincoln that closed with these words:*

The marches, battles, sieges, and other military operations that have signalized the campaign must render it famous in the annals of war, and have entitled those who have participated therein to the applause and thanks of the nation.

Lincoln himself had a special reason for being thankful. He was running for a second term, with his management of the war the leading issue, and the war had been going poorly. His great Eastern army, the Army of the Potomac, was stalled before Richmond and Petersburg, a vigorous drive southward from the Rapidan River having deteriorated into a frustrating siege. True, Admiral David G. Farragut had just defeated the Confederate naval squadron in Mobile Bay, Alabama, but this was a success of only moderate significance. Now the President had a major victory to his credit.

"The fall of Atlanta," wrote Horace Greeley in the New York Tribune,

comes at an opportune moment. Let the loyal North take heart. . . . Let us grow stronger in resolve, more unalterable in purpose, more religiously confirmed in faith, that the Rebellion shall be utterly crushed and the Free Union of these States be reestablished forever.

Horace Greeley

No one was more pleased with Sherman's victory than General Ulysses S. Grant. Though Grant made his headquarters with the Army of the Potomac in Virginia, he was supreme commander of all the Union armies, and it was he who had placed Sherman in charge of the troops in the West and who bore top responsibility for the campaign from Chattanooga.

In a telegram sent from his siege lines east of Richmond and Petersburg, Grant informed Sherman:

In honor of your great victory I have ordered a salute to be fired with *shotted* guns from every battery bearing upon the enemy. The salute will be fired . . . amid great rejoicing.

General Sherman ordered both Lincoln's and Grant's telegrams to be read before every unit of his army, some being in Atlanta and others in the city's environs. According to Adjutant Fenwick Y. Hedley of the Thirty-second Illinois Infantry Regiment:

And now that the troops . . . learned with what joy the news was received at home, they gave way to a protracted jubilee. The brass and martial bands, which had been silent all the long way from Chattanooga to Atlanta, now played their most exultant airs; and the men vied with the instruments in making noise expressive of great joy.

All were happy and smiling, from the commander in chief to the humblest private in the ranks, and even the bray of the half-starved government mule seemed mellow and melodious as it added to the din.

For the tall, lean, deeply wrinkled, and red-bearded commander in chief, this was the greatest moment in the entire forty-four years of his life. No small part of his pleasure arose from the fact that his progress toward the moment, from his earliest years, had often been painfully difficult.

Born in Ohio into a large family of modest means, "Cump" Sherman was only nine years old when his father died. A neighbor and well-to-do attorney and businessman, Thomas Ewing, who had been a close friend of Cump's father, took the child into his home to raise, saying later:

There was nothing specially remarkable about him, except that I never saw so young a boy who would do an errand so correctly and promptly as he did. He was transparently honest, faithful, and reliable. . . .

Cump was also bright, and he did well in school. When he was sixteen, his foster father, having become a United States Senator, arranged for his admittance to West Point. Though the youth had little trouble mastering all aspects of the training, he disliked being required to sacrifice his individuality to the discipline. His fellow cadets found him to be filled with nervous energy, to have a genial and sociable nature peppered with moments of irritability, to be fond of a good joke, and to be an excellent conversationalist in spite of a habitual outspokenness.

Cump was always ready, according to one classmate, "for a lark of any kind," and, at the risk of expulsion, would sometimes slip away in the night to an off-limits tavern "to eat oysters and drink beer."

Sherman himself relates:

I went through the regular course of four years, graduating in June, 1840, number six in a class of forty-three. These forty-three were all that remained of more than one hundred which originally constituted the class. At the Academy I was not considered a good soldier, for at no time was I selected for any office, but remained a private throughout the whole four years. . . .

Neatness in dress and form, with a strict conformity to the rules, were the qualifications required for office, and I suppose I was found not to excel in any of these. In studies I always held a respectable reputation with the professors . . . especially in drawing, chemistry, mathematics, and natural philosophy. My average demerits, per annum, were about one hundred and fifty, which reduced my final class standing from number four to six.

Among the numerous other cadets of this period who were destined for Civil War fame was Ulysses Grant, who began his first year as Sherman

Ulysses S. Grant

began his last. The institute's caste system kept their acquaintance casual.

Upon his graduation, Sherman was made a second lieutenant of artillery. He saw his first service in Florida, where he took part in some minor expeditions against the Seminole Indians. He found no pleasure in "hunting and harassing a poor set of people," yet favored severe measures in order that the uprising be ended quickly.

The summer of 1842 found the young lieutenant stationed at Fort Moultrie, in the harbor of Charleston, South Carolina. Fort Sumter, to become so famous nineteen years later, was then only in the process of construction. Spending several years at Fort Moultrie, Sherman participated with delight in Charleston society and he became deeply devoted to the South and its people. Since he regarded slavery as being an indispensable part of the Southern economy, he saw no point in weighing its morality. He gave considerable thought, however, to the issue of states' rights:

Charleston . . . assumed a leadership in the public opinion of the South far out of proportion to her population, wealth, or commerce. On more than one occasion previously, the inhabitants had almost inaugurated civil war by their assertion and professed belief that each state had, in the original compact of government, reserved to itself the right to withdraw from the Union at its own option, whenever the people supposed they had sufficient cause.

We used to discuss these things at our own mess tables, vehemently and sometimes quite angrily; but I am sure that I never feared it would go further than it had already gone.

These years in the South saw Sherman make two extended trips, one a furlough and the other an army assignment, that gained him a knowledge of terrain he would one day traverse as a conqueror. Much of the knowledge stayed fresh in his mind, for he had a prodigious memory.

Many of Sherman's spare moments at Fort Moultrie were spent in reading, in painting landscapes and portraits that his friends considered to be very good, and in writing long letters that revealed him to have considerable literary talent.

In 1846, the first year of the Mexican War, Sherman was assigned to an artillery company destined for California. The unit made the trip by sea, the ship swinging around Cape Horn, the southern tip of South America. An unnamed passenger, meeting Sherman for the first time, was later to say:

Grave in his demeanor, erect and soldierly in his bearing, he was especially noticeable for the faded and threadbare appearance of his uniform. . . . He was characterized . . . by entire devotion to his profession in all its details. His care for both the comfort and discipline of his men was constant and unwearied.

Sherman's duties in California were strictly occupational; he saw no action. In 1848 he wrote home:

I feel ashamed to wear epaulettes after having passed through a war without smelling gunpowder. But God knows I couldn't help it. . . .

This disappointment was soon partly assuaged, for Sherman played a leading role in the army's investigation of the discovery of gold at John Sutter's sawmill in the Sacramento Valley, and he wrote the report his commanding officer sent to Washington. Sherman explains:

The President made it the subject of a special message, and thus became "official" what had before only reached the world in a very indefinite shape. Then began that wonderful development, and the great emigration to California, by land and sea, of 1849 and 1850.

When Sherman returned to the East in 1850 he found his foster family, lately of Ohio, living in Washington. Thomas Ewing was serving as Secretary of the Interior. On May 1 of that year, Cump married his foster sister, Ellen Ewing, she being twenty-six and he thirty. Among the many notables who attended the wedding were President Zachary Taylor, his cabinet, and those two aging principals of the slavery issue, Senators Daniel Webster and Henry Clay.

Cump's views on religion cast at least a small shadow over Ellen's satisfaction with the wedding. She was a devout Catholic, while he held to no particular creed:

I believe in good works rather than faith, and believe them to constitute the basis of true religion, both as revealed in Scripture and taught by the experience of all ages and common sense.

That autumn, now ten years out of West Point, Sherman was finally promoted to captain. His record included no real distinguishment. He remained in uniform for two more years, then decided to try to make his way in civilian life. During the next seven years, with his family growing apace, Sherman failed at three professions: banker, lawyer, and farmer. To his intense mortification, he had to accept aid from Thomas Ewing to make ends meet.

Sherman's failures were the result of ill luck and not of a lack of ability or determination. A Kansas newspaper writer who met him during this period termed him "the most remarkable intellectual embodiment of force" he had ever encountered. Looking into Sherman's eyes, the newsman found them filled with "smoldering fire."

His temperament is nervous-sanguine, and he is full of crochets and prejudices, which, however, never stand in the way of practical results. The idea, or rather object, which rules him, for the time, overrides everything else.

But in 1859 Sherman wrote:

I am doomed to be a vagabond, and shall no longer struggle against my fate. . . . I look upon myself as a dead cock in the pit, not worthy of further notice, and will take my chances as they come.

By this time the nation was dangerously divided over the issues of slavery and states' rights, but Sherman was hopeful that reason would prevail. Late in the year he accepted a commission from the State of Louisiana to aid with the establishment of a new military college and become its first superintendent. This offered him residence in his beloved South and, as he put it, "solitude and banishment enough to hide from the misfortunes of the past." Going to his new post alone, he planned to send for his family when he was suitably established. Early in 1860 he wrote his small daughter Minnie:

I will soon have a good house, so next year you and Mama, Lizzie, Willy, Tommy and the baby will all come down to Louisiana, where, maybe, we will live all our lives.

The family never made the trip. In January, 1861, when it became obvious that Louisiana was about to secede from the Union, the sixth state to do so, Sherman informed Governor Thomas O. Moore:

If Louisiana withdraws from the Federal Union, I prefer to maintain my allegiance to the Constitution as long as a fragment of it survives, and my longer stay here would be wrong in every sense of the word. . . . I beg you to take immediate steps to relieve me as superintendent the moment the state determines to secede, for on no earthly account will I do any act or think any thought hostile to, or in defiance of, the old Government of the United States.

Rejecting all pleas that he continue at the school, where he had come to be considered irreplaceable, Sherman soon went north. But a personal interview with Abraham Lincoln, arranged for him by his brother John Sherman, who had become a United States Senator, failed to gain Cump

John Sherman

reentry into the Federal army, for the President did not yet consider war a certainty.

Cump told John: "You politicians have got things in a hell of a fix, and you may get them out as best you can." In need of money, for Ellen was pregnant for the sixth time, Cump took a job as president of a street railway company in St. Louis, Missouri. But soon after the war began at Fort Sumter he reentered the army as a colonel and was put in charge of a brigade of infantry. He was deeply troubled, seeing himself as a man with a large family to support in a nation headed for ruin.

At First Bull Run, fought on July 21, 1861, Sherman made a good showing. According to a newspaper correspondent:

His coolness and efficiency surprised friends familiar with his excitable temperament.

But the Union defeat in this battle confirmed for Sherman his fears that the war would be a long one and was probably unwinnable. He now entered a period dominated by spells of irritability and acute depression.

Nonetheless, thanks to the vigor he had shown in combat and to the influence of his brother the senator, Sherman was quickly promoted to brigadier general. Late in the summer of the war's first year he was sent to Kentucky, one of the states that lay between the Union and the Confederacy and was divided in its sympathies, a state the North wanted very much to hold.

Mistakenly believing that the Confederate troops who had entered the southern part of the state were very strong, Sherman predicted disaster for the Union defenders. Soon made their top commander, with his headquarters in a Louisville hotel, he came under the critical eye of the town's war correspondents.

Sherman was unpopular with both reporters and editors, for he repeatedly accused them of publishing too much information that aided the enemy and he strove to restrict their work. Now a correspondent noted that the general

paced the corridor outside his rooms for hours, absorbed. The guests whispered about him. . . . He . . . could not rid himself of the apprehension that he was due for defeat if the rebels attacked.

Visited by a delegation from Washington headed by Secretary of War Simon Cameron in October, Sherman gave full voice to his apprehensions, claiming he needed reinforcements in enormous numbers. This earned him a new round of newspaper criticism. At the same time, he admitted in a

Henry W. Halleck

letter to Ellen that his worries had him "almost crazy."

In mid-November Sherman was transferred to the Department of Missouri, farther to the west, but the change did nothing to ease his mind. He wrote his brother John:

Some terrible disaster is inevitable. . . . Could I now hide myself in some obscure corner I would do so, for my conviction is that our Government is destroyed and no human power can restore it.

In Missouri Sherman came under the command of a friend of his days at West Point and his service in California, Major General Henry W. Halleck. Ignoring the things the newspapers were saying about Sherman, Halleck assigned him to active duty.

The pace Sherman set for himself was a frantic one. A newsman who saw him in St. Louis reported that "his eye had a half-wild expression" and that he smoked cigars in a continuous chain:

Sometimes he works for twenty consecutive hours. He sleeps little. Nor do the most powerful opiates relieve his terrible cerebral excitement.

According to another correspondent, Sherman "spoke despondingly" and "talked of a thirty years' war."

Early in December, General Halleck sent Sherman on a twenty-day leave to his home in Lancaster, Ohio, hoping that a rest would "restore him." The rest, however, was quickly sundered. On December 11, the Cincinnati Commercial *carried an item that bore the headline* GENERAL WILLIAM T. SHERMAN INSANE:

The painful intelligence reaches us, in such form that we are not at liberty to disclose it, that Gen. William T. Sherman . . . is insane. It appears that he was, at the time while commanding in Kentucky, stark mad. . . . He has of course been relieved altogether from command. The harsh criticisms that have been lavished on this gentleman, provoked by his strange conduct, will now give way to feelings of deepest sympathy for him in his great calamity.

The blow this announcement dealt to Sherman was compounded when his small son Tommy came running into the house saying that a boy in the street had told him, "Your papa is crazy."

Sherman's fortunes had hit bottom. His trouble was not insanity but a critical lapse of self-confidence, quite understandable in the light of his list of failures through the years. Ellen wanted Cump to remain at home until spring, but, jarred into pulling himself together, he returned to St. Louis and General Halleck. The situation was embarrassing:

I could not hide from myself that many of the officers and soldiers . . . looked at me askance and with suspicion.

To his brother John he wrote:

I am so sensible now of my disgrace from having exaggerated the force of our enemy . . . that I do think I should have committed suicide were it not for my children. I do not think I can again be entrusted with a command.

But with his wife at home retaining her faith in him, with John Sherman and Thomas Ewing speaking for him in Washington, and with Halleck helping him, in easy stages, toward heavier duties, Sherman's career soon began to flourish.

He became a close and trusted friend to General Grant, who had a Western command at this time, not yet having been promoted to supreme commander of the Union armies. Sherman headed a division under Grant when the Confederates made their surprise attack at Shiloh, Tennessee, in April, 1862. Fighting with great skill and courage, and being twice wounded, Sherman had much to do with saving the army. This gained him the trust and admiration of his men and a promotion to major general of volunteers.

Curiously, Sherman was found to be an entirely different person when under fire. As explained by an officer who knew him:

At such times his eccentricities disappeared, his grasp of the situation was firm and clear, his judgment was cool and based upon sound military theory as well as upon quick practical judgment; and no momentary complication or unexpected event could move him from the purpose he had based on full previous study of contingencies. His mind seemed never so clear, his confidence never so strong, his spirit never so inspiring, and his temper never so amiable as in the crisis of some fierce struggle. . . .

Many Northerners believed that the Confederate army's failure at Shiloh had crushed the Southern spirit and that another battle would end hostilities. Sherman, though not the pessimist he was at first, still expected the war to last "for a long, long time."

Two and a half months after Shiloh, he became military administrator of the Confederate city of Memphis, on the Mississippi River, the city having been captured by a Union naval force.

"I found the place dead," he states. "No business doing, the stores closed, churches, schools, and everything shut up."

It appeared to Sherman that the citizens were undergoing hardships not necessary to the progress of the Union cause. On the contrary, the city seemed about to become a liability. Sherman continues:

I caused all the stores to be opened, churches, schools, theaters, and places of amusement to be reestablished; and very soon Memphis resumed its appearance of an active, busy, prosperous place. I also restored the mayor . . . and the city government. . . .

He even set up a program of aid for the poor. At the same time, he made the city a Union base. But when he was obliged to destroy a number of build-

ings to emplace his fortifications, he authorized compensation for the owners. He felt he was being as fair to the city as circumstances allowed.

But soon he began to realize that many citizens were giving secret assistance to Confederates under arms. While maintaining the liberal system he had established, he began to exact stern retribution for specific acts against the Union. When a party of guerrillas in the town of Randolph, north of Memphis, fired on an unarmed Union steamboat carrying civilian passengers, he ordered the town burned, stipulating that a single house be left standing "to mark the place."

It was during his stay at Memphis that Sherman began to regard the rebellion more as a matter of "collective responsibility" than as a simple uprising of armed men.

"It is about time the North understood the truth," he wrote his brother in Washington, "that the entire South, man, woman, and child is against us. . . ."

If the South's fighting spirit was to be extinguished, Sherman decided, civilians as well as soldiers had to be regarded as enemies. The war had to be made "terrible."

To his daughter Minnie, then in school at Notre Dame, Indiana, Sherman lamented the fact that he was obliged to be harsh with people he liked, some of them actually personal friends of his years in the South:

Think of . . . how cruel men become in war when even your papa has to do such acts. Pray every night that the war may end. Hundreds of children like yourself are daily taught to curse my name, and every night thousands kneel in prayer and beseech the Almighty to consign me to perdition.

The fate of the Southern blacks caught up in the war gave Sherman no particular concern. "Up to that date," he explains,

neither Congress nor the President had made any clear, well-defined rules touching the Negro slaves, and the different generals had issued orders according to their own political sentiments, Both Generals Halleck and Grant regarded the slave as still a slave, only that the labor of the slave belonged to his owner if faithful to the Union, or to the United States if the master had taken up arms against the Government or adhered to the fortunes of the rebellion.

Therefore in Memphis we received all fugitives, put them to work on the fortifications, supplied them with food and clothing, and reserved the question of payment of wages for future decision. No force was allowed to be used to restore a fugitive slave to his master... but if the master proved his loyalty he was usually permitted to see his slave, and, if he could persuade him to return home, it was permitted.

Black prostitutes who gathered on the fringes of Sherman's camps were allowed to remain. One soldier averred that these women "felt loving toward us because they thought we were bringing them freedom, and they wouldn't charge us a cent."

When Sherman learned, in the early autumn of 1862, that President Lincoln had issued the preliminary draft of his Emancipation Proclamation, he did not approve: "Are we to feed all the Negroes? Freedom don't clothe them, feed them, and shelter them."

Sherman's command was in Grant's department, and Grant had come to consider Sherman his right-hand man. These two friends of the Western theater made an arresting picture. Grant was small in stature, habitually calm and reserved; Sherman was tall, nervous, restless, loquacious; both were careless dressers and both smoked cigars one after the other, their every conference being canopied by a blue haze. Sherman says of the relationship:

We were as brothers—I the older man in years, he the higher in rank. We both believed in our heart of hearts that the success of the Union cause was not only necessary to the then generation of Americans, but to all future generations. We both professed to be gentlemen and professional soldiers, educated in the science of war... for the very occasion which had arisen. Neither of us by nature was a combative man....

Now, aided by Admiral David Dixon Porter, dashing commander of the Mississippi Squadron, Grant and Sherman undertook their long and difficult campaign against Vicksburg. Victory came in July, 1863. This gave the Federals control of the entire length of the Mississippi River; the Confederacy was cut in two. Sherman got his "first glimpse of daylight in this war."

The Vicksburg campaign was accompanied by the widespread destruction of Confederate property. Sherman himself devastated a great part of Jackson, the capital of Mississippi. He was now convinced that the best way to cripple the South and break its morale was to take every opportunity to destroy property connected in any way with its military efforts. Such a policy, he reasoned, would shorten the war and save many lives, thus proving beneficial to the South as well as the North.

In practice, however, the policy could not be kept in hand. The Union soldiers abused their instructions to destroy only war-related property and to be moderate with private citizens when they had to resort to foraging to obtain food. Jackson was not only burned without discrimination but was also sacked. Sherman lamented to Grant:

The amount of plundering and stealing done by our army makes me ashamed of it. . . . I fear we are drifting to the worst sort of vandalism. I have endeavored to repress this class of crime, but you know how difficult it is to fix the guilt among the great mass of the army.

Sherman entertained this worry for a brief time only. To the anguished Southerners who complained to him of their losses he responded that the blame lay not with his men and himself but with the leaders of secession. The way to stop the outrages, he said, was to stop the war.

Sherman's duties underwent a lull at this point, and Ellen and the four oldest children came to visit him at his camp near Vicksburg. Ellen took great pride in the stature Cump had achieved since his critical bout with depression two years earlier. Cump was happy, having just been promoted to brigadier general in the regular army. His major generalship of volunteers was only a temporary commission. The promotion put Sherman's financial future on a sound footing. No longer would he have to seek help from his foster father to keep his family comfortable.

A particular joy to Cump was his son Willy, nine years old, who spent much of his time with the troops. According to one man: "The little fellow . . . won all hearts by his winning ways and his fondness for playing soldier." Willy was made an honorary sergeant in the Thirteenth Battalion of United States regulars.

Then tragedy struck. The boy came down with typhoid fever and died. He was given a military funeral by the men of the Thirteenth, and his heartbroken mother took him northward for burial. Alone in the night after Ellen's departure, a sleepless Sherman wrote a letter to the commander of the Thirteenth:

The child that bore my name, and in whose future I reposed with more confidence than I did in my own plan of life, now floats a mere corpse, seeking a grave . . . with a weeping mother, brother, and sisters clustered about him.

For myself I ask no sympathy. On, on I must go, to meet a soldier's fate or live to see our country rise superior to all factions, till its flag is adored and respected by ourselves and by all the powers of the earth.

But Willy was, or thought he was, a sergeant in the Thirteenth. I have seen his eye brighten, his heart beat, as he beheld the battalion under arms and asked me if they were not *real* soldiers. . . . God only knows why he should die thus young. . . .

Please convey to the battalion my heartfelt thanks, and assure each and all that if, in after years, they call on me or mine and mention that they were of the Thirteenth Regulars when Willy was a sergeant, they will have a key to the affections of my family that will open all it has; that we will share with them our last blanket, our last crust.

Sherman was obliged to make a quick rise from his grief, for Grant needed him at Chattanooga. A three-day battle in November, 1863, placed this city, "the Gateway to the Deep South," firmly in Union hands. Grant became the North's "man of the hour."

The beginning of 1864 found Sherman back at Vicksburg. From here he led a raid eastward through Mississippi to Meridian, a Confederate railroad center and supply base. The army's route was marked by destruction, with much of the town itself being burned. Upon his return to Vicksburg, Sherman reported: "We bring in some 500 prisoners, a good many refugees, and about ten miles of Negroes." The blacks had followed the army to the freedom granted them by Lincoln's Emancipation Proclamation, and they regarded Sherman as their savior.

The expedition had resulted in little bloodshed, and this pleased Sherman: "Of course I must fight when the time comes, but whenever a result can be accomplished without battle I prefer it."

He made the following pronouncement regarding his failure to safeguard private property:

The people of the South, having appealed to war, are barred from appealing for protection under our Constitution, which they have practically and publicly defied.

That spring Grant was summoned to Washington to become the Union's top commander, and Sherman took Grant's place as commander in the West. Far from swelling with pride over the expansion of his authority, Sherman wrote Washington that he preferred not to be nominated for another advancement in rank:

I now have all the rank necessary to command, and believe all here concede me that ability, yet accidents may happen and I don't care about increasing the distance of my fall. The moment another appears on the arena better than me, I will cheerfully subside. . . . I know my weak points. . . . I will try to hold my tongue and pen and give my undivided thoughts and attention to the military duties devolving on me.

2

GEORGIA BECOMES A BATTLEGROUND

AS THE UNION'S *chief commander in the West, Sherman soon made his headquarters at Chattanooga, the Gateway to the Deep South.*

The Confederacy had two major armies, one covering its capital at Richmond, Virginia, and the other lying at Dalton, Georgia, about twenty-five miles southeast of Chattanooga, where it was recuperating from its defeat the preceding November. General Robert E. Lee commanded in Virginia, General Joseph E. Johnston in Georgia.

Grant felt that he could deliver a deathblow to the Confederacy by attacking these two armies simultaneously, he himself leading in the East, and Sherman in the West. The twin campaigns were launched in May, 1864.

Grant's effort against Lee, as already explained, succeeded only in driving him into the fortifications of Richmond and Petersburg. Grant resorted to a siege, setting up a great semicircle of works just to the east of these cities. With the siege threatening to become a long one, Grant counted on Sherman to do better with his half of the grand operation.

Sherman's army was in first-rate condition, largely the result of his personal efforts. "The least part of a general's work," he was heard to say, "is to fight a battle." He had overseen the preparations of all departments: his infantry, artillery, and cavalry, his medical corps, his telegraphers and signalmen, his engineers and pioneers.

Included with his pioneers, or laborers, were units of blacks, slaves who had fled the Southern plantations to become freemen. Orders had issued from Washington that blacks be made also full-fledged soldiers, but Sherman had deferred action in this direction. Earlier, he had confided in a letter to his wife:

I would prefer to have this a white man's war, and provide for the Negroes after the time has passed.... With my opinions of

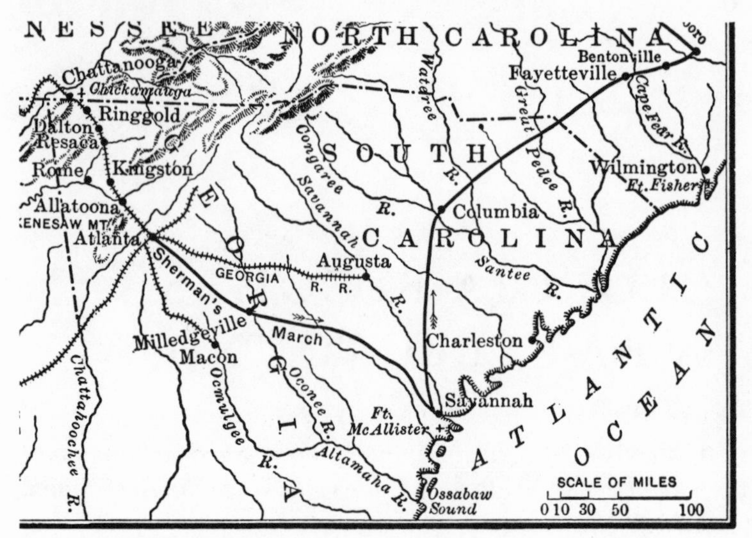

General map of Sherman's campaigns from Chattanooga, Tennessee, to Raleigh, North Carolina

Negroes and my experience, yea, prejudice, I cannot trust them yet.

Sherman knew of Napoleon's boast that he had overrun Europe with the bivouac, that is, with his encampments providing only the barest necessities, mobility being the main consideration. Catching the same inspiration, Sherman reduced his supply wagons to the smallest possible number.

When a delegation of regimental chaplains requested room for the transportation of Bibles and tracts, Sherman said, "Bibles and tracts are very good in their way, gentlemen, but rations and ammunition are much better."

Sherman intended to be sparing even with medical stores, but an opposing view was held by Mary A. Bickerdyke, a middle-aged widow who had attached herself to the army as a volunteer nurse. Sherman was very fond of "Mother Bickerdyke." Says one observer:

There was something in her character akin to his own. Both were restless, impetuous, fiery, hard-working, and indomitable.

Sherman liked to pretend that Mary's repeated solicitations on behalf of his medical department were a great nuisance to him. One day while he was writing a dispatch at his headquarters, she pushed her way past the aides at the door.

"Good morning, general. May I come in?"

"I should think you had got in!" Sherman growled. "What's up now?"

Mary began to remonstrate in her peppery way about the restrictions he had placed on medical stores.

"I'm busy today," said Sherman. "I will see you some other time."

And he returned to his writing, his brow stern but the corners of his mouth twitching into the beginnings of a smile.

"General!" snapped Mary. "Have some sense about this!"

Sherman threw down his pen, leaned back in his chair, and broke out laughing. He granted Mother Bickerdyke her added supplies, which she was to use to good advantage all through the campaign.

As for the personal equipment of the individual soldiers:

Each man [explains Adjutant Fenwick Hedley of the Thirty-second Illinois] carried his gun and accoutrements, 40 rounds of ammunition in his cartridge box and 160 more in his pockets, knapsack, or haversack. His blanket and light rubber blanket were made into a long roll, the ends tied together, so as to admit of being carried upon the shoulder. This roll generally contained an extra shirt, a pair of socks, and a half section of a "dog tent," . . . which, when buttoned to the half carried by a comrade, made a very fair shelter for two men. . . .

The provision issued to the soldier was a much abridged ration, but it brought up the total weight of his burden to a good 30 pounds or more, no light load to carry for days at a time, in all weather, and over all kinds of roads. He habitually had a three-

Mary A. Bickerdyke

days' supply of hard bread and fat pork, and this was to last from seven to ten days in case of necessity.

The distance from Chattanooga to Atlanta was about 120 miles. Even though Sherman had more than 100,000 men and Joe Johnston had only 65,000, it took all of Sherman's skill to make the drive. Johnston had the advantage of being on the defensive. He could choose his own battlefields. He was also operating in friendly territory, and his supply lines were short. Moreover, Johnston was an able general.

The fifty-six-year-old Virginian was a graduate of West Point who won his first laurels fighting the Seminole Indians in Florida, and added to his record during the war with Mexico. In 1861 he resigned the Federal service to become a senior general in the Confederate army. He was top commander at First Bull Run and was in charge of the defense of Richmond during the early days of the Peninsula Campaign, his service there being terminated by a musket ball and a shell fragment, taken very nearly at the same time. These wounds raised the number of his battle scars to nine, the others having been acquired in Florida and Mexico.

Though Johnston was a small man, his presence was impressive. One of his soldiers described him as having

an open countenance with a keen restless eye that seemed to read your inmost thoughts.... He ever wore the finest clothes that could be obtained.... His hat was decorated with a star and feather, his coat with every star and embellishment, and he wore a

Joseph E. Johnston

bright new sash, big gauntlets, and silver spurs.

Said a Confederate news correspondent:

General Johnston . . . is the bravest and most cool man under fire that I ever saw. He is almost reckless with his own life, but is exceedingly careful with the lives of his men.

The contest between Sherman's bluecoats and Johnston's men in gray began with several weeks of maneuvering and cautious fighting. The terrain ranged from flat to mountainous, the days from bright and chokingly dusty to wet and abundant with clinging mud. The gunfire waxed and waned, seldom stopping entirely. A Confederate officer wrote in his diary:

It does seem strange that we cannot have one quiet Sabbath. Sherman has no regard for the Fourth Commandment ["Remember the Sabbath day, to keep it holy."]. I wish a Bible society would send him a prayer book instead of shipping them all to a more remote heathen [the Western Indian], but it would be the same in either class. The one is uncivilized by nature—the other, I fear, becoming so from habit. Perhaps "Tecumseh" [an Indian name] has something to do with it.

Though Sherman had a health complaint, chronic asthma, he gave the impression of having an iron constitution. As noted by one of his staff officers:

Exposure to cold, rain, or burning heat seems to produce no effect upon his powers of endurance and strength. Under the most harassing conditions I have never seen him exhibit any symptoms of fatigue. In the field he retires early, but at midnight he may be found pacing in front of his tent, or sitting by the campfire smoking a cigar. His sleep must be light and unrestful, for the galloping of a courier's horse down the road instantly wakes him, as well as a voice or a movement in his tent. . . .

When sounds of musketry or cannonading reach his ears, the general is extremely restless until he has been satisfied as to the origin, location, and probable results of the fight in progress. At such moments he usually lights a fresh cigar, and smokes while walking to and fro; stopping now and then to listen to the increasing rattle of musketry; then, muttering "Forward," will mount Old Sam, a horribly fast-walking horse, which is as indifferent to

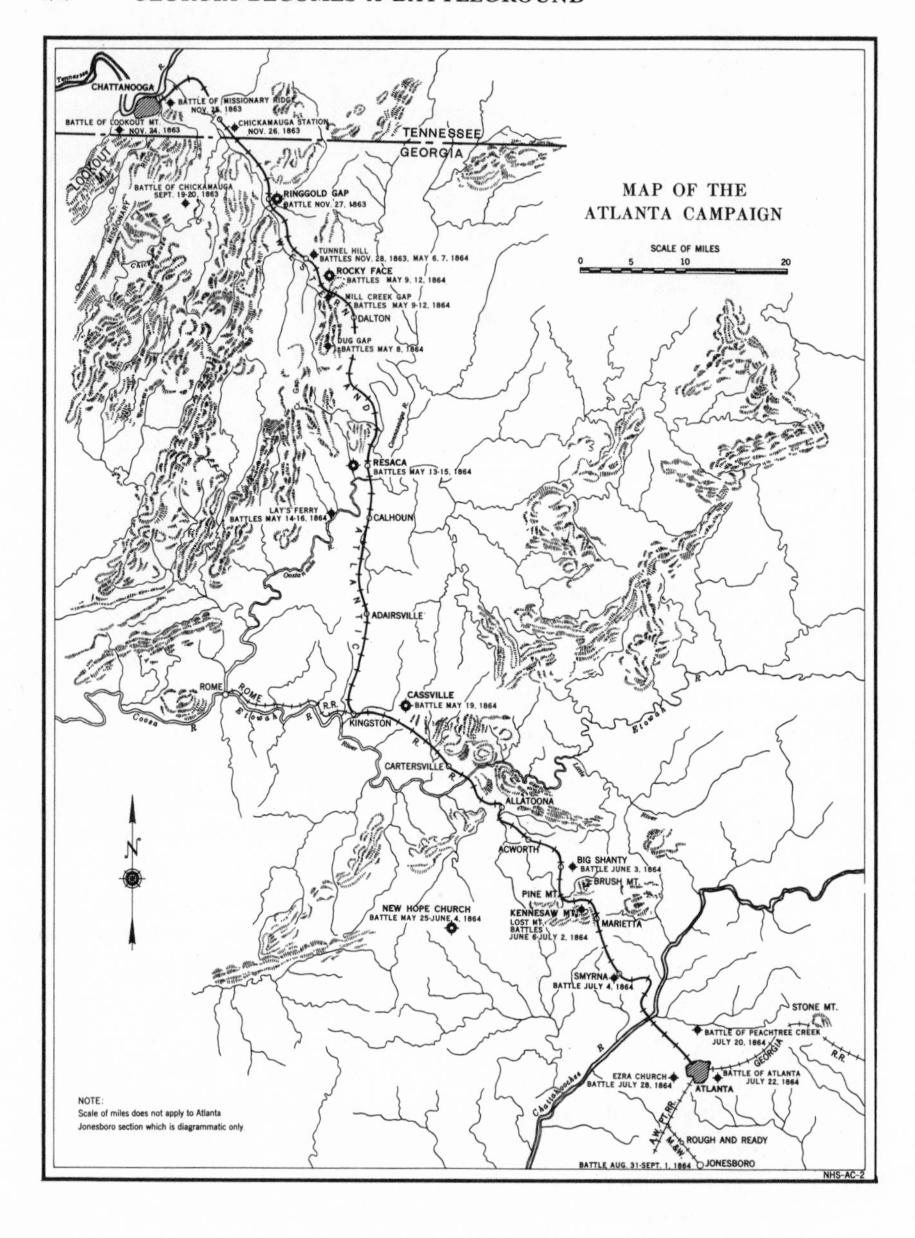
MAP OF THE
ATLANTA CAMPAIGN
SCALE OF MILES
0 5 10 20
CHATTANOOGA
BATTLE OF MISSIONARY RIDGE
NOV. 25, 1863
BATTLE OF LOOKOUT MT.
NOV. 24, 1863
CHICKAMAUGA STATION
NOV. 26, 1863
TENNESSEE
GEORGIA
LOOKOUT MT.
MISSIONARY
RIDGE
BATTLE OF CHICKAMAUGA
SEPT. 19-20, 1863
RINGGOLD GAP
BATTLE NOV. 27, 1863
TUNNEL HILL
BATTLES NOV. 28, 1863, MAY 6, 7, 1864
ROCKY FACE
BATTLES MAY 9, 12, 1864
MILL CREEK GAP
BATTLES MAY 9-12, 1864
DALTON
DUG GAP
BATTLES MAY 8, 1864
WESTERN AND ATLANTIC
RESACA
BATTLES MAY 13-15, 1864
LAY'S FERRY
BATTLES MAY 14-16, 1864
CALHOUN
ADAIRSVILLE
ROME
ROME R.R.
Coosa R
Etowah R
CASSVILLE
BATTLE MAY 19, 1864
KINGSTON
CARTERSVILLE
ALLATOONA
ACWORTH
BIG SHANTY
BATTLE JUNE 3, 1864
BRUSH MT.
PINE MT.
KENNESAW MT.
LOST MT.
BATTLES
JUNE 6-JULY 2, 1864
MARIETTA
NEW HOPE CHURCH
BATTLE MAY 25-JUNE 4, 1864
SMYRNA
BATTLE JULY 4, 1864
STONE MT.
BATTLE OF PEACHTREE CREEK
JULY 20, 1864
GEORGIA R.R.
EZRA CHURCH
BATTLE JULY 28, 1864
BATTLE OF ATLANTA
JULY 22, 1864
ATLANTA
Chattahoochee R
A.W. PT. RR.
M.&W.
ROUGH AND READY
BATTLE AUG. 31-SEPT. 1, 1864
JONESBORO
NOTE:
Scale of miles does not apply to Atlanta
Jonesboro section which is diagrammatic only.
NHS-AC-2

Sherman in Georgia

shot and shell as his master, and starts off in the direction of the fire.

Dismounting near the battle line, he will stride away into the woods, or to the edge of a creek or swamp, until some officer, fearful of the consequences, respectfully warns him that he is in a dangerous position, when, perhaps, he retires.

Sherman's strategy, according to Adjutant Hedley of the Thirty-second Illinois, was "marvelous" but inconclusive against his "worthy adversary."

Move succeeded move, like rook and pawn on the chessboard, one giving a check here, the other there. Sherman maneuvered so as to gain position after position with the minimum loss of men and material; Johnston retreated so skillfully before him that he scarcely lost a tin cup.

Sherman's general route was along the railroad that led from Chattanooga to Atlanta, which became his link with the North, his all-important supply line.

As for the Georgia people of the farms and towns in the army's path, many of them fled as the long columns approached, carrying away what possessions they could. The abandoned properties were looted and ravaged, with many newly freed blacks taking part in the sport. Some of the families who remained in their homes were lucky enough to escape serious molestation, while others were driven away. Billowing flames and towering smoke were a common sight, and at night the horizons were often an angry red.

"To realize what war is," Sherman wrote Ellen, "one should follow our tracks."

David P. Conyngham, a correspondent for the New York Herald *who was serving in the army as a volunteer aide-de-camp with the rank of captain, states that he saw*

frenzied groups of affrighted, starving women and children huddled together in the woods.... Such sad pictures of old and young, gray-haired matrons and timid girls, clinging together in hopeless misery, may be imagined but cannot be described.

Newsman Conyngham, an uncommonly keen and impartial observer, had joined Sherman's forces at Chattanooga the preceding March. He explains:

The instructions of the *Herald* to its army correspondents were brief but comprehensive. They were simply these: To obtain the most accurate information by personal observation, and forward it with the utmost despatch, regardless of expense, labor, or danger. Guided by these concise instructions—with his horse, his revolver, his fieldglass, his notebook, blanket, and haversack—the army correspondent of the New York *Herald* started forth to share the vicissitudes and hardships of the camp, the fatigues of the march, and the perils of the battlefield, to contribute his narrative to the history of the great war.

Some of the regions in Sherman's wake lay both devastated and depopulated. Wrote a correspondent for the Indianapolis Journal:

So startling is the utter silence that even when a wild bird carols a note you look around surprised that amid such loneliness any living thing should be happy.

It was during this campaign that Sherman began to acquire a black name in all parts of the South. His old friends could hardly believe that this was the same man who had taken such an obvious pleasure in sharing their way of life. He assured one woman who wrote him a letter that his affection for his Southern friends was as great as ever:

And yet they call me barbarian, vandal, a monster, and all the epithets that language can invent that are significant of malignity and hate.

All I pretend to say: On earth, as in heaven, man must submit to an arbiter.... Had we declined battle, America would have

Confederates at
Kennesaw Mountain

sunk . . . meriting the contempt of all mankind. . . .

I would not subjugate the South in the sense so offensively assumed, but I would make every citizen of the land obey the common law. . . .

Even yet my heart bleeds when I see the carnage of battle, the desolation of homes, the bitter anguish of families; but the very moment the men of the South say that instead of appealing to war they should have appealed to reason, to our Congress, to our courts, to religion, and to the experience of history—then will I say peace, peace.

Sherman was soon about three-quarters of the way to Atlanta, the stiffest clashes taking place at Resaca (May 14–15) and at New Hope Church

(May 25-28). A dozen miles from New Hope Church was Kennesaw Mountain. Here, on June 27, Sherman launched a major attack. Johnston hurled it back, the bluecoats suffering sharp losses.

"Next day," says Union newsman David Conyngham,

General Johnston sent a flag of truce to Sherman in order to give time to carry off the wounded and bury the dead, who were festering in front of their lines. A truce followed, and Rebels and Federals freely participated in the work of charity.

It was a strange sight to see friends, to see old acquaintances, and in some instances brothers, who had been separated for years, and now pitted in deadly hostility, meet and have a good talk over old times and home scenes and connections. They drank together, smoked together, appeared on the best possible terms, though the next day they were sure to meet in deadly conflict again....

Under the shelter of a pine I noticed a huge gray Kentuckian rebel with his arm affectionately placed around the neck of a Federal soldier, a mere boy. The bronzed warrior cried and laughed by turns, and then kissed the young Federal.

Attracted by such a strange proceeding, I went over to them and said to the veteran, "Why, you seem very much taken by that boy. I suppose he is some old friend of yours."

"Old friend, sir! Why, he is my son!"

New maneuvers on Sherman's part soon obliged Johnston to continue his withdrawal toward Atlanta.

Founded less than thirty years earlier but having grown to a population of nearly 20,000, Atlanta was one of the most important cities of the Confederacy. In addition to being a railroad center, it held factories, machine shops, foundries, and storehouses filled with military supplies, both hardware and rations.

"Atlanta must be held at all hazards," declared President Jefferson Davis. And a Southern newspaper added:

Its fall would open the way for the Federal army to the Gulf on the one hand, and to Charleston on the other, and close up those rich granaries from which Lee's armies are supplied. It would give them control of our network of railways and thus paralyze our efforts.

The people of Atlanta and its environs were now greatly agitated. Since the

Jefferson Davis

Battle of Kennesaw Mountain they could hear the sound of the fighting.

"Distant roar of cannon and sharp report of musketry," says one woman, "spoke in language unmistakable the approach of the enemy."

Church bells were rung, sometimes to give an alarm, and again to call the people to a special service. Atlanta was filled with military traffic. As reported by the Daily Intelligencer:

Hundreds of horsemen and footmen are dashing hither and thither.... The roar of wagons rolling on the streets and the cracking of whips, the screeching and grinding of wheels, the shouts of drivers, the braying of mules, and the rapid footfalls of couriers congregate a medley of sounds that seem strange and almost bewildering to the citizen.

Somewhat pathetic in appearance were the units of Georgia militiamen, mostly gray-haired men and smooth-faced boys, who were hastily assembled in the city and marched to the front. Joe Johnston needed every soldier he could get.

Trains that came puffing down the line from the front brought great numbers of sick and wounded who were placed in private homes, in public buildings, and in tent camps thrown up in parks and on the fairgrounds. Since doctors and nurses were few, much of the ministering was done by

Atlanta's women. Men died at such a rate that undertakers and coffin makers scarcely had time to sleep. The pace of the military funerals made a strange contrast with the busier traffic.

Civilian refugees poured into the city from the north even as others were leaving for points to the south. Among those who left was the seventeen-year-old daughter of a Confederate senator, Louise Wigfall, who was later to recount:

I shall never forget the horrors of that journey from Atlanta to Macon. We left in a hospital train, filled with wounded, sick, and dying soldiers, in all imaginable stages of disease and suffering.... I never imagined what a hideous, cruel thing war was until I was brought into direct contact with these poor victims.... I reached Macon sick at heart over the suffering I had witnessed....

On July 10, Joe Johnston took up a position just north of Atlanta. Sherman moved in cautiously, for the Confederates now had excellent cover. For the past few weeks hundreds of slaves had been busy strengthening the fortifications that encircled the city.

A good many of Atlanta's blacks, both men and women, were now in a curious situation. Though eager for Sherman to take the city, they were at the same time devoted to their Confederate owners.

A few miles east of Atlanta was the village of Decatur, where lived Mary Ann Harris Gay, a young white woman whose family owned many slaves, some of whom were hired out to businessmen in the city. Mary cites a

View of Atlanta's defenses

revealing episode that began one day when she was standing on the portico of her home:

I saw, approaching, one of my mother's faithful servants, who was hired to Dr. Taylor, a well-known druggist of Atlanta. Ever apprehensive of evil tidings from "the front," and "the front" being the portion of the army that embraced my brother, I was almost paralyzed. I stood as if riveted to the floor, and awaited developments.

King, for that was the name of the ebony-hued and faithful servant whose unexpected appearance had caused such a heart-flutter, came nearer and nearer. . . . I asked in husky voice, "Have you heard anything from your Marse Thomie, King?"

"No, ma'am. Have you?"

The light of heaven seemed to dispel the dark clouds which had gathered over and around my horizon, and I remembered my duty to one who, though in a menial position, had doubtless come on some kind of errand.

"Come in, King, and sit down and rest yourself," I said, pointing to an easy chair on the portico.

"I am not tired, Miss Mary, and would rather stand," he replied. And he did stand, with his hat in his hand. . . .

The suspense was becoming painful, when it was broken by King asking: "Miss Mary, is Miss Polly at home?" ["Miss Polly" was Mary's mother and King's mistress.]

"Yes, King, and I will tell her you are here."

Miss Polly . . . soon appeared and gave him a genuine welcome. King now lost no time in making known the object of his visit, and thus announced it: "Miss Polly, don't you want to sell me?"

"No. Why do you ask?"

"Because, Miss Polly, Mr. Johnson wants to buy me, and he got me to come to see you and ask you if you would sell me."

"Do you want me to sell you, King? Would you rather belong to Mr. Johnson than me?"

"Now, Miss Polly, you come to the point, and I am going to try to answer it. I love you, and you have always been a good mistress to us all, and I don't think there is one of us that would rather belong to someone else. But I tell you how it is, Miss Polly, and you mustn't get mad with me for saying it. When this war is over, none of us are going to belong to you. We'll all be free. And I would a great deal rather Mr. Johnson would lose me than you. He is always bragging about what he will do. Hear him talk, you would think he was a bigger man than Mr. Lincoln is, and had more to back him. But I think he's a mighty little man myself, and I want him to lose me. He says he'll give you his little old store on Peachtree Street for me. It don't mean much, I know, but, much or little, it's going to be more than me after the war."

And thus this unlettered man, who in the ordinary acceptance of the term had never known what it was to be free, argued with his mistress the importance of the exchange of property of which he himself was a part, for her benefit and that of her children.

"Remember, Miss Polly," he said, "that when Marse Thomie comes out of the war, it will be mighty nice for him to have a store of his own to commence business in, and if I was in your place I would take it for me, for I tell you again, Miss Polly, when the war's over we'll all be free."

But the good mistress, who had listened in silence to these arguments, was unmoved. She saw before her a man who had been born a slave in her family, and who had grown to man's estate under the fostering care of slavery, whose high sense of

Federals crossing the Chattahoochee

honor and gratitude constrained him to give advice intelligently, which, if followed, would rescue her and her children from impending adversity; but she determined not to take it. She preferred rather to trust their future well-being into the hands of providence....

She told King that when our people became convinced that the troubles between the South and North had to be settled by the sword, that she, in common with all good citizens, staked her all upon the issues of war, and that she would not now, like a coward, flee from them, or seek to avert them by selling a man, or men and women, who had endeared themselves to her by service and fidelity.

Not all of the blacks in Atlanta and vicinity favored the Northern cause. Again in the words of Decatur resident Mary Gay:

On the way to the post-office early one morning ... to mail a number of letters ... I was accosted as follows by "Uncle Mack," the good Negro blacksmith, whose shop was situated immediately upon the route:

"Did you know, Miss Mary, that the Yankees have crossed the

John B. Hood

river, and are now on this side of the Chattahoochee?"

"Why, no!" I said....

With an imprecation more expressive than elegant that evil should overtake them before getting here, he resumed hammering at the anvil....

For failing to stop Sherman, Joe Johnston now lost his command to General John Bell Hood, this by order of President Davis. A Kentuckian with a West Point education, Hood had been a fine-looking man when he entered the Confederate army. He was more than six feet tall, broad-chested, light of hair and beard, and had blue eyes with a wistful look that appealed to women. But Gettysburg had left Hood with a crippled arm, and Chickamauga had cost him a leg. These days he had to be strapped to his horse, and his blue eyes were often darkened by pain. But Hood was still a fighter. He wasn't a skilled tactician like Johnston, being known, rather, for his aggressiveness.

The Battle of Atlanta

Hood managed to hold Atlanta for six weeks, during which time its environs were almost daily the scene of skirmishing and fighting. According to Mary Gay:

The constant roaring of cannon and rattling of musketry; the thousands—yea, tens of thousands of shots blending into one grand continuous whole . . . told in thunder tones of the fierce contest . . . being waged without intermission for the possession of Atlanta.

Sherman brought the city itself under fire. One of the residents, Noble C. Williams, who was a small, wide-eyed boy at the time, was later to describe the ordeal:

Shells were frequently exploding in the main business portion of the city, and when they would come in contact with the hard paving stones there was no calculating what course they would take. Both soldiers and citizens were maimed and killed in the streets almost daily.

Most of the citizens constructed on their premises what were known as bombproofs, which were holes dug in the earth eight or ten feet deep, and of a desirable width and length to suit the builder, covered overhead with heavy beams which contained a covering of boards or tin to keep out the rain, and then covered with earth from three to five feet deep. The entrance to the small door was dug out in the shape of the letter L [to prevent the entry of shell fragments]. . . .

Night and day . . . shells were constantly being thrown into the city, adding to the death-rate daily, and setting fire often to the houses, which kept the firemen very busy extinguishing the flames.

There was certainly a strange fascination connected with the nightly bombardment, for there could be seen at almost any time numbers of lighted shells which brightly illuminated the sky with their fiery trails as they sped onward on their mission of death and destruction.

There were many stone and brick houses situated on the outskirts of the city, which seemed to have been made as special targets for practice, which were almost completely battered down by the vicious shells.

The citizens . . . were in constant fear of the city being taken by the Federals.

General Hood initiated three major battles at points about the city: the battles of Peach Tree Creek (July 20), Atlanta (July 22), and Ezra Church (July 28). The Confederates were repulsed all three times.

These battles threw many of Atlanta's citizens into a state of wild excitement. Riding into the city on the day of Peach Tree Creek, a major with the Ninth Kentucky Cavalry, J. P. Austin, observed citizens "running in every direction":

Terror-stricken women and children went screaming about the streets seeking some avenue of escape from hissing, bursting shells. . . . Perfect pandemonium reigned near the Union Depot. Trunks, bedclothing, and wearing apparel were scattered in every direction. People were striving in every conceivable way to get out of town with their effects [the routes southward as yet being open].

As the month of August began, Hood still held Atlanta. But he launched no more battles.

"On the 12th of August," says Sherman,

I heard of the success of Admiral Farragut in entering Mobile

Federals destroying the railroad at Jonesboro

Bay, which was regarded as a most valuable auxiliary to our operations at Atlanta; and learned that I had been commissioned a major-general in the regular army, which was unexpected, and not desired until successful in the capture of Atlanta. These did not change the fact that we were held in check by the stubborn defense of the place. . . .

Sherman finally marched to cut off Hood's railroad communications running southward from the city, and the move brought on the Battle of Jonesboro (August 31–September 1), another Union victory. This ended nearly four months of fighting that had cost each side upwards of 30,000 casualties.

Hood evacuated Atlanta, leaving the prize to Sherman, during the night of September 1. The Confederate troops marched out with the sad strains of "Lorena" on their lips: "A hundred months have passed, Lorena, since last I held that hand in mine. . . ." Mixed with the units of infantry, artillery, and cavalry were departing civilians, some trudging along on foot and others riding in wagons heaped with goods from their homes.

Left behind by the army were perhaps eighty carloads of ammunition that were set afire. Among those who witnessed the result was an Atlanta writer, Wallace P. Reed:

The infernal din of the exploding shells sent a thrill of alarm through the city. . . . The flames shot up to a tremendous height, and the exploding missiles scattered their red hot fragments right and left. The very earth trembled as if in the throes of a mighty earthquake. The houses rocked like cradles, and on every hand was heard the shattering of window glass and the fall of plastering and loose bricks. . . . Fortunately all the citizens in the vicinity . . . had been ordered to leave their houses before the work of destruction commenced. Every building for a quarter of a mile around was either torn to pieces or perforated with hundreds of holes. . . . Day was dawning when the last shell and the last keg of powder exploded.

"In the dread silence of that memorable morning," Reed goes on to say, "ten thousand helpless people looked into each other's faces for some faint sign of hope and encouragement, but found none."

Then came the awful hours of waiting. . . . Men with wives and daughters stayed at home to be ready for any emergency. But the center of the town was filled with the riffraff, with stragglers or deserters, with Negroes delirious over their strange sense of freedom, and with lean and haggard men and women of the lowest class who were going through the stores, picking up such odds and ends as had been left behind by their owners. . . . Atlanta, worn out and shattered by the storm of war, lay panting between two flags . . . abandoned by one, and with no hope of mercy from the other.

Allowing Hood to retreat with little molestation, the Federals advanced to seize the city. The first troops to draw near were met by a delegation led by Mayor James M. Calhoun and bearing a white flag. Calhoun handed the Yankee commander a note that read:

The fortune of war has placed Atlanta in your hands. As mayor of the city, I ask protection of noncombatants and private property.

3

ATLANTA UNDER MARTIAL LAW

*A*MONG THE ATLANTA CITIZENS *who watched the bluecoats march in was the small boy Noble Williams. He almost missed the sight, for his first reaction to the approach had been to run upstairs and hide under a bed. Coaxed down by his elders "under promise of protection," he went to a window and peered out.*

A Federal officer and his staff were seen riding down the street in front of the house, a fact which assured all that the enemy had taken possession of the city. An hour later the tramp, tramp, tramp of... General Sherman's army could be heard as they passed down the street.... This continuous motion was kept up for several hours, when the command was given a halt to rest.

No sooner had they broken ranks than hundreds of soldiers' faces could be seen peering through the fence which separated the street from the garden, and as the grape arbor, filled with temptingly luscious grapes, appeared before their vision, their mouths fairly watered and their stomachs seemed to contain an aching void that could only be filled by a speedy and vigorous assault upon them; which in less than five minutes was accomplished, greatly to the damage of both grapes and arbor. Perched as they were on every available inch of slat, they were reminders of a flock of hungry bluebirds....

"The city," says the New York Herald *correspondent, David Conyngham,* had suffered much from our projectiles.... In some places the streets were blocked up with rubbish. The suburbs were in ruins, and few houses escaped without being perforated. Many of the citizens were killed, and many more had hair-breadth escapes.... One woman pointed out to me where a shell dashed through her

house as she was sitting down to dinner. It upset the table and things, passed through the house, and killed her neighbor in the next house. . . .

Almost every garden and yard around the city had its cave. . . . All along the railroad, around the intrenchments and the bluff near the city were gopher holes where soldiers and citizens concealed themselves. . . .

Near the depot were several slave marts, with their glaring signs announcing "Slaves Bought and Sold Here," "Slave Auction Rooms," "The Great Slave Mart," and such like. As the soldiers passed these they read them with a mocking laugh. As the poor Negro passed . . . his heart became light, for he no longer dreaded . . . the auctioneer's hammer that was to consign him to a new master. . . .

Conyngham noted that Sherman's personal entry into the town was made without parade or ostentation—no beating of drums, no flaunting

Sherman's headquarters in Atlanta

of colors, no firing of salutes to humble the pride of the conquered. Sherman and staff, accompanied by several general officers, simply rode through to his headquarters. There was not even a shout or huzza to welcome him.

The citizens looked out from their doors and windows, eager to catch a glance of the man whose name had now become so famous. The soldiers lined the sidewalks, quietly looked on, and passed their own remarks on "Old Billy."

Officers mounted on prancing steeds looked far more consequential than the great conqueror himself, and cast their eyes from window to balcony to see if any fair eyes were admiring their gracious selves. The fair eyes had fled, and those remaining would fain wither them. . . .

Conyngham goes on to point out that Sherman placed the administration of the city under General Henry W. Slocum, whose troops had been the earliest to enter:

The people, after awakening from the first shock inspired by the terrible barbarities they heard of the Federal soldiers, seemed to welcome the new order of things. They were now protected, and could walk abroad in security. General Slocum's administration of Atlanta was so impartial and rigidly enforced that life and property there were as secure as in the city of New York.

Henry W. Slocum

A Union camp in Atlanta's city hall square

But the captured city's serenity was brief. Sherman explains:

I peremptorily required that all the citizens and families resident in Atlanta should go away, giving to each the option to go south or north, as their interests or feelings dictated. I was resolved to make Atlanta a pure military garrison or depot, with no civil population to influence military measures.

I had seen Memphis, Vicksburg, Natchez, and New Orleans all captured from the enemy, and each at once was garrisoned by a full division of troops, if not more; so that success was actually crippling our armies in the field by detachments to guard and protect the interests of a hostile population.

Sherman told of his aim to depopulate Atlanta in a letter to his old friend General Halleck, now serving as chief of staff in Washington, the letter closing with these words:

If the people raise a howl against my barbarity and cruelty, I will answer that war is war and not popularity-seeking. If they want peace, they and their relatives must stop the war.

Halleck replied:

Not only are you justified by the laws and usages of war in removing these people, but I think it . . . your duty. . . . The safety of our armies and a proper regard for the lives of our soldiers require that we apply to our inexorable foes the severe rules of war. . . . We have fed this class of people long enough. . . . I have endeavored to impress these views upon our commanders for the last two years. You are almost the only one who has properly applied them.

Again in Sherman's words:

I knew, of course, that such a measure would be strongly criticized, but made up my mind to do it with the absolute certainty of its justness, and that time would sanction its wisdom. I knew that the people of the South would read in this measure two important conclusions: one, that we were in earnest; and the other, if they were sincere in their common and popular clamor "to die in the last ditch," that the opportunity would soon come.

Another consideration had taken shape in Sherman's mind. His operations in the Deep South and his punitive measures against the people, especially if sustained, were bound to have a strong effect on the morale of General Robert E. Lee's Army of Northern Virginia, entrenched in opposition to Grant at Richmond and Petersburg. Many of Lee's troops were from areas that Sherman now held or was threatening. These men, Sherman reasoned, had to be deeply worried about their homes and families. Lee's desertion rate, known to be already serious, was almost certain to rise.

General Hood and his battered army were at this time recuperating in the vicinity of Lovejoy Station, about twenty miles south of Atlanta. In a letter to Hood, Sherman stated:

I have deemed it to the interest of the United States that the citizens now residing in Atlanta should remove, those who prefer it to go south, and the rest north. For the latter I can provide food and transportation to points of their election in Tennessee, Kentucky, or farther north. For the former I can provide transportation by cars as far as Rough and Ready [seven or eight miles south of Atlanta], and also wagons. . . .

If you consent, I will undertake to remove all the families in Atlanta who prefer to go south to Rough and Ready, with all their movable effects, viz., clothing, trunks, reasonable furniture, bedding, etc., with their servants, white and black, with the proviso that no force shall be used toward the blacks [at this end]. . . . If they want to go with their masters and mistresses they may do so; otherwise they [are to] be sent away. . . . Men . . . may be employed by our quartermaster.

Atlanta is no place for families or noncombatants, and I have no desire to send them north if you will assist in conveying them south. If this proposition meets your views, I will consent to a truce in the neighborhood of Rough and Ready....

Hood said in his reply:

I do not consider that I have any alternative in this matter. I therefore accept your proposition to declare a truce ... and shall render all assistance in my power to expedite the transportation of citizens in this direction....

And now, sir, permit me to say that the unprecedented measure you propose transcends, in studied and ingenious cruelty, all acts ever before brought to my attention in the dark history of war.

In the name of God and humanity, I protest....

Sherman responded that it wasn't necessary for Hood to look back into the history of war for examples of its cruelty:

Modern examples are so handy. You yourself burned dwelling houses along your parapet, and I have seen today fifty houses that you have rendered uninhabitable because they stood in the way of your forts and men....

In the name of common sense, I ask you not to appeal to a just God in such a sacrilegious manner. You who, in the midst of peace and prosperity, have plunged a nation into war—dark and cruel war—who dared and badgered us to battle, insulted our flag, seized our arsenals and forts ... turned loose your privateers to plunder unarmed ships; expelled Union families by the thousands, burned their houses, and declared, by an act of Congress, the confiscation of all debts due Northern men....

Talk thus to the marines, but not to me, who have seen these things, and who will this day make as much sacrifice for the peace and honor of the South as the best-born Southerner among you!

If we must be enemies, let us be men, and fight it out as we propose to do, and not deal in such hypocritical appeals to God and humanity.

Hood wrote back that he was quite willing to fight it out: "Better die a thousand deaths than submit to live under you or your Government and your Negro allies!"

In a final letter, Sherman assured Hood that there were no armed blacks in his army.

Following the custom of the times, the two men closed each of their spirited missives with, "Respectfully, your obedient servant."

Privately, Sherman said: "To be sure, I have made war vindictively. War is war, and you can make nothing else of it. But Hood knows as well as anyone I am not brutal or inhuman."

The Sherman-Hood correspondence was widely published in the newspapers. Sherman's rebukes to Hood infuriated many Southerners, but were applauded in the North. The Cincinnati Commercial, *whose editor had once called Sherman insane, now praised the power of his writing.*

A young scholar in Grant's Army of the Potomac exclaimed in a letter home:

What a "buster" that man is! He really seems to be the most earnest and straightforward of the whole war. In him and in him alone we seem to get the glimpse of real genius.

Even while he was corresponding with Hood, Sherman received a letter signed by Atlanta's mayor and two councilmen, a delineation of the suffering his evacuation order would inflict on the city's people:

Many poor women are in advanced state of pregnancy, others now having young children, and whose husbands for the greater part are either in the army, prisoners, or dead.

Some say: "I have such a one sick at my house...."

Others say: "What are we to do? We have no house to go to, and no means to buy, build, or rent any; no parents, relatives, or friends to go to."

... We only refer to a few facts to try to illustrate in part how this measure will operate in practice. As you advanced, the people north of this [city] fell back; and before your arrival here a large portion of the people had retired south, so that the country south of this is already crowded and without houses enough to accommodate the people, and we are informed that many are now staying in churches and other outbuildings.

This being so, how is it possible for the people still here—mostly women and children—to find any shelter? And how can they live through the winter in the woods—no shelter or subsistence in the midst of strangers who know them not, and without the power to assist them much if they were willing to do so?

This is but a feeble picture of the consequences of this measure. You know the woe, the horrors, and the suffering cannot be described by words; imagination can only conceive of it, and we ask you to take these things into consideration....

What has this helpless people done that they should be driven from their homes, to wander strangers and outcasts and exiles, and to subsist on charity?

... In conclusion, we most earnestly and solemnly petition you to reconsider this order ... and suffer this unfortunate people to remain at home....

Sherman replied:

I ... give full credit to your statements of the distress that will be occasioned, and yet shall not revoke my orders, because they were not designed to meet the humanities of the case but to prepare for the future struggles in which millions of good people outside of Atlanta have a deep interest....

I assert that our military plans make it necessary for the inhabitants to go away, and I can only renew my offer of services to make their exodus in any direction as easy and comfortable as possible.

You cannot qualify war in harsher terms that I will. War is cruelty, and you cannot refine it. And those who brought war into our country deserve all the curses and maledictions a people can pour out. I know I had no hand in making this war, and I know I will make more sacrifices today than any of you to secure peace. But you cannot have peace and a division of our country....

You might as well appeal against the thunderstorm as against these terrible hardships of war. They are inevitable, and the only way the people of Atlanta can hope once more to live in peace and quiet at home is to stop the war, which can only be done by admitting that it began in error and is perpetuated in pride.

We don't want your Negroes or your horses or your houses or your lands, or anything you have. But we do want, and will have, a just obedience to the laws of the United States ... and if it involves the destruction of your improvements, we cannot help it....

By the original compact of Government, the United States had certain rights in Georgia, which have never been relinquished and never will be.... The South began the war by seizing forts, arsenals, mints, custom-houses, etc., etc.... I myself have seen ... hundreds and thousands of women and children fleeing from your armies and desperadoes, hungry and with bleeding feet....

Now that war comes home to you, you feel very different. You deprecate its horrors; but did not feel them when you sent carloads of soldiers and ammunition, and moulded shells and shot, to carry war into [Unionist areas of] Kentucky and Tennessee, to desolate the homes of hundreds and thousands of good people who only asked to live in peace at their old homes and under the government of their inheritance.

But these comparisons are idle. I want peace, and believe it can only be reached through union and war, and I will ever conduct war with a view to perfect an early success. But, my dear sirs, when peace does come, you may call on me for anything. Then will I share with you the last cracker, and watch with you to shield your homes and families against danger from every quarter.

Now you must go, and take with you the old and feeble, feed and nurse them, and build for them in more quiet places proper habitations to shield them against the weather until the mad passions of men cool down and allow the Union and peace once more to settle over your old homes at Atlanta.

This letter, also, was published in the newspapers. Though it sounded very sensible to Northerners, it found no favor with dyed-in-the-wool rebels such as Mary Gay of Decatur. By implementing the evacuation order, she fumes,

the Nero of the nineteenth century, alias William Tecumseh Sherman, was put upon record as the born leader of the most ruthless, godless band of men ever organized in the name of patriotism. . . .

Sherman's order made no exception for citizens who claimed loyalty to the Union. It would have been difficult and time-consuming to sort the genuine claims from the false.

Newsman David Conyngham talked with a sad-faced old man who told him:

"At the breaking out of the war I owed large sums to Northern merchants, and I paid them. I had neither hand nor voice in bringing on this war. I wanted to live under the old flag. During the war I gave every assistance in my power to relieve Union prisoners, and my only son was caught aiding one of them to escape, and shot. The rebels then stripped me of my property and called me a damned Yank. . . ."

". . . I think you are a Union man," I replied.

"I have given proofs enough, at least. And now what's my

Provost marshal's headquarters. Citizens are applying for passes in compliance with Sherman's evacuation order

reward? . . . I have the alternative of going north and starve, or going into the rebel lines and being hung."

Alas! He spoke the truth. There were hundreds like him. But war makes no distinction.

Numerous citizens came to Sherman's headquarters with special problems related to their departure. One man declared later that most of the appellants found Sherman "patient, gentlemanly, and obliging—as much so as he could be . . . consistently with his prescribed policy."

[A] lady with whom I conversed . . . represents him as being very kind and conciliatory in his deportment towards her and others who visited him. He expressed much regret at the necessity which compelled him to order the citizens of Atlanta from their homes; but stated in justification of his course . . . that it was impossible for him to subsist his army, and feed the citizens too, by a single line of railroad. . . .

He took the little child of my friend in his arms and patted her rosy cheeks, calling her a "poor little exile" and saying he was sorry to drive her away from her comfortable home, but that war was a cruel and inexorable thing, and its necessities compelled him to do many things which he heartily regretted.

Mary Gay of Decatur came into the city at this time to join the refugees moving southward, which made up the majority. In front of many homes, Mary noted, were wagons being loaded with effects to be taken to the depot, where strings of cars awaited. Atlanta was "a veritable pandemonium."

Those who have studied mythical lore and dwelt in imagination upon the attributes of mythical characters, especially those of an evil nature, can perhaps form some idea of the confusion and disquiet of an entire city yielding its possession to an alien army, which, now that success had been achieved by brute force, was bent upon the utter impoverishment of the people, and their extreme humiliation.

Curses and imprecations too vile to repeat, and boisterous laughter and vulgar jests resounded through the streets of Atlanta. Federal wagons followed in the tracks of Confederate wagons [in front of the houses], and after a few light articles were placed in the latter for southern destination, the former unblushingly moved up to receive pianos and other expensive furniture which found its way into every section of the North.

David Conyngham, in the role of an observer, rode one of the refugee trains southward to Rough and Ready:

The cars . . . were loaded with miscellaneous cargo. In some

Citizens loading their goods and leaving the city

were crowded together tottering old age and maidens in their youthful bloom.... In addition... were... a heterogeneous medley of poodle dogs, tabby cats... household furniture... squalling, wondering children—all of which, huddled together, made anything but a pleasant travelling party....

We were kindly received by... the rebel party. Everything went on in the most friendly way—visits paid between Federals and Confederates... friendly intercourse kept up. One could scarcely realize that these laughing chattering groups were deadly enemies....

The plight of the refugees accumulating in the truce area appalled Mary Gay:

I opened wide my eyes and took in the situation in all its horrible details. The entire Southern population of Atlanta, with but an occasional exception, and that of many miles in its vicinity, were dumped out upon the cold ground without shelter and without any of the comforts of home, and an autumnal mist or drizzle was slowly but surely saturating every article of clothing upon them; and pulmonary diseases in all stages were admonishing them of the danger of such exposure. Aged grandmothers tottering upon the verge of the grave, and tender maidens... and little babes not three days old in the arms of sick mothers, driven from their homes, were all out upon the cold charity of the world....

When one of the long trains from Atlanta rolled in with its living freight and stopped at the terminus, a queenly girl, tall and lithe in figure and willowy in motion, emerged from one of the cars and stood, the embodiment of feminine grace, for a moment upon the platform.... The pretty, plain debeige dress, trimmed with Confederate buttons and corresponding ribbon, all conspired to make her appear, even to a casual observer, just what she was—a typical Southern girl who gloried in that honor.

She stood only a moment, and then, as if moved by some divine inspiration, she stepped from the car, and, falling upon her knees, bent forward and kissed the ground. This silent demonstration of affection for the land of Dixie touched a vibrating chord, and a score or more of beautiful girlish voices blended in sweetest harmony while they told in song their love for Dixie.

I listened spellbound, and was not the only one thus enchanted. A United States officer listened and was touched to tears. Approaching me, he asked if I would do him the favor to tell him the name of the young lady who kissed the ground.

"I do not think she would approve of my telling you her name, and I decline to do so," I said in reply.

Not in the least daunted by this rebuff, he responded: "I shall learn it; and if she has not already become the wife or the affianced of another, I shall offer her the devotion of my life."

The Confederate authorities soon took many of the homeless people southeastward to Macon. Stated one of the city's newspapers:

Refugees report generally kind personal treatment from General Sherman and his officers. Whatever exceptions may have occurred have been in violation of orders—instances of individual pilfering, which cannot always be prevented in an army, and in many cases have been detected and punished.

A friend, whose wife was left an invalid in Atlanta and came within our lines a day or two since, says that at her request General Sherman came to see her, and finding her unable to attend to the arrangement of her moveables for transportation, had them all bound up nicely and transported to our lines, even to her washtub.

"By the middle of September," relates Sherman,

matters and things had settled down in Atlanta, so that we felt perfectly at home. The telegraph and railroads were repaired, and we had uninterrupted communication to the rear [i.e., northward to Chattanooga]. The trains arrived with regularity and dispatch, and brought us ample supplies.

While Sherman was considering what his next move should be, Confederate President Davis, rocked by the loss of Atlanta, was trying to revitalize the sagging Southern spirit. In a speech delivered at Macon he declared:

Sherman cannot keep up his long line of communication, and retreat, sooner or later, he must. And when that day comes, the fate that befell the army of the French Empire in its retreat from Moscow will be reenacted. Our cavalry and our people will harass and destroy his army as did the Cossacks that of Napoleon, and the Yankee general, like him, will escape with only a bodyguard.

When the news of this speech reached General Grant in Virginia, he remarked, "Mr. Davis has not made it quite plain who is to furnish the snow for this Moscow retreat."

Grant's situation remained virtually unchanged, with Lee's lines before Richmond and Petersburg showing no signs of breaking. Using the military mails, Grant had entered into a discussion with Sherman regarding his next campaign. Now Grant sent one of his letters west by the hand of an aide, Colonel Horace Porter, who recounts:

I reached Chattanooga on the afternoon of September 19.... Being anxious to reach General Sherman with all despatch, I started forward that night on a freight train. Rumors of approaching guerrillas were numerous; but, like many other campaign reports, they were unfounded, and I arrived in Atlanta safely the next forenoon....

I went at once to General Sherman's headquarters. My mind was naturally wrought up to a high pitch of curiosity to see the famous soldier of the West, whom I had never met. He had taken up his quarters in a comfortable brick house... opposite the Courthouse Square.

As I approached I saw the captor of Atlanta on the porch, sitting tilted back in a large armchair, reading a newspaper. His coat was unbuttoned, his black felt hat slouched over his brow, and on his feet were a pair of slippers very much down at the heels.... He was just forty-four years of age.... With his... tall, gaunt form, restless hazel eyes, aquiline nose, bronzed face, and crisp beard, he looked the picture of "grim-visaged war."

My coming had been announced to him by telegraph, and he was expecting my arrival at this time. I approached him, introduced myself, and handed him General Grant's letter. He tilted forward in his chair, crumpled the newspaper in his left hand while with his right he shook hands cordially, then pushed a chair forward and invited me to sit down. His reception was exceedingly cordial, and his manner exhibited all the personal peculiarities which General Grant, in speaking of him, had so often described.

After reading General Grant's letter, he entered at once upon an animated discussion of the military situation East and West, and as he waxed more intense in his manner the nervous energy of his nature soon began to manifest itself.

He twice rose from his chair and sat down again, twisting the newspaper into every conceivable shape, and from time to time drew first one foot and then the other out of its slipper, and followed up the movement by shoving out his leg so that the foot could recapture the slipper and thrust itself into it again.

He exhibited a strong individuality in every movement, and there was a peculiar energy of manner in uttering the crisp words and epigrammatic phrases which fell from his lips as rapidly as shots from a machine gun.

I soon realized that he was one of the most dramatic and picturesque characters of the war. . . .

After a while lunch was announced, and the general invited me to his mess, consisting of himself and his personal staff. . . . The general's mess was established in the dining room of the house he occupied, and was about as democratic as Grant's. The officers came and went as their duties required, and meals were eaten without the slightest ceremony. . . .

After lunch we repaired to a room in the house which the general used for his office, and there went into an elaborate discussion of the purpose of my visit.

He said: "I am more than ever of the opinion that there ought to be some definite objective point or points decided upon before I move farther into this country. Sweeping around generally through Georgia for the purpose of inflicting damage would not be good generalship. I want to strike out for the sea. . . .

"I can subsist my army upon the country as long as I can keep moving; but if I should have to stop and fight battles the difficulty would be greatly increased.

"There is no telling what Hood will do, whether he will follow me and contest my march eastward, or whether he will start north with his whole army, thinking there will not be any adequate force to oppose him, and that he can carry the war as far north as Kentucky. I don't care much what he does. I would rather have him start north though; and I would be willing to give him a free ticket and pay his expenses if he would decide to take that horn of the dilemma. I could send enough of this army to delay his progress until our troops scattered through the West could be concentrated in sufficient force to destroy him. . . .

"With the bulk of my army I could cut a swath through to the sea . . . and be able to move up in the rear of Lee, or do almost anything else that Grant might require of me. Both Jeff Davis, according to the tone of his recent speeches, and Hood want me to fall back. That is just the reason why I want to go forward."

Sherman was later to present the following thoughts as his moral and military justification for planning further punitive measures against the Confederates:

When we took Atlanta . . . they were bound by every rule of civilized warfare to surrender their cause. It was then hopeless. . . . But they continued the war, and then I had a right, under the rules of civilized warfare, to commence a system that would make them feel the power of the Government and cause them to succumb to our national authority. . . .

The question then arose in my mind how to apply the power thus entrusted by my Government so as to produce the result—the end of the war—which was all we desired; for war is only justifiable among civilized nations to produce peace.

Grant's aide, Horace Porter, stayed with Sherman for two or three days, then returned to Virginia. He gave Grant a letter from Sherman that closed as follows:

I admire your dogged perseverance and pluck more than ever. If you can whip Lee, and I can march to the Atlantic, I think Uncle Abe will give us twenty days' leave of absence to see the young folks.

About the same time as the arrival of this letter, Grant engaged in a discussion about Sherman with a clergyman who had met him.

"Sherman," said Grant, "is a most superior general. A good, kind man, too."

"But very unrelenting," replied the clergyman, "in walking the path marked out for himself."

"Yes," agreed Grant. "That is his character."

4

THE MARCH TO THE SEA BEGINS

IN EARLY OCTOBER, *1864, even as Sherman continued to exchange messages with Grant regarding the merits of his new proposal, Confederate General John Hood, his army renewed, moved against the Federal railroad communications running northward to Chattanooga. Sherman was obliged to march from Atlanta to meet the threat.*

A sharp battle at Allatoona, some thirty miles above Atlanta, resulted in Hood's repulse, though he tore up a section of the road. After hitting several other spots farther to the north he retreated westward into Alabama. Sherman pursued him across the border, then desisted.

Hood was expected next to launch an invasion of Tennessee in an effort to draw Sherman northward, but Sherman had no intention of following. This was the direction he preferred Hood to go. It would make the march to the sea less of a gamble. Leaving a suitable force under Major General George H. Thomas, the famed "Rock of Chickamauga," to defend Tennessee against Hood, Sherman turned back toward Atlanta.

Neither President Lincoln nor General Grant was enthusiastic about Sherman's plan to march to the sea, viewing it as too ambitious, but Grant finally telegraphed: "Go on as you propose." Sherman himself was confident: "I can make this march, and make Georgia howl!"

According to the adjutant of the Thirty-second Illinois Infantry Regiment, Fenwick Hedley:

Events during the last week in October and the first ten days in November, 1864, were stirring enough. The railroad . . . was repaired from Chattanooga to Atlanta, where the bulk of Sherman's army was assembling. Every train going north was loaded to its utmost capacity with the wounded and infirm, with surplus artillery, and, in fact, almost everything that the men could not carry on their backs. Returning trains brought only the most needed articles—hard bread, pork, coffee, sugar, and ammunition. It was evident even to those in the ranks that some important, if not desperate, undertaking was at hand.

On November 8 Sherman issued the following announcement:

The general commanding deems it proper at this time to inform the officers and men of the Fourteenth, Fifteenth, Seventeenth, and Twentieth Corps that he has organized them into an army for a special purpose, well known to the War Department and to General Grant. It is sufficient for you to know that it involves a departure from our present base, and a long and difficult march to a new one.

All the chances of war have been considered and provided for, as far as human sagacity can. All he asks of you is to maintain that discipline, patience, and courage which have characterized you in the past; and he hopes, through you, to strike a blow at our enemy that will have a material effect in producing what we all so much desire, his complete overthrow.

Read before the various units of the army, this announcement was greeted with expressions of approval. The men, says newsman David Conyngham,

The Battle of Allatoona. Confederates in foreground

George H. Thomas

knew not whither [they were going], nor did they care. All they knew was, "it was all right; Old Billy knew what he was about."

Conyngham goes on to explain that it now became necessary for Sherman to publish in Atlanta

an order for its immediate evacuation by all citizens who had not left in compliance with his first order. A great many, of thorough Unionist sentiments, had remained. . . .

It was generally understood that the city was to be evacuated and destroyed. It was pretty well known that Sherman was going to cut loose from all communications, and to destroy all the factories, foundries, railroads, mills, and all [railroad] property between Atlanta and Chattanooga, thus preventing the rebels from using them in his rear. . . .

The depot presented a scene of confusion and suffering seldom witnessed. Women and children were huddled together, while men . . . were . . . frantically rushing about, trying to procure transportation, and forced to give their last dollar to some exacting conductor or railway official.

An order had been issued . . . providing all these people with free transportation; but several . . . employees and railroad officials could not see it in that light. They saw that the thing could be made to pay, and they did make it pay. . . .

[The citizens] were afraid to complain. They were too anxious to get off. . . . In some cases they gave all they had to be let go . . . though all the time provided with free passages.

Had Sherman known of this extortion, he would have put a stop to it. But he had no deep sympathy for Southern Unionists in general. He felt that most had not done enough to resist the rebellion, having been more concerned with their comfort and security than with making sacrifices.

When Sherman spoke of the sacrifices he himself was making for the cause he wasn't referring to the hardships and dangers he had to face. These rather appealed to the restless and venturesome side of his nature.

Railway destruction as a military art

He had in mind the long periods he was obliged to spend apart from his wife and children, whom he missed acutely.

Now, with another campaign about to begin, Sherman was burdened with the knowledge that his youngest son—a baby he had never seen—was sick and was not expected to live.

To his daughters Minnie and Lizzie, Sherman wrote: "I want to see you very much. Indeed, I cannot say how much."

Writing also to his son Tommy, he explained that the North now considered him a great general, and that if he came home he would be met by band music and cheering crowds, but that he would prefer to come home quietly. "I would rather . . . have you and Willy meet me."

"Willy," he added, "will never meet us again in this world, and you and I must take care of the family."

Sherman's work of destruction prior to launching his march began with the railroad property between Atlanta and Chattanooga. Buildings and bridges were fired, and the rails torn up. Says Adjutant Hedley:

A regiment would scatter along one side of the road, each man picking up the end of a tie; then, at the word of command, all would throw the ties end over end, the fall breaking the rails loose. Then ties and telegraph poles were piled up and fired, and the rails thrown across them. The latter were soon red-hot in the middle, and the men would pick them up and wrap them around trees [forming what came to be known as "Sherman's neckties"], or twist them with cant hooks into a corkscrew pattern which it was impossible to straighten. . . .

The men worked with a will, seeming to take a savage delight in destroying everything that could by any possibility be made use of by their enemies. They attained great proficiency in these methods, and, after this fashion, they absolutely destroyed three-fourths of the railroad between Chattanooga and Atlanta. . . . Each detachment, immediately upon accomplishing the work in its own vicinity, marched rapidly toward Atlanta.

On the night of the 14th, the [last detachment] . . . followed the remainder of the army. There was now not a Federal soldier between Atlanta and Chattanooga, and the hills and plains, which had lately echoed the fearful din of artillery and musketry, and had been alive with masses of fiercely contending human beings, were as still and desolate as if a demon of destruction had passed over.

But there were monuments testifying to the fearful struggle—

trees riven by cannon shot, and broken-down caissons [i.e., ammunition wagons]. Here, there, and everywhere were graves of those who wore the blue and those who wore the gray, each surmounted by a board upon which were rudely cut by knives of comrades the name, company, and regiment of him who lay beneath.

By the time the last detachment from the north reached Atlanta, the destruction of the city was well under way. The torch became the chief expedient of destruction on the afternoon and evening of November 15. According to David Conyngham:

Winship's iron foundry and machine shops were early set on fire. This valuable property was calculated to be worth about half a million of dollars. An oil refinery nearby next got on fire and was soon in a fierce blaze. Next followed a freight warehouse. . . . The depot, turning-tables, freight sheds, and stores around were soon a fiery mass. . . .

Some ruffians ran with brands to fire the churches. . . . The Roman Catholic minister, Father [Thomas] O'Reiley, who was the only minister that remained in town, met them and upbraided them for their impious sacrilege. Even these hardened men of war shrank before virtue and truth, and the good priest not only saved his own church but also [some of] those of his fellow Christians.

The Atlanta Hotel, Washington Hall, and all the square around the railroad depot were soon in one sheet of flame. Drugstores, drygoods stores, hotels, Negro marts, theaters, and grog shops were all now feeding the fiery element. Worn-out wagons and camp equipage were piled up in the depot and added to the fury of the flames.

A stone warehouse was blown up by a mine. . . . The men plunged into the houses, broke windows and doors with their muskets, dragging out armfuls of clothes, tobacco, and whiskey. . . . The men dressed themselves in new clothes, and then flung the rest into the fire.

It was nighttime now, and many of the soldiers were drunk. More and more of the private homes that Sherman's evacuation orders had emptied were looted and burned.

"All sorts of discordant noises rent the air," states a Union officer. "Drunken soldiers on foot and horseback raced up and down the streets, while the buildings on either side were solid sheets of flame."

Sherman says that one of the machine shops that was fired
had been used by the rebels as an arsenal, and in it were stored piles of shot and shell, some of which proved to be loaded, and the night was made hideous by the bursting of shells, whose fragments came uncomfortably near Judge Lyon's house, in which I was quartered.

Major George Ward Nichols, an aide-de-camp to Sherman, wrote in his diary:

A grand and awful spectacle is presented to the beholder in this beautiful city, now in flames. . . . The heaven is one expanse of lurid fire; the air is filled with flying, burning cinders; buildings covering two hundred acres are in ruins or in flames; every instant there is the sharp detonation or the smothered booming sound of exploding shells and powder concealed in the buildings, and then the sparks and flames shoot away up . . . scattering cinders far and wide.

These are the machine shops where have been forged and cast the Rebel cannon, shot and shell that have carried death to many a brave defender of our nation's honor. These warehouses have been the receptacle of munitions of war, stored to be used for our destruction. The city which, next to Richmond, has furnished more material for prosecuting the war than any other in the South, exists no more as a means for injury to be used by the enemies of the Union.

A brigade of Massachusetts soldiers are the only troops now left in town. They will be the last to leave it.

These troops soon marched out. As they did so, explains Adjutant Hedley:
the fine silver band of the 33rd Massachusetts . . . played "John Brown." The men took up the words wedded to the music, and high above the roaring flames, above the crash of falling walls, above the fierce crackling of thousands of small-arms cartridges in the burning buildings, rose the triumphant refrain, "His truth is marching on!"

Sherman and his staff remained at his headquarters in the city until morning. He relates:

About 7 A.M. of November 16 we rode out of Atlanta by the Decatur Road, filled by the marching troops and wagons of the

Oliver O. Howard

Fourteenth Corps; and reaching the hill just outside of the old rebel works, we naturally paused to look . . . upon the scenes of our past battles. We stood upon the very ground whereon was fought the bloody battle of July 22d. . . .

Behind us lay Atlanta, smouldering and in ruins, the black smoke rising high in the air and hanging like a pall over the ruined city. Away off in the distance, on the McDonough Road, was the rear of [General Oliver O.] Howard's column, the gun barrels glistening in the sun, the white-topped wagons stretching away to the south; and right before us the Fourteenth Corps, marching steadily and rapidly, with a cheery look and swinging pace that made light of the thousand miles that lay between us and Richmond.

Again, a band struck up the "John Brown" march, and Sherman had never heard the chorus of "Glory, glory, hallelujah!" sung "with more spirit, or in better harmony of time and place."

"Then," he says, "we turned our horse's heads to the east. Atlanta was soon lost behind the screen of trees, and became a thing of the past."

The city was still a thing of the present to about fifty families who, in spite of Sherman's evacuation orders, had remained in their homes until the very end. Their determined occupancy had helped to keep the men with torches at a distance. This morning these citizens walked about in groups and soberly inspected the vast areas of destruction and chaos, the women experiencing an extra pang at sight of the scorched and trampled flower gardens. The hovering smoke filtered the sun's rays, giving the distressing scenes a curious amber hue.

According to a Georgia militia officer who soon rode into the city:

The crowning act of all their wickedness and villainy was committed by our ungodly foe in removing the dead from the vaults in the cemetery and robbing the coffins of the silver name plates and tippings, and depositing their own dead in the vaults.

Among the observers on the morning Sherman left was the boy Noble Williams. Along with two or three friends, he tramped to the city's outskirts:

The country for miles around presented a scene of almost unequalled desolation. Many trees had fallen by the army woodman's ax, and those left standing were but the shattered remnants of their former selves, for cannon ball, shell, and Minié had vied with each other in their attempts at relieving the mighty oaks and pines of their limbs and trunks. The woods and fields were strewn with the carcasses of dead and decaying animals, most of which had performed valuable service but, becoming disabled, were shot or left to die of starvation.

These carcasses, the boy adds, gave off a "sickening stench" and were surrounded by "numbers of buzzards."

Sherman and his columns were soon through this belt of desolation and in farm country that was fresh and clean. As Sherman tells it:

The day was extremely beautiful, clear sunlight with bracing air, and an unusual feeling of exhilaration seemed to pervade all minds. . . . Even the common soldiers caught the inspiration, and many a group called out to me as I worked my way past them, "Uncle Billy, I guess Grant is waiting for us at Richmond!"

Indeed, the general sentiment was that we were marching for Richmond, and that there we should end the war; but how and when they seemed to care not. Nor did they measure the distance or count the cost in life, or bother their brains about the great rivers to be crossed, and the food required for man and beast that had to be gathered by the way.

There was a devil-may-care feeling pervading officers and men that made me feel the full load of responsibility; for success would be accepted as a matter of course, whereas, should we fail, this march would be adjudged the wild adventure of a crazy fool.

5

MAKING GEORGIA HOWL

SHERMAN HAD NO THOUGHT *of marching directly for Richmond, designing to reach the seacoast first. He had his eye on Savannah, Georgia, about 500 miles south of Richmond and a march of nearly 300 miles from Atlanta. Armed resistance to his advance was not a major concern. With Hood out of the way, he expected to encounter no more than cavalry and militia units.*

A native Georgian, Colonel Charles C. Jones, Jr., explains that, in truth, the only forces available to oppose the march were

the cavalry corps of Major General Joseph Wheeler, and the Georgia State troops led by Major Generals Howell Cobb and Gustavus W. Smith. . . . In the interior of the Commonwealth remained only old men and boys to shoulder their fowling pieces and assist in disputing the passage of swamps.

Sore-pressed at every point, the once puissant armies of the Confederacy had been sadly depleted by diseases, wounds, and death. Supplies of every kind were well-nigh exhausted, and no helping hand was extended [to Georgia] in this hour of supreme need.

Sherman's chief problem was that of keeping his army in food, for he had given up all contact with the North. He had issued the following orders:

The army will forage liberally on the country. . . . To this end, each brigade commander will organize a good and sufficient foraging party, under the command of one or more discreet officers, who will gather, near the route traveled, corn or forage of any kind, meat of any kind, vegetables, cornmeal, or whatever is needed by the command, aiming at all times to keep in the wagons at least ten days' provisions . . . and three days' forage.

Soldiers must not enter the dwellings of the inhabitants . . . but, during a halt or camp, they may be permitted to gather

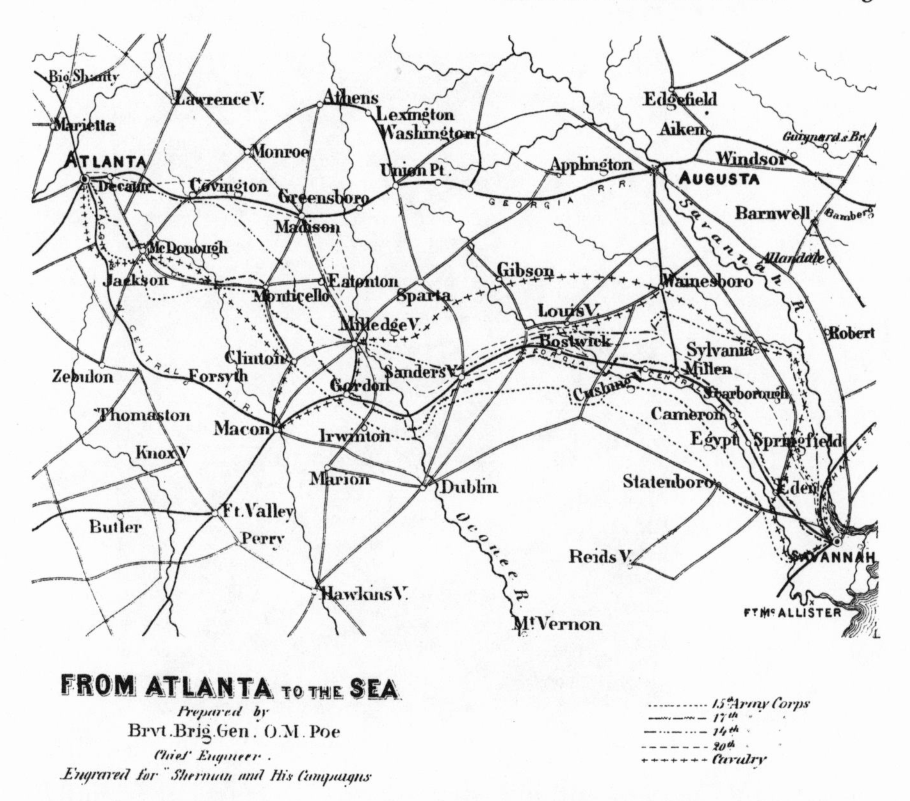

turnips, potatoes, and other vegetables, and to drive in stock in sight of their camp. To regular foraging parties must be intrusted the gathering of provisions and forage at any distance from the road traveled.

To corps commanders alone is intrusted the power to destroy mills, houses, cotton gins, etc.; and for them this general principle is laid down:

In districts and neighborhoods where the army is unmolested, no destruction of such property should be permitted; but should guerrillas or bushwhackers molest our march, or should the inhabitants burn bridges, obstruct roads, or otherwise manifest local hostility, then army commanders should order and enforce a devastation more or less relentless, according to the measure of such hostility.

As for horses, mules, wagons, etc., belonging to the inhabitants, the cavalry and artillery may appropriate freely and without limit, discriminating, however, between the rich, who are usually

Joseph Wheeler

hostile, and the poor and industrious, usually neutral or friendly. Foraging parties may also take mules or horses. . . .

In all foraging, of whatever kind, the parties engaged will refrain from abusive or threatening language . . . and they will endeavor to leave with each family a reasonable portion for their maintenance.

Sherman's army numbered about 60,000 men. Adjutant Hedley explains that they were "veterans who had served an apprenticeship of more than three years at their profession and learned nearly all that was worth knowing."

Each soldier was practically a picked man. . . . He was fertile of resources, and his self-confidence was unbounded. . . . His confidence in the long-headedness of "the old man" (General Sherman) was such that he did not disturb himself on that score. He was heading south[east] instead of north, and this was ample assurance that Thomas was taking care of Hood, and that Grant was "holding Lee down."

... This army, which had been marching light from Chattanooga to Atlanta, was now simply reduced to what it had on, and that was not much.... What few tents had been smuggled as far south as Atlanta were now entirely discarded, and only a few "flies" for the various headquarters, and one to each regiment to shelter the field desks of the adjutant and quartermaster, were retained....

Each soldier was supposed to carry half of a shelter tent, which, combined with the counterpart carried by a comrade, made reasonable protection for two, but many of the men regarded them with contempt. The average soldier cared only for a blanket, and this he carried in a roll swung over his shoulder, the ends being tied together, meeting under the opposite arm.

A majority of the men discarded knapsacks altogether. Those who yet clung to them carried only a shirt and a pair or two of socks. Each soldier had 40 rounds of ammunition in his cartridge box and 160 elsewhere upon his person. His cooking utensils were a tin oyster can in which to make his coffee, and sometimes one half of a canteen to serve as a skillet or frying pan. His haversack [a satchel-like bag with a shoulder strap] contained a liberal amount of coffee, sugar, and salt, a very small fragment of salt pork, and three days' rations of hard bread....

Howell Cobb

The soldier's outfit was not complete without a deck of cards, and these were carried in the pocket so as to be convenient at any halt on the road. Frequent thumbing had so worn these treasured pasteboards that in many instances it was an absolute impossibility for one to tell what card he held. . . .

To sum up, no army ever marched with less impedimenta, and none adapted itself so completely or cheerfully to its conditions.

The army marched in four columns, the various corps pursuing parallel roads. These columns were sometimes five, sometimes fifteen miles apart. Their combined front was from forty to sixty miles. . . . The skirmishers and flankers of each corps spread out until they met those of the corps next to them on either side. . . . In front of each corps marched a regiment of cavalry or mounted infantry. . . . A cavalry brigade under the dashing [General Hugh J.] Kilpatrick, with a few light guns, moved on this flank [of the army] or that, as the emergency required.

The outset of the march found Sherman riding with one of the central columns. "The first night out," he relates, "we camped by the roadside near Lithonia."

Stone Mountain, a mass of granite, was in plain view, cut out in clear outline against the blue sky. The whole horizon was lurid with the bonfires of rail ties, and groups of men all night were carrying the heated rails to the nearest trees and bending them around the trunks. . . . I attached much importance to this destruction of the railroad. . . .

The next day we passed through the handsome town of Covington, the soldiers closing up their ranks, the color bearers unfurling their flags, and the bands striking up patriotic airs. The white people came out of their houses to behold the sight in spite of their deep hatred of the invaders, and the Negroes were simply frantic with joy. Whenever they heard my name they clustered about my horse, shouted and prayed in their peculiar style, which had a natural eloquence that would have moved a stone.

One of the town's white citizens, a young woman named Allie Travis, was later to recount:

The street in front of our house was a moving mass of bluecoats—infantry, artillery, and cavalry—from 9 o'clock in the morning to a late hour at night. All during the day squads would

Hugh J. Kilpatrick

leave their ranks, rush into the house, and demand something to eat, seize what they could get, then go to the yard and garden to chase chickens and pull up turnips. . . .

Our nearest neighbor locked up one of her turkeys in a large room in the house. The light and noise kept it so uneasy that it paced the floor uttering its "gobble! gobble! gobble!" every few minutes. It proved to be a regular apple of Tantalus to a squad of Yankees in the yard. As it would change its position in the room and its cry would come from different directions, they would rush from corner to corner of the house, exclaiming, "Oh, it's right under here, and I'll have it directly!"

As their search afforded such amusement to the family, and proved to be so fruitless, they finally gave it up, perhaps deciding that it was either a phantom turkey or the work of a ventriloquist. . . .

But I must not forget to mention the conduct of a colored girl of ours while the Yankees were passing. She was standing in the yard, viewing with apparent indifference the passing pageant, when she recognized some of her clothing in the hands of a soldier. . . . She immediately investigated the matter, and found that they had broken open her house and were appropriating all that she prized. She soon filled the yard with her shrieks and lamentations.

A Dutchman [i.e., a Yankee of German origins] in our house at the time inquired, "What's de matter wid dat nigger?"

"Your soldiers," I replied, "are carrying off everything she owns, and yet you pretend to be fighting for the Negro."

"Fight for de nigger! I'd see 'em in de bottom of a swamp before I'd fight for 'em," he answered angrily.

The girl was afraid to say anything to the white men, but when she saw a colored soldier [i.e., a pioneer, or laborer] wearing her newest style hat her wrath knew no bounds. Going up to him and shaking her fists in his face, she exclaimed: "Oh! If I had the power like I've got the will, I'd tear you to pieces!"

Once during the day she was standing by my mother, who was telling a crowd of soldiers that "the Lord would be revenged upon them for their treatment of us."

One of them answered, "Oh, yes, you talk about the Lord now, but there is no Lord for the poor Negro when you've got him tied up, giving him six or seven hundred lashes a day."

The colored girl instantly replied, "I've never got that much yit."

He answered, "Oh, you'll tell any lie now," then added, "Will you allow your race to live in bondage all their days when you could be free?"

"Well, of course," she said slowly, "if the whole universal was free I'd want to be free, but I expect to live in the Confederick as long as there's a Rebel."

Later in the day she was standing by the front gate when a soldier marching down the street said to her, "Oh, yes, the Rebs said we never could get to Atlanta, but you tell 'em I say the Yanks can go anywhere."

"Thank God you can't go to Heaven," burst from her lips, while she quickly moved back from the fence.

Stopping a moment and looking as if at a loss what to say, he asked, "Why, do you think you'll get there?"

"I don't know about it if you don't quit coming through here kicking up such a fuss," she answered. "You won't give me time to pray."

... Knowing the strength of my Rebel sentiments, my mother ... had exhausted every argument to convince me of the rashness of expressing them.... She succeeded so well in frightening me that for several hours after the arrival of Sherman's army I was so silent that I might have been taken for a probationary disciple of Pythagoras.

"Knitting socks for the Rebs?" elicited no reply as my sister and I sat quietly knitting from balls whose hearts were gold watches.

But, alas, when greatly provoked it is hard to preserve self-control, and, after witnessing the depredations of the raiders... and when an officer came in and attempted to reconstruct me by arguments to prove the sin of Secession and the certainty of our subjugation, my tongue was loosed and my heart was fired.

During the long controversy that followed, devotion to our cause and fears for my personal safety produced such a conflict of emotions in my heart that I would frequently rise to my feet as some answer to his arguments would come to me. . . . Then, at the entreaties of my sister, I would recollect myself, sit down, and endeavor to be calm.

At length unable to answer, he rushed from the room, saying, "I see it is no use to argue with you!"

"Nor I with you," I called after him, for

"If you convince a man against his will,
He's of the same opinion still."

I heard afterward that a soldier went to the house across the street and said to some comrades: "Boys, you had better not go to that house over yonder. There is one of the rankest Secesh gals there you ever saw. She used us up, and looked like she might lick us, too. . . ."

The remark was not very flattering, but still I liked the idea of being thought true to the South.

In the afternoon a young friend insisted so much on my going to the front door with her to hear the music that I consented. When we reached the door the band was playing "Dixie." I smiled and remarked to her that "they must be at a loss for tunes, as they were playing one of ours."

If they had heard me they could not have changed the tune quicker to "Yankee Doodle." Taking my friend by the hand, I led her in immediately, saying, "We will not listen to that tune."

Many of Covington's citizens failed to get a look at Sherman. To escape the congestion, he dropped out of the main line of march and resorted to a back street:

I . . . rode on to a place designated for camp, at the crossing of the Ulcofauhachee River, about four miles to the east of the town. Here we made our bivouac, and I walked up to a plantation house close by, where were assembled many Negroes, among them an old, gray-haired man, of as fine a head as I ever saw.

I asked him if he understood about the war and its progress. He said he did; that he had been looking for the "angel of the Lord" ever since he was knee-high, and though we professed to be fighting for the Union he supposed that slavery was the cause, and that our success was to be his freedom.

I asked him if all the Negro slaves comprehended this fact, and he said they surely did. I then explained to him that we wanted the slaves to remain where they were, and not to load us down with useless mouths, which would eat up the food needed for our fighting men; that our success was their assured freedom; that we could receive a few of their young, hearty men as pioneers; but that, if they followed us in swarms of old and young, feeble and helpless, it would simply load us down and cripple us in our great task. . . .

It was at this very plantation that a soldier passed me with a ham on his musket, a jug of sorghum molasses under his arm, and a big piece of honey in his hand, from which he was eating, and, catching my eye, he remarked *sotto voce* and carelessly to a comrade, "Forage liberally on the country," quoting from my general orders. . . . I reproved the man, explaining that foraging must be limited to the regular parties properly detailed. . . .

The skill and success of the men in collecting forage was one of the features of this march. Each brigade commander had authority to detail a company of foragers, usually about fifty men, with one or two commissioned officers selected for their boldness and enterprise. This party would be dispatched before daylight with a knowledge of the intended day's march and camp; would proceed on foot five or six miles from the route traveled by their brigade, and then visit every plantation and farm within range. They would usually procure a wagon or family carriage, load it with bacon, cornmeal, turkeys, chickens, ducks, and everything that could be used as food or forage, and would then regain the main road, usually in advance of their train [i.e., their brigade's wagon train]. When this came up, they would deliver to the brigade commissary the supplies thus gathered by the way.

Often would I pass these foraging parties at the roadside, waiting for their wagons to come up, and was amused at their strange collections—mules, horses, even cattle, packed with old saddles and loaded with hams, bacon, bags of cornmeal, and poultry of every character and description.

Unfortunately for Georgia, the army's raids were not to be confined to official foraging and to the regulated destruction of property specified in Sherman's published orders. Already in and around Covington minor infractions had occurred. By the third day of the march, the orders were breaking down. According to Union newsman David Conyngham:

A new spirit began to animate the men. They were as busy as so many bees about a honey pot, and commenced important voyages of discovery. . . . Foragers, bummers [unauthorized foragers], and camp followers scattered over the country for miles, and black clouds of smoke showed where they had been. Small lots of cotton were found near most of the plantation houses. These, with the gins and presses, were burned, oftentimes firing the houses and offices. . . .

The 20th Corps encamped near Madison that night. The cavalry had the advance, burned the depot and cleared out the town pretty well. . . .

Our troops entered the town next morning, and a brigade was detailed to destroy all the works around the depot and railroad track, also to burn a pile of nearly two hundred bales of cotton in a hut near.

While this work was being executed, the stragglers, who manage to get in front when there is plunder in view, and vagabonds of the army crowded into the town, and the work of pillage went on with a vengeance. Stores were ripped open; goods, valuables, and plate, all suddenly and mysteriously disappeared. I say mysteriously, for if you were to question the men about it, not one of them admitted having a hand in it.

Grinning Negroes piloted the army, and appeared to be in their element. They called out, "Here, massa; I guess we gwine to get some brandy here." The doors would at once be forced open, the cellars and shelves emptied, and everything tossed about in the utmost confusion.

If a good store chanced to be struck, the rush for it was immense. Some of those inside . . . would fling bales of soft goods, hardware, harness, and other miscellaneous articles through the windows. . . .

A piano was a much-prized article of capture. I . . . witnessed the ludicrous sight of a lot of bearded, rough soldiers capering about the room in a rude waltz, while some fellow was thumping away unmercifully at the piano, with another cutting grotesque capers on the top-board. . . .

The wreck of Madison was pretty effective. . . . All the stores were gutted, and the contents scattered and broken around. Cellars of rich wine were discovered, and prostrate men gave evidence of its strength. . . .

A milliner's establishment was sacked, and gaudy ribbons and artificial flowers decorated the caps of the pretty fellows that had done it. Their horses and the Negro wenches, too, came in for a share of the decorative spoils.

One fellow created a great deal of amusement by riding down the street, kissing and embracing a female form, which he hugged before him on the saddle, and then squeaked and cried [in the manner of a ventriloquist] as if she was kicking up a rumpus at such liberties.

"I say, Ned, where did you catch the prize?" called out one of his comrades.

". . . Up there [in the milliner's store]. There is a little colony of them in it. Go get one for yourself."

"I guess not, Ned, if she makes such a fuss as that one about it."

"Isn't there anyone in the crowd will protect a poor, lone female from such violence?" squeaked Ned for the figure. "Oh, oh! Is there any man here at all?"

. . . An officer who heard the appeal, riding up to Ned with a cocked pistol, demanded, "Halt, you scoundrel, and let go that lady!"

"Now, captain, I reckon I'm no more a scoundrel than you. And as to the lady, you may take her with pleasure."

Ned bobbed her around in a most helpless way.

"Dear me," exclaimed the captain, "she is in a faint."

"By hell, she hasn't a word," said Ned.

"Ruffian, hand her to me tenderly!" And the captain alighted to take down the poor lady.

Ned handed her to him, and then rode off. Fancy the captain's indignation when he found that it was only a wire and wax figure,

Black refugees in wake of Sherman's army

richly dressed for a show window. He soon let it drop, mounted his horse, said some very hard prayers, and rode off amidst the suppressed titters of the delighted crowd.

This scene lasted until . . . General Slocum arrived, when the town was at once cleared out of these marauders, and guards placed while the troops were passing.

The left wing [of the army] had destroyed the Augusta line along their march. The right wing had moved by McDonough to Jackson without encountering an enemy. The Rebels were making some little show to the cavalry on our flanks, but did not as yet attempt to give battle.

The Negroes were joining us in crowds. Near every crossroad and plantation, we would meet groups of old men and women and young children who received us with shouts of joy, exclaiming, "Glory be to de Lord! Bress de Lord! The day of jubilou is come! Dis nigger is off to glory!" and fell in with their sable friends in the rear, without even asking where we were going or what we would do with them.

According to Adjutant Hedley, whose regiment was a part of the army's right wing:

A corduroy road through the mire

November 18th the troops marched eighteen miles, crossing the Ocmulgee River on pontoons. Here some extensive cotton factories were destroyed. On both sides of the stream, for many miles, the roads lay through low, flat ground, sodden with recent rains, and the heavy wagon trains soon converted them into almost bottomless abysses of mud, entailing upon the men severe labor in corduroying [i.e., in making roadbeds by placing logs side by side] and extracting artillery and wagon trains. . . .

The next day the troops passed through the beautiful town of Monticello. No male inhabitants were to be seen, except young boys and infirm old men. The rebel conscription act literally "robbed the cradle and the grave," . . . driving into the ranks all who could possibly do any manner of military service, whether in the field, in garrison, or guarding prisoners. A few women occasionally peered curiously from their windows, but usually kept themselves well hidden from sight. The Negroes turned out in full force to hail their deliverers.

6

ON TO MILLEDGEVILLE

SHERMAN'S *first major objective was Milledgeville, nearly one hundred miles southeast of Atlanta. This town was of special importance because it was then Georgia's capital.*

In an unnamed village along the last leg of the route to Milledgeville lived Miss A. C. Cooper, a refugee from Atlanta. She and two friends, "Jennie" and "Kitty," were boarding at a house along the main street. It was not known in the village that Sherman's whole army had left Atlanta, the belief being that only a large raiding party was approaching. In Miss Cooper's words:

Thick and fast the rumors flew, no one knowing exactly from whence or whom they came. For three days there was a regular uproar. The whole country was roused; convicts from the penitentiary were taken out and armed; cadets, mere beardless boys, taken from school, brought out to resist the invader. The capital of the state was threatened, and these boys, etc., were to protect it at all hazards.

The excitement increased; we could neither eat nor sleep. Scouts were sent out up this road, down that, across the country. Everywhere the roads teemed with foam-flecked, hard-run horses bestrode by tired, excited men; and the greater part of these men were disabled soldiers who had come home to rest and recover, if possible, from grievous wounds. These scouts would ride into the village almost exhausted, and, not dismounting, take their food from the willing hands that would carry it out to them, then ride off again in the direction from which it was thought the raiding party would come.

Reports varied. One would be that the enemy would be upon us ere long, as a few bluecoats had been seen in the distance; and we women were advised to pack up and flee. But there was blank silence when we asked, "Where shall we flee?"

Ah, heavens! The hurry, the worry, the excitement! So much to be done, and no time in which to do it. Hurry, scurry, run here, run there, run everywhere. Cram this into an open trunk, ram that into a goods box, no matter if it does break in the ramming process.

Women cried and prayed, babies yelled and . . . went off to sleep with a sob, dogs howled and yelped, mules brayed, Negro drivers swore while Negro girls giggled, more from excitement and fright than from any mirth-provoking cause, and could not be made to do anything at all.

Our pretty Jennie ran about with her head tied up in a towel and packed her gray travelling dress with its jaunty plume of snow-white goose feathers into the box with the teakettle and stew pan, then rammed the molasses jug . . . into the hatbox . . . where it incontinently tipped up and emptied its contents all over her dainty lingerie laces and ribbons, cherished relics of her . . . attire before the war.

Kitty became angry and discouraged, and flopped down on a pile of half-wrapped bedding . . . and declared: "Yanks or no Yanks, raid or no raid," she would do "not another thing."

Just then Zip—one of the quarter Negroes—came running in . . . declaring that "Mars Jim Phillips wus out dar, an' his horse wus all of a lather, and he sed as how us all had better be a-gittin', fur he had seed de Yanks a-cummin', and dey had sot fire to all de houses, and wus just a-killin' all de fo'kes—wimmen and chillun, white fo'kes and niggers—an' you could hear their guns a hundred miles—'sides which some of 'em had horns!"

Of course, we knew much of this report was exaggeration, yet this fact did not tend to allay the excitement. Kitty jumped off the pile of bedding and began to work again, doing everything wrong, while tears streamed down her cheeks and her teeth chattered with fright.

Finding it impossible to work—even to pack anything—we rushed out on the front veranda and listened for the guns. We could not have heard [even] a cannon, for from every house in the village came the sound of weeping and heartrending cries. The streets were filled by crowds of frightened Negroes who, having no one to oversee them, had dropped the shovel and the hoe and were sharing in the general excitement. Some believed that death was imminent—these prayed and cried. Others had heard that they would be freed—these laughed and were insolent, obeying the orders of no one. . . .

Only one set of these Negroes were doing anything, and they were a part of the force belonging to the man with whom we refugees boarded, and they were burying the syrup—ten barrels—which had just been received; and the spades were flying fast in order to get it in and covered before the enemy came in.

Many of the white women were using the spade and hoe, burying their treasures—not gold and silver but pieces of home-spun jeans and factory cloth, intended to be made up for the soldiers; also home-knit socks, pieces of bacon, etc. The scene would have been laughable, had it not been so pathetic.

We heard no guns, though every ear was strained; saw no smoke from burning homes, though our eyes scanned every point of the horizon. "Mars Jim Phillips" had galloped away to take another look at the Yankees—if he could see any—for when his story was sifted he had seen none, only heard that they were expected. . . .

Ere long another courier—one who had served well and was at home with a useless arm—trotted in reporting the raid all a false alarm, so far as he could see. He had been out ten miles and heard nor seen anything. . . .

How we laughed and jested! How relieved we were! We had had all our packing for nothing.

But why did not the other scouts come in? There were eight or ten scattered about.

Very soon another drifted in—"No Yanks in sight." Another long hour dragged its slow length away, when the next scout galloped in with the news that two or three of the enemy had been sighted. Then the excitement began again, and the three scouts galloped off again.

Only two returned after a lapse of time, bringing with them a wounded Yankee! My God! It was true! The enemy were near!

Just then a train of cars steamed in filled with refugees as badly frightened as were we. We had some few friends among them who implored us to come on board. But how could we? Where could we go? We had but little money at this time, and we had no friends further south to whom we could go.

We decided to stay, and if worse came we could but endure it; and we watched the train steam out of sight, not knowing if we should ever see our friends again—if the truth be told, not much caring, for anxiety, care, and excitement had rendered us somewhat stolid and indifferent.

Only a few minutes had the train stopped. Then we turned to our scouts and the bleeding enemy. We hauled out a mattress, washed his wound, made him as comfortable as possible, and then turned to hear the particulars of his capture.

He had been captured by these scouts while brutally mistreating a defenseless woman . . . and had been shot—not by them, for they were bringing him unharmed to town, but by "Mars Jim Phillips," who suddenly coming upon them in the turn of the road, and who, under the influence of "pine-top whiskey" and fright combined, fired at them, thinking the whole posse were the enemy. The ball passed through the sleeve of one of our own men and buried itself in the enemy.

Then we learned the truth, the fearful truth! We were not threatened with a mere raiding party. It was Sherman—Sherman on his "march to the sea," and we lay in the course of his march.

We were indeed paralyzed. Had we not all heard of him? Like a huge octopus he stretched out his long arms and gathered everything in, leaving only ruin and desolation behind him. Had not the very heavens glowed with the reflection of the fires lit by his orders? Were there not among us, even then, those whose homes had been laid in ashes by his soldiers, and they themselves turned out without a second suit of clothing?

Sherman was near us. There were not twenty men, all told, to protect us. What, what should we do? We had packed for nothing. There was not a place to which we could flee, for that army would spread for miles. . . . There was nothing to be done but to clinch the hands till the nails cut the flesh, grate the teeth together hard, and wait. . . .

One by one the scouts came galloping in hot haste, verifying the truth of the near approach of the enemy. And—besought with tears and entreaties by the women . . . to save themselves, for we did not wish to see them shot down in cold blood—they galloped off.

We gathered in the street and watched the road down which the enemy would come. For some time we saw nothing, so we drifted back to the house and stood on the veranda. One man stayed with us, but he remained on the street.

All at once he threw up his hands and exclaimed: "All hell's turned loose! Save yourselves!" then turned and went down the street.

Just then we heard loud shouts, and the air was rent with pistol shots. Three of our scouts, their horses white with foam, flashed by shouting a good-bye. Bullets thick as hail whistled past and around us, burying themselves in the pillars and back of the veranda where we stood so paralyzed we could not move. Yet fortunately none struck us.

Then came a blue streak of yelling men, firing as they came—Sherman's cavalry in hot pursuit of the almost disabled couriers. While a part of them kept on in the chase, part of them rode their horses at the palings [of our front fence] and, bearing them down, rode up to the veranda, some of them even riding their horses up the steps. While these came in front, others had swept around to the back. And when we regained the use of our limbs and senses and went in, we were confronted by squads of bluecoats, who even then were commencing to search the house, their sabres clattering dismally up and down the steps.

This happened at sunset, and ere the shades of night had fallen . . . we women and the little ones were left at the mercy . . . of Sherman's army!

Since Miss Cooper ends her account at this point, it must be assumed that the women and the little ones were not seriously mistreated, and, further, that the village as a whole got by at least tolerably well. Miss Cooper surely would have appended any gross abuses.

On November 22, near the town of Griswoldville, one of the columns of the army's right wing was approached by a body of perhaps 3,000 Confederates, mostly inexperienced militiamen. With their combat-wise commander, General Gustavus Smith, being temporarily absent, the Confederates hastened to launch an attack. It resulted in what Sherman's aide-de-camp, Major Nichols, called "the most serious fight of the campaign . . . up to this date."

The enemy . . . advanced upon our troops, who had thrown up temporary breastworks with a section of [artillery] battery in position. . . . The Rebels . . . with the ignorance of danger common to new troops . . . rushed upon our veterans with the greatest fury. They were received with grapeshot and musketry at point-blank range, our soldiers firing coolly, while shouting derisively to the quivering columns to come on, as if they thought the whole thing a nice joke. The Rebels resumed the attack, but with the same fatal results. . . .

At the close of this fight the Union side counted less than fifty men killed or wounded, while, as General Smith laments, the Confederate loss

was a little over 600, being more than one-fourth of the effective muskets we had in the engagement. Several of the best field officers of the command were killed or wounded.

Union Major Nichols felt that the Confederate militiamen had received "a pretty severe lesson" and were not likely to try anything so heedless again.

Major Nichols, as a member of Sherman's staff, had begun to realize that he was in a unique position, that his observations were likely to gain historical significance. The entries in his diary, he explains,

were written during the midday rest of the army, on fences and stumps by the wayside, by the light of the campfires in the night bivouac, in cities or towns at which we halted, wherever or when-

A rail fence becomes fuel for campfires

ever a moment's release from pressing official duties afforded leisure to jot down the fleeting impressions of our long and wonderful march.

The Confederate cavalry corps under the young and energetic General Joseph Wheeler kept almost constantly active against Sherman's front and flanks. Not that Wheeler and his few thousand men were able to accomplish much. As one Confederate cavalryman put it: "The daily skirmishing . . . had no more effect than a fly would have on the back of a sea turtle."

It happened that Joe Wheeler and red-haired Hugh Kilpatrick, the commander of Sherman's cavalry corps, had been acquainted at West Point when both were preparing for service under the Stars and Stripes, and now the two men made a great game of their maneuvers and confrontations under rival flags.

The evening of the day of the fight near Griswoldville was unusually raw and cold, and General Sherman, traveling with one of the other columns, now nearing Milledgeville, sought shelter for the night in a log house where some of his officers had built a fire:

In looking around the room, I saw a small box, like a candle-box, marked "Howell Cobb," and, on inquiring of a Negro, found that we were at the plantation of . . . one of the leading rebels of the South, then a general in the Southern army, and who had been Secretary of the United States Treasury in Mr. Buchanan's time. Of course, we confiscated his property, and found it rich in corn, beans, peanuts, and sorghum molasses. . . .

That night huge bonfires consumed the fence rails, kept our soldiers warm; and the teamsters and men, as well as the slaves, carried off an immense quantity of corn and provisions of all sorts. . . .

After supper I sat on a chair astride, with my back to a good fire, musing, and became conscious that an old Negro with a tallow candle in his hand was scanning my face closely.

I inquired, "What do you want, old man?"

He answered, "Dey say you is Massa Sherman."

I answered that such was the case, and inquired what he wanted. He only wanted to look at me, and kept muttering, "Dis nigger can't sleep dis night."

I asked him why he trembled so, and he said that he wanted to make sure that we were in fact Yankees, for on a former occasion some rebel cavalry had put on light blue overcoats, impersonating Yankee troops, and many of the Negroes were deceived thereby, himself among the number—had shown them sympathy, and had in consequence been unmercifully beaten. . . .

This time he wanted to be certain before committing himself; so I told him to go out on the porch, from which he could see the whole horizon lit up with campfires, and he could then judge whether he had ever seen anything like it before.

The old man became convinced that the Yankees had come at last. . . .

Sherman left Cobb's comfortable cabin the next morning, having ordered the troops on the plantation to "spare nothing."

By this time the leading column of the army's left wing had reached Milledgeville, the state capital. Newsman David Conyngham witnessed the occupation:

General Slocum was received by the mayor, who surrendered the city, requesting that life and private property might be respected. The troops entered playing national airs, and their ban-

The capitol at Milledgeville under the Union flag

ners flying. Soon after, the Stars and Stripes floated from the State House.

Governor [Joseph E.] Brown had delivered a very inflammatory speech to the legislators on Saturday the 19th, telling them that the Yankee Vandals were approaching the capital to destroy, pollute, and devastate all before them. He exhorted and entreated every member here present to seize his musket and meet the ruthless invaders. As for himself, he was resolved to defend his home to the last.

His glowing philippic seemed to infuse a spirit of patriotism into the legislative body. The members loudly cheered, and went home to furbish their arms. A report ran through the city that the Yankee cavalry were approaching; and then all their courage . . . ran through their fingers' ends. They hastily packed their traps, and fled—Governor Brown heading the runaways—to Macon.

This was followed by a regular stampede, which was greatly accelerated next day by the appearance of . . . some ten scouts who made a dash into the town, scaring away all the men except the poor craven mayor. . . .

The women, of course, remained, but were saucy and indignant enough to fight it out themselves. One lady, whose lord had joined the retreat, and who felt very bitter at such a mean piece of cowardice, informed us how it all took place.

"The cowardly, mean set!" she exclaimed. "I tell you, I'd sooner see my husband dead at my feet than such a skunk. Some Yankee scouts came dashing pellmell into the town, when the men—the mean, craven-hearted wretches—skedaddled, leaving our baby mayor to surrender the town unconditionally to five greasy Yankees, ten miles in advance of the army! Faugh on them! The chicken-hearted wretches! And the mayor a puffed up old fool! Had I been in town I'd have collected all the women and driven the skunks out with mop-handles and broomsticks!"

Milledgeville, the capital of Georgia, is rather a pleasant-looking town, with a population of about three thousand. It is situated on a bluff in the midst of a fine cotton-growing country, on the west side of the Oconee River. Some of the residences are very fine, and built of brick. Delightful gardens, tasteful lawns, and spacious streets give the whole place an air of comfort and elegance. The Capitol, which is a very imposing brownstone building, is built on a ten-acre square in the center of the town, and is

Joseph E. Brown

flanked on each corner by a small but tasteful church.

Trophy-hunters, boisterous Negroes who did not know what to do with themselves and their freedom, drunken soldiers, all revelled now about the State House. The library was ransacked by the literati, and archives and books carried off in loads. . . .

Stacks of Georgia state money were found in the treasurer's office. There were millions of dollars there, the most of it not signed. The men loaded themselves with it. The Negroes fought over it, and "bressed de Lord—dey were richer dan poor massa now!"

. . . The fright of the honorable body of legislators must have been amusing. They scarcely knew where to run or what to do [since Sherman had marched his different columns in such a way as to spread confusion regarding his intentions]. They heard that our left wing was moving on Augusta, and they felt secure. Then Howard threatened them from McDonough, and they shivered again. Then our cavalry and right wing were striking for Macon, and they became valiant again and made fiery speeches of the last-ditch style.

News came that a column was moving right on the capital and the cavalry were in sight of the city. This was too much for the Falstaff heroes, and they fled in such confusion that the railroad cars became crowded to excess with furniture, private property, and goods; and fabulous sums were given for any kind of conveyances.... Buggies, barouches, and other vehicles fetched thousands of dollars....

General Sherman took up his quarters uninvited at the executive mansion, Governor Brown, with very bad grace, not waiting to receive him.

Sherman found the mansion in a curious condition. He says that Brown had hastily stripped it of carpets, curtains, and furniture of all sorts... even the cabbages and vegetables from his kitchen and cellar—leaving behind muskets, ammunition, and the public archives.

Again in Conyngham's words:

General Slocum had placed a provost guard through the city, with strict orders to arrest anyone found pillaging, and to protect all private property.

Colonel [William] Hawley, of the 3d Wisconsin, was appointed commandant of the post, and established his headquarters in the State House, after which all scientific and literary investigation [i.e., theft and vandalism] were put a stop to.

The only property destroyed were the magazines, arsenals, depots, factories, the penitentiary, which some lawless soldiers had fired... and storehouses, with near two thousand bales of cotton. No private property was destroyed, and the people began

Burning of the penitentiary at Milledgeville

to think that the devil was not so black as he was painted, after all.

As Governor Brown and the congregated wisdom of Georgia had taken a French leave of absence, and as striking events were developing, it was thought advisable that an extraordinary meeting of the house should be convened. In pursuance of said call, a full house was assembled. The halls and chambers were crowded with honorable members in blue. The meeting was held in the Senate Chamber; the subject under discussion was the reorganization of the State of Georgia.

Colonel J. C. Robinson was elected president; Lieutenant Colonel H. C. Rogers, clerk; Captain W. W. Mosely was appointed sergeant-at-arms to assist the pages . . . and others in keeping order and decently laying out under the table any member seized with Bourbon fits, which disease was rather prevalent among the honorable members.

The honorable body took their seats in the usual riotous, scrambling manner of such bodies in general, and with the strictest observance of legislative usages.

The business of the house was opened by a general drink, and a Committee on Federal Relations appointed . . . who retired and were soon engaged discussing the merits of a strong bottle of brandy. Snatches of song and laughter, which floated up from the committee room, proved that the honorable gentlemen were liberally and cheerfully engaged.

Pending their return, General Kilpatrick [Sherman's cavalry commander] regaled the convention with a full and highly embellished account of a very dashing raid he had made on a cellar.

"Though," said the honorable gentleman, "I am a very modest man that never blows his own horn—like other gentlemen whom I could name—I must honestly tell you that I am Old Harry on raids. My men, too, have strongly imbibed the spirit and are always full of it.

"I must confess that my fellows are very inquisitive. Having come so far to visit the good people of Georgia, who are famed for their hospitality, they live in the free and easy style among them. And if, perchance, they discover a deserted cellar, believing that it was kindly left for their use by the considerate owner, they take charge of it. It sometimes happens, too, that they look after the plate and other little matters.

"Coming to my own particular raid, it was one of the handsomest and most brilliant affairs of the war. I—"

"Mr. Speaker, I must raise a point of order. I believe it is always the custom to treat the speaker." This interruption came from a lobby member. . . . "Yes, I believe it's customary to treat the speaker."

And he produced a huge brandy flask. "I beg to inform this honorable body that I am going to treat the speaker." And he gravely put the bottle to his mouth and seemed to enjoy most lovingly its contents.

This interruption was received by cheers from some, and cries of "Order! Order!" from others.

Before the honorable gentleman [Kilpatrick] could resume his address, the committee returned, some humming, "We won't go home until morning" and "Marching, marching along."

A noisy debate ensued, everyone edging in his own words, the chief tenor of which was a strong wish of cultivating a closer acquaintance with [Governor] Joe Brown and Company, and regretting their unparliamentary absence from the meeting.

After several calls to order, the chairman of the Committee on Federal Relations read the following set of resolutions:

1. That [Georgia's] ordinance of secession was highly indiscreet and injudicious, and ought to be discouraged.

2. That the aforesaid ordinance is a damned farce, and always was, and is hereby repealed and abrogated.

3. That Sherman's columns will play the devil with the ordinance and the state itself.

4. As the Federal relations with the state are not very friendly, that a committee be appointed to kick Joe Brown and Jeff Davis, and also to whip back the state into the Union.

A lobby member suggested that Sherman's committee of safety, comprising Uncle Sam's bluejackets, would do that, and proposed that the reconstruction of the state be left in their hands.

The resolutions and amendments were submitted to the house, and were loudly ratified, *nem. con.*

The legislature rather hastily adjourned, after the style of Governor Brown, first regaling itself with Bourbon and brandy smashers.

Thus terminated the sittings of this important body of Yankee representatives, who had brought back the state into the Union *vi et armis.*

"I was not present at these frolics," says Sherman, "but heard of them . . . and enjoyed the joke." He goes on:

At Milledgeville we found newspapers from all over the South, and learned the consternation which had filled the Southern mind at our temerity; many charging that we were actually fleeing for our lives and seeking safety at the hands of our fleet on the seacoast.

All demanded that we should be assailed, "front, flank, and rear"; that provisions should be destroyed in advance, so that we would starve; that bridges should be burned, roads obstructed, and no mercy shown us. Judging from the tone of the Southern press . . . the outside world must have supposed us ruined and lost.

General Grant explains that the papers from the South

got to the North and had more or less effect upon the minds of the people, causing much distress to all loyal persons—particularly to those who had husbands, sons, or brothers with Sherman.

Sherman had no way of getting a reassuring word through to Washington, and President Lincoln himself was worried, sometimes to the point of preoccupation. According to an observer at a White House reception:

He was shaking hands with a host of visitors passing him in a continuous stream. An intimate acquaintance received the usual conventional handshake and salutation, but perceiving that he was not recognized, kept his ground instead of moving on, and spoke again. . . .

The President, roused to dim consciousness . . . perceived who stood before him, and seizing his friend's hand, shook it again heartily, saying, "How do you do? How do you do? Excuse me for not noticing you. I was thinking of a man down South."

Again in Grant's words:

Mr. Lincoln . . . had a letter written asking me if I could give him anything that he could say to the loyal people that would comfort them. I told him there was not the slightest occasion for alarm; that with 60,000 such men as Sherman had with him, such a commanding officer as he was could not be cut off. . . . He might possibly be prevented from reaching the point he had started out to reach, but he would get through somewhere . . . and even if worst came to worst he could return North.

I heard afterwards of Mr. Lincoln's saying to those who would inquire of him about the safety of Sherman's army that Sherman was all right: "Grant says they are safe with such a general, and that if they cannot get out where they want to, they can crawl back by the hole they went in at."

7

PASSING THE HALFWAY POINT

DURING THESE DAYS *in latter November, 1864, while the people of the North worried and speculated, a spell of Indian summer pervaded Georgia, and Sherman's columns advanced buoyantly on all fronts. According to Major Nichols:*

Thanksgiving Day was very generally observed in the army, the troops scorning chickens in the plenitude of turkeys with which they had supplied themselves. Vegetables of all kinds, and in unlimited quantities, were at hand, and the soldiers gave thanks as soldiers may, and were merry as only soldiers can be. In truth, so far as the gratification of the stomach goes, the troops were pursuing a continuous Thanksgiving.

Two of Sherman's columns, the Fourteenth Corps and the Twentieth Corps, were now marching along roads that would bring them together at Sandersville, about twenty-five miles southeast of Milledgeville.

Living with her mother-in-law in Sandersville was a seventeen-year-old girl, unnamed except for the initials "L.F.J.," to whom the war had brought an almost incredible amount of woe. Two of her soldier brothers had died of sickness. A third lost his right arm to gunfire. A fourth, only fourteen years old, came home with his nerves shattered. Her father-in-law and a brother-in-law both died on the battlefield. The youth she married in 1863 grew sick while campaigning, came home to recuperate (getting his first glimpse of a baby son), returned to duty, grew sick again, and died while she was on her way to his side.

Now, only a month after this last and hardest blow, this "poor little weary and worn child-wife," as she calls herself, was awakened in the dawn by a Confederate courier galloping through the streets of Sandersville crying, "Sherman is coming!"

Solemn and sad rose that November sun. Breakfast passed, untasted. Confederate soldiers were stationed in battle lines, even up to our front doors. Sitting in the parlor window, I could put out my hand and touch the files of the soldiers.

Soon the skirmish fighting began. Volley after volley was poured forth and returned by the advancing army. Now a horse came wildly dashing through the ranks. See—a dying soldier in gray is being dragged at the stirrup! Oh, God, how horrible that sight! Here falls a man—yonder others.

Wildly beats my heart, and regardless of danger I spring into the window, and would have sprung into the ranks below, when a Confederate soldier rushed into the room saying, "For God's sake, ladies, go into your cellar! Don't you know these bullets will kill you?"

For the first time I thought of danger, and told him we had no cellar.

"Go into the back rooms, then, and stand in front of your middle chimney. Here, take your poor baby and put him on a pillow in that fireplace."

Soon mother, myself [and baby], and the little Negroes were all huddled up at the fireplace, while the bullets rattled like hailstones against the house.

The fighting had continued but a short while when a second soldier rushed into the room where we were and exclaimed, "My God, ladies, we are fighting the whole of Sherman's army! We thought we were fighting a skirmishing party, but it's the whole army! Take care of yourselves, ladies. We'll have to run . . . or we will be captured."

"Oh, what shall we do? What shall we do? Please stay with us!" I cried.

"I would gladly do so, if I could do you any good, but they will take us prisoners right off. Lock your doors. Keep inside. If the Yankees come to the doors, unlock them and stand in them. Be sure to ask for a guard. Be polite, and you will not be mistreated—I hope. Good-bye! God bless you, ladies! It is the hardest thing I ever did—to run!"

I now looked out. Over the fences and fields our Confederates were flying. The last horse I saw leap the fences was that rode by the kind soldier who had come in to speak to us. One wave of his cap, and he was gone. . . .

The fighting was now over, so I ventured to a front window. These windows faced the two roads leading to the capital of Georgia. . . . Looking out, I screamed in horror. It seemed to me the whole world was coming.

Here came the woodcutters . . . clearing the way before the army [i.e., removing trees the Confederates had felled across the roads]. Men with axes . . . men with spades. . . . Men driving herds of cattle—cows, goats, hogs, sheep. Men on horseback with bunches of turkeys, bunches of chickens, ducks and guineas swinging on both sides the horses like saddle-bags. Then the wagons—oh, the wagons! In every direction, wagons, wagons!

"What does it mean? Have they stripped the whole country?" I thought. "Oh, we will perish!"

Then they began to stop, and I saw they would camp in our town. Now came the soldiers—cavalry and infantry. . . . I could easily be excused if I thought it was the world. Certainly the world was well represented.

Now the rush of Yankee ruffians! Our doors were well barred and locked, but they shook them so we knew they would soon break them down. So mother and I went to open them. Fierce-looking men confronted me. The veranda was full!

"Please, gentlemen, you will not harm women and children, will you?" I said—remembering that our soldier-friend had told us to be polite.

I don't know why, but they shrank back, while the man nearest me stammered as he pulled out a five-dollar greenback and said, "We want provisions. We'll pay you for something to eat."

Mother was indignant. She told him to put up his greenback, that he well knew they would take all they wanted—it was useless to sham.

But the fellow offering the money did really look ashamed.

All day long the men and wagons poured into the town. "Rip! Rip!" went the yard and garden fences, as they tore them down and pitched their white-winged tents at our very doorsteps. No yards, no gardens were spared in our ill-fated village.

Now the soldiers, with hateful leers from their red eyes, would walk up to the steps of the back veranda on which we stood, and, throwing down the hams and shoulders of our meat, which they had found, would cut them up with savage delight, in our very faces!

Next they found the sugar, flour, lard, salt, syrup, which mother had stored away in a cellar dug beneath one of the Negro houses.... The significant nods which they gave us as they brought out these things said plainly as words, "You see, you can't hide anything from Yankees."

Like statues mother and I stood looking on, and saw them take all the provisions we had, then kill the milk cows and other stock about the lot—saw them find the wheat and grain we had hidden in the attics behind the walls; stood silent and sad as we saw the "potato hill" robbed, and knew that now our last hope for food was gone.

Yet even in the midst of our sorrow and distress a laughable incident occurred. One of the officers had ordered some little Negro boys, who were following the camps, to catch mother's chickens. As they were running them down in the back yards, mother stood on the veranda looking at them. Involuntarily she sprang down the steps, ran through the midst of the soldiers out into the garden spot, broke some peach-tree switches, and started full-tilt for the Negro boys.

"You little black thieves!" she cried. "Put my chickens down! If I don't know what to do with Yankees, I do know what to do with niggers. I'll switch you good!"

The soldiers roared with laughter and clapped their hands in a hearty cheer as they saw the crestfallen look of the little darkies, who stood tremblingly holding out the chickens to mother.

An officer stepped up. Taking the chickens in his hands, he gallantly presented them to mother, saying, "Madam, had you treated my soldiers as you have these little Negroes, they would have been conquered too."

Mother blushed as she took an old rooster and several hens from the officer. But, nevertheless, she carried them into the house and pushed them under an elegant bed. There the old rooster and frightened hens sat, mute as mice....

That night we went to bed supperless. All day long we had fasted, for our breakfast was untasted because of excitement, and dinner we had none. What to do I did not know. Sadly I had seen the rice, sugar, coffee, and lard taken from the storerooms on the back veranda, but sadder now was the thought, "The cows are killed. I will be so hungry I cannot nurse Baby!"

I remembered that a sugar dish, full of nice sugar, sat in the china closet. So, I thought, I will get a stocking, pour this sugar into it, and put it, "a la bustle," around my waist. Then, if the Yankees remain after tomorrow night, I can get sassafras roots and make tea for poor Baby, like I had seen the Negroes make it. "To purify de blud," Maum Hannah had told me when a little girl.

Just as I had finished fixing up my sugar, one of the housemaids ran in, crying and wringing her hands.

"Oh, Missy, de bu'ful courthouse is all burnin' up. And dem soldiers say dey is gwine to burn dis town dis berry night. Please, Missy, you and ole Miss go out to de plantation. Dey will shorely burn you all up!"

Poor Betsy wrung her hands and wept bitterly. Now I shut my mouth firm and hard, packed some of Baby's clothes in a small carpet sack, and placed it behind the door, where I could easily put my hand upon it if I must go.

I had told the Masonic officers [on the premises] . . . that I was a Mason's daughter, had asked them for a guard, and they had placed one at either door. I now went to one of these guards and asked him if the town would be burned.

"Not tonight," he answered. "The courthouse is a signal fire."

Lonely and sad, mother and I sat around the little handful of coals in the fireplace that dreary night. . . . Husbands, father and sons, brothers—all slept under the blood-red turf, while their widows, clothed in weeds, sat hungry and cold at their hearthstones. . . . I hushed poor Baby to sleep on my exhausted bosom. . . .

Old Black Tom . . . had told us, at dark, that he would keep watch round the house and come to a certain window and tap every few hours.

"I'll tell you what's gwine on outside," he said, "and if anyt'ing berry serious am a gwine to happen, den I'll git you off to de plantation somehow."

About every two hours during that fearful night he would come under the fig tree which hid this window, and, tapping softly, say, "Don't be skeered, Missy. Dere's notting serious gwine to take place. Be easy and sleep, ef you kin. I'm keepin' watch."

. . . Dear old Tom!

. . . All . . . the second [day] of their coming, the army ravaged the town. Houses were entered, property destroyed or carried off, until mother and I had to divide even our clothing. Somehow we fared better than most of our neighbors. It might have been mother's peach-tree switches.

All over our town the campfires burned, until the stench of the garbage was intolerable, while the smoke was so dense we could not see across the streets.

At the close of the second day, as I stood on the veranda near our guard, my babe's low wail [from within the house] fell on our ears.

"Why does that baby cry so?" asked the guard—a boyish fellow.

"He is hungry," I replied. "I have had nothing which I could eat in two days now, and I cannot nurse him."

Tears filled the guard's eyes.

"I will be relieved soon," he said. "I draw my rations this evening, and I will bring them to you."

Sure enough, about sundown this guard came to our back door, tapped softly, and said, "Here is some flour and ground coffee. . . . Do have some food cooked at once."

I called our cook, gave her the provisions, told her to borrow some cooking utensils from the camps and prepare as good a supper as she could with this material. She hastened to comply, and in about an hour brought in hot biscuits and coffee. We had set the table as nicely as we could, and when the supper was ready I asked mother to let me invite my little friend, the guard, to eat with us.

"Certainly," she replied.

I went out to the back steps, on which he sat again keeping guard, and asked him to come in and take supper with us. Without a word of comment, he spoke to an officer in a tent nearby, asking permission to go to supper with me. Permission was granted, he was instantly relieved, and came to our table. So a Boy in Blue supped with the widow of a Boy in Gray right in the midst of the enemy's land, surrounded by the Federal army!

The young widow goes on to say that when the Yankees departed, only one of the family servants joined the procession of blacks in the army's wake:

This one was old Tom's daughter. He pursued her to the next town, found her, gave her a sound thrashing, and brought her home. . . .

If a whirlwind had swept over our beautiful village its streets could not have appeared more desolate, save that its homesteads were spared, though ransacked and pillaged. . . .

Our horses and cattle were all taken, our provisions all destroyed, a number of servants were to be fed. We could not dismiss these "faithful friends." Even though we knew they were free, [they were] homeless and penniless, [and] we could not send them from us.

It was now winter, too late for crops. What were we to do? The prospect was truly appalling to two delicate women. But we lived through it all. . . .

Sherman's columns were now about halfway to Savannah. For many units, the advance had become a more-or-less routine operation. As explained by Adjutant Hedley of the Thirty-second Illinois:

Soon after day dawns, the bugler sounds the reveille, and the sleeping army bestirs itself for another day's march. The men turn out unwillingly, half-dressed, to roll call, and then gather in little knots to prepare the morning meal. One reawakens the all-but dead embers of last night's campfire and piles on fresh wood. Others take a bunch of canteens and go in search of water.

Each man makes his own pot of coffee. The berry is laid inside a piece of cloth and broken on a stone under the blows from the butt of a musket; and the delicious beverage is soon brewing in the old tin oyster-can held over the fire at the end of a ramrod.

If the foragers have been successful the day before, sweet potatoes are baking in the ashes and a piece of beef, well salted, is broiling upon the glowing embers. Meat thus cooked would satisfy the appetite of the veriest gourmand. Scorching by immediate contact with the fire imparted a delicious flavor; besides, all the natural juices were retained within. . . .

An hour later the bugle sounds the assembly, and the troops fall in on their color line. Each regiment, brigade, and division has its appointed place in the column, and all move in an orderly way. The head of the column marches out promptly at the appointed hour. . . .

Well in the advance is a small detachment of cavalry, or mounted infantry, moving at a good pace. But they are argus-eyed, and frequently halt to ascertain the occasion of a suspicious circumstance, or to reconnoiter the road. Two or three ride in advance, their reins held in the left hand, their repeating carbines or Henry rifles resting across the pommel of the saddle, or held at the side, muzzle downward, ready for instant pulling to the shoulder.

A detachment of the enemy, also mounted, is discovered, and

Graves by the wayside

the main body of the Union [horsemen] are notified. Down the road the regiment charges, at a sharp trot, then at a gallop, until well within range of the enemy, when they break into a wild rush, urging their horses to the utmost speed, firing as they go.

The enemy turns and retreats until he reaches his supports, and then the Federal advance is checked. The Union skirmishers dismount, seek such shelter as the ground will afford, and keep up a sharp fire until the infantry supports hurry forward and seek the enemy's flanks. Meanwhile a few pieces of artillery open fire down the road. . . .

In half an hour the enemy vanishes. The Union troops resume their place in the column. An ambulance drives rapidly forward and receives a load of bleeding sufferers. A grave or two is hastily dug under the shadow of the trees, and the march is resumed until the next turn in the road, a small stream, a swamp, or a clump of timber offers opportunity for a repetition of the scene.

These events do not disturb the main column. At the halt the men scatter to the sides of the road. Some drop into a doze, others reach into their haversacks and munch a piece of hardtack, while here and there little knots engage in the mysteries of euchre or seven-up.

Presently a general and his staff, or a mounted officer passes by, and a running fire of interrogatories is discharged [by the troops]: "How far is it to camp? What's up ahead? What in the hell are we stopping here for?"

... The enemy in front has been brushed away by this time, and the column is again put in motion. The men plod along in a go-as-you-please fashion. Conversation, quip and badinage, interspersed with fragments of song and school-day recitations, enliven the hour.

There is no such place to learn character as here. Every man is weighed by his comrades, and his true value ascertained. His weaknesses may be concealed in society—here they stand fully revealed. Any peculiarity, good or bad, physical or mental, is detected, and fastens upon him some significant appellation from which he cannot escape. A particularly tall man goes by the name of "Fence rail" or "Ramrod"; a short one by that of "Stunch" or "Shorty"; while one of square build is known as "Chunky" or "Fatty."

But traits of character are more readily recognized than those of person. Here is "Shakespeare," so called from his habit of interloading his reflections upon current events with quotations from books read in boyhood. There is the "Professor," who at home was a country school teacher and crossroad lyceum debater. He commits the unpardonable sin in the eyes of his comrades—that of using a big word where a small one will answer equally well....

Here, too, is "Grunty," whose life is a perpetual torment to himself, for [as the result of his idiosyncrasies] he becomes a butt for the jeers and pranks of all his comrades.... "Hog" cares only for himself. Never a cracker or piece of tobacco will he divide with a comrade, and a dying man could scarcely hope for a drink of water from his canteen. "Slouchy" never carries a blanket or overcoat on the march, but depends upon stealing one or both when he reaches camp. He is intolerably filthy, and has not a friend who would sleep under the same blanket with him.

But these are the exceptions. The great majority have been formed in other moulds. Among them is "Old Bully," generally a boy—and who otherwise belies his name by not being a quarrelsome or overbearing brawler but the personification of companionability.... Here, too, is "Old Reliable," a slow-but-sure sort of a fellow, usually older and more staid than most of his comrades.... He is never without a needle or button, or piece of tobacco that cannot be had elsewhere in the regiment, and is ever willing to do a kind turn for a comrade and make no fuss about it.

Here, also, is "Firecracker," a lighthearted chap with ... a ready wit, full of quaint conceits, firing his jokes and repartee at his companions from one end of the day to the other. One such man in a company does better service in keeping his fellows in good health—so much does health depend upon animal spirits—than a dozen surgeons. . . .

Now the column descends from the high land into the swampy bottom, which tells of the nearness of a formidable stream. A small but well-equipped pioneer corps, generally composed of Negroes, has worked manfully to put the road in repair, but here the greater part of the army must lend a helping hand. Entire brigades stack arms and tear down miles of rail fences and carry them to make a corduroy road where the bottom has dropped out of the country—or fell trees by the roadside if rails are wanting.

The heavy army wagons and trains of artillery rumble across, the poor animals suffering cruelly as their feet plunge between the rails. Soon the extemporized road disappears in the soft ooze, and a second, and even a third roadway is laid. . . . Meanwhile, other large detachments are struggling with wagons or guns whose teams are exhausted, or which are sunk in the mud almost beyond recovery—lifting them out by main strength.

Farther on is the river. The skirmishers are exchanging shots with the enemy on the other shore. Now a couple of pieces of artillery are hurried forward and pitch shells across. The pontoon train is brought up, and under the protection of this fire the pontooniers launch their canvas boats, one after another, and connect them, until they reach the other side. The skirmishers run across, an infantry battalion close at their heels, and drive the enemy from the river bank. Planking is then laid upon the boats, upon which troops and trains pass over.

On the other shore the ascent is steep and the roadway is through thick, sticky clay. Hundreds of men apply themselves to the wheels of the heavy wagons and guns, while the army teamster cracks his whip and urges forward his weary animals with the choicest oaths known to the language. . . .

Nothing that ever fell upon human ears is to be likened to the complexity and comprehensiveness of the vocabulary of the army teamster. He knows the pedigree and performance of the mule, and every detail of its anatomy; and he anathematizes it from one end to the other. . . . He runs the gamut of oaths in every key, and with every possible inflection of voice, and then profanely apostrophizes himself because of his inability to express himself as vigorously as he thinks circumstances justify.

So the day wears away. There is no halt made for the noonday meal. The men eat as they march, or when there is a stop because of the road being blocked. . . . As evening comes on, the steps of the men grow laggard. . . . The jibes and jokes which have been bandied from man to man have died out, and there is only sullen silence or profane complaint.

Then the foragers rejoin the column, and their treasures of eatables unloose the tongues of the men and cause them to chirrup gleefully in anticipation of the feast to come with camp and night. Anon the martial music strikes up, a tremendous shout is raised, and the column regains its buoyancy of spirit and elasticity of gait.

At length the camping ground for the night is reached. . . . Turkeys, chickens, beef, and pork, vegetables of all descriptions, sorghum and honey, make a toothsome meal, and the severity of their labor gives to the men the heartiest of appetites. . . .

[Afterward] the men gather in little knots about their campfires . . . variously engaged. Some repair garments falling into pieces through long and hard service. Many beat the sand and dust of the march out of their shoes, and patch up, as best they can, the stockings which are so worn and ragged as to be little protection for their blistered, travel-worn feet. Others cook a fragment of meat or potato for the midday meal on the morrow, while not a few industriously thumb a deck of cards. . . .

The men produce their pipes and tobacco . . . and discuss the events of the day. In this symposium, the Bummer, who has been out foraging that day, occupies a conspicuous position. He is the gazette of the army. His rambles have led him among comrades belonging to other commands traveling far distant roads, and he knows all about what Slocum or Kilpatrick has been doing. This narrative, and his encounters with citizens on plantations he has visited, he relates in a graphic manner. . . .

The conversation turns upon the morrow—which way are we going, and what will we do when we get there?

. . . This subject disposed of, the boys would fill up the evening with such anecdotes and song as grew naturally out of the conversation. . . .

Meanwhile the men drop away gradually to their shelter-tents and blankets, each one seeking such a spot as may suit his convenience, preferably snug up against the root of a great tree. . . .

The campfires now die down; and, environed by hundreds of vigilant sentinels, the army sleeps upon another of its countless bivouacs.

Adds Major Nichols, writing in his diary:

As we journey on from day to day, it is curious to observe the attention bestowed by our soldiers upon camp pets. With a care which almost deserves the name of tenderness, the men gather helpless, dumb animals around them: sometimes an innocent kid whose mother has been served up as an extra ration, and again a raccoon, a little donkey, a dog, or a cat. . . .

The favorite pet of the camp, however, is the hero of the barnyard. There is not a regiment nor a company, not a teamster nor a Negro at headquarters, nor an orderly, but has a rooster of one kind or another. When the column is moving, these haughty gamecocks are seen mounted upon the breech of a cannon, tied to the pack-saddle of a mule among the pots and pans, or carried lovingly in the arms of a mounted orderly; crowing with all his might from the interior of a wagon, or making the woods reecho with his triumphant notes as he rides perched upon the knapsack of a soldier.

These cocks represent every known breed, Polish and Spanish, Dorkings, Shanghais, and Bantams—high-blooded specimens, traveling with [others] of their species who may not boast of noble lineage. They must all fight, however, or be killed and eaten.

Hardly has the army gone into camp before these feathery combats begin. The cocks use only the spurs with which Nature furnishes them; for the soldiers have not yet reached the refinement of applying artificial gaffs, and so but little harm is done. . . .

Cock-fighting is not, perhaps one of the most refined or elevating of pastimes, but it furnishes food for a certain kind of fun in camp; and as it is not carried to the point of cruelty, the soldiers cannot be blamed for liking it.

By this stage of the march to the sea, the term "bummer" had come to cover all the army's foragers, authorized or unauthorized. Years later, Sherman was to speak of even himself as "an old bummer."

Adjutant Hedley knew a man he considered to be a bummer of "the most perfect type."

Snipe . . . was a square-built fellow with light complexion and a

One of Sherman's "bummers"

tuft of red beard on his chin. He did duty as an orderly for the adjutant of an Illinois regiment. When rations became scarce, Snipe, of his own motion, and from a real love of adventure, added to the duties of his position.... As soon as the troops left camp in the morning, he would strike out for the day's excursion.... Snipe was often absent a couple of days... and when it came to be believed that he had fallen victim to his own venturesomeness, he would bob up serenely with an unusually large and excellent supply of provisions.

On one of these excursions, Snipe's absence was protracted into the third day. A short time before this, some of the bummers had been killed by the enemy's cavalry and their bodies left on the road.... Taken in connection with this incident, Snipe's demise was commented upon as a matter of fact, and a new orderly was duly installed in his stead.

About midnight the voice of Snipe was heard arousing the camp. Seen in the flickering light of the pine-knot campfires, he and his outfit presented a ludicrously striking appearance. He had six animals, horses and mules, strung together [in front of a wagon] with a motley assortment of improvised harness.... He bestrode one of the wheelers, and swayed in the saddle with an excitement which was in some degree the exhilaration of victory, but in greater part the effects of applejack.

His wagon was an immense box . . . high at each end and low in the middle . . . loaded to the guards with the choicest of wines and liquors. And, by fortunate chance, there was in the cargo a small box of glass goblets. Snipe at once had his wagon unloaded, with the boxes extemporized a bar, and grandiloquently called upon all hands to walk up and take a drink.

It is curious to note that every man in the regiment at once awoke and accepted the invitation. If they had been wanted for guard duty or fatigue it would have taken the sergeant-major, an orderly-sergeant, and a stout pair of boots to have awakened the very same men.

Samples of the wine were sent to corps headquarters, and the general [i.e., the corps commander] pronounced them excellent, at the same time intimating that a further supply [sent at once] would be acceptable. Snipe, however, failed to discover any reason for complying with the request, and by the assistance of some men from a couple of neighboring regiments, his stock was exhausted before daylight.

"It is impossible," states David Conyngham, "to enter into the details of the many ways an army can live on the country."

I . . . had a Negro servant—a very pious Negro, by the way. He was a kind of preacher, collected his "bredern" at night, and with them shouted out psalms lustily enough to take heaven by storm. . . .

"I'm gwine out [foraging], massa, wid de boys, and I want money." This was one morning when we were preparing to march.

"For what, Moses?"

"Well, you, massa, hain't a chicken nor butter for dinner."

"Moses, why can't you forage like the rest? I declare, our mess is costing us a pile, while others are living on the country."

"Dat's true, massa," said Moses, with a look of offended virtue, "but dis chil' never steal his neighbor's goods."

I stood rebuked by this unsophisticated son of the wilderness, and, feeling ashamed of myself, handed him a five-dollar bill.

In the course of the day, passing a poor shanty, I heard a great uproar in the yard and the voice of a woman in angry remonstrance. I dismounted in time to see Moses and our cook charge out of the yard [and ride away], both flanked with chickens and roosters tied to their saddles.

"Oh, the murthering thieves!" exclaimed the woman. "They hain't left me a morsel. They have even taken my blanket, and a little crock of butter, and a few pieces of bacon an officer left me; and myself and children will starve. And here is what they gave me." And she showed me a twenty-dollar Confederate note.

At night Moses had a very nice dinner for me. . . . The chickens were elegantly done, the bacon was rich and juicy. I could have enjoyed the thing immensely at any other time, but somehow the widow and orphans seemed to look on upbraidingly.

Moses, however, took it very complacently, and even rebuked me because I sat down without saying grace.

"Any change [from the five-dollar bill] for me, Moses?"

"Change, massa? I declare, dese 'ere things was dreadfully dear. Cost a heap!"

"Indeed! What did you pay?"

"You see, massa, she was a lone woman, so I gave her ten dollars."

"So I owe you five." And I took out a Confederate bill for that amount.

"This 'ere thing no good," said Moses, handing it back to me in disdain.

The treasure seekers

"You hypocrite!" I exclaimed. "It is as good as the one you gave the widow. And by Jove, if you practice any more on me I'll have you tied up and well flogged!"

Moses was quite crestfallen, and never asked me for money again. . . .

This is a mild case, and gives but a poor notion of the exploits of the grand army of foragers and bummers.

War is very pleasant when attended by little fighting and good living at the expense of the enemy.

To draw a line between stealing, and taking and appropriating everything for the subsistence of an army would puzzle the nicest casuist. Such little freaks as taking the last chicken, the last pound of meal, the last bit of bacon, and the only remaining scraggy cow from a poor woman and her flock of children, black or white not considered, came under the order of legitimate business. Even crockery, bed-covering, or clothes were fair spoils. As for plate, or jewelry, or watches, these were things rebels had no use for. They might possibly convert them into gold, and thus enrich the Confederate treasury.

[I saw] men with pockets plethoric with silver and gold coins; soldiers sinking under the weight of plate and fine bedding materials; lean mules and horses with the richest trappings of Brussels carpets and hangings of fine chenille; Negro wenches, particularly good-looking ones, decked in satins and silks, and sporting diamond ornaments; officers with sparkling rings that would set Tiffany in raptures. . . .

This rampant thievery, Conyngham goes on to say, was often accompanied by the wholesale vandalism of household goods and furnishings that could not be carried off; and, worse yet:

After all was cleared out, most likely some set of stragglers wanted to enjoy a good fire, and set the house, debris of furniture, and all the surroundings in a blaze.

This is the way Sherman's army lived on the country. They were not ordered to do so, but I am afraid they were not brought to task for it much either.

"It must not be supposed," Major Nichols reported in his diary,

that we do not meet many persons who claim to have been Unionists from the beginning of the war. . . . Almost every old man, when he sees his pigs and poultry killed in his very dooryard and gazes with mournful eyes upon the wagons that are filled with his corn, protests that he always was a Union man.

It seems hard, sometimes, to strip such men so clear of all eatables as our troops do . . . but, as General Sherman often says to them, "If it is true that you are Unionists, you should not have permitted Jeff Davis to dragoon you until you were as much his slaves as once the Negroes were yours."

. . . General Sherman is terribly in earnest in his method of conducting war. . . . He once said to a Methodist preacher in Georgia who had, by voice and example, helped to plunge the nation into war:

"You, sir, and such as you, had the power to resist this mad rebellion; but you chose to strike down the best government ever created—and for no good reason whatsoever. You are suffering the consequences, and have no right to complain."

While the General was speaking, his soldiers were rapidly emptying the preacher's barns of their stores of corn and forage.

On November 28, Nichols recorded:

Last night we camped near the house of a Mr. Jones, who has represented his district in the Legislature of Georgia. Mr. Jones may have been a good legislator, but he was certainly neither a

Bummers returning to camp and exhibiting their private plunder

valiant nor extremely affectionate man, for he ran away at the approach of our army, leaving behind him a sick wife and a child only a few days old.

He also carried away with him all his ablebodied slaves, leaving some fifteen or twenty helpless blacks, kindly informing the latter that "they were welcome to their liberty."

Several of these Negroes—old, decrepit, and destitute—came to see General Sherman soon after our arrival, soliciting his advice. One of them had lost a leg; another was bent with rheumatism; another was suffering under chronic chills and fever. All were ill from diseases contracted during the long period of their hard work and no pay.

These poor creatures said to our General, "We un'stan' dere is perfec' freedom to everybody, and dat we'se free wid de rest. Massa told us we might go along wid you. . . . But you see, Mister Sherman, we'se not well. We shall only be an encumbrance on you'se. You has a mighty long road to go ober, and we should be in de way. We'se cum to you for advice and opinion."

The General answered them with the utmost kindness. He said: "I approve of your resolution. It is excellent. As you said, you are already free. Yet, in your condition, if you are well treated, you had better remain where you are until the means of transportation are more complete. We hope to remove all of you one of these days. Meanwhile, do your work cheerfully and honestly, and you will be much happier for so doing."

Other groups were daily joining the caravan of black refugees in rear of the army. According to Conyngham:

Colonies, squads, whole families, from the feeble old folks, supported on their canes and tottering under heavy bundles, down to the muling infant in the mother's arms, while her back was burdened with a heavy bundle, fell in. The young and the old left home, at a moment's notice, to go they knew not where . . . in search of freedom.

Black children of all ages and sizes, I might add . . . toddled along in rags and filth, urged on by the application of the maternal rod. Babies squealed in their mothers' laps [in] old buggies and wagons that they took from massa. . . . Galled and jaded mules and horses carried hampers and bags, stuffed with children and wearables, balanced on each side. It was no unusual sight to see a black head, with large staring eyes, peeping out of a sack at one side, and a ham of bacon or a turkey balancing it at the other. . . .

At night . . . the men lighted large campfires of rails and fallen trees, and around these they collected in circles and partook of their frugal meal, if they had any. Then they all joined in a kind of hymn, "bressin' de Lord." Their finely modulated voices, chiming in one solemn chorus, rang through the still camp.

These blacks had little enough to be thankful for. Only those who could be of service as pioneers, servants, mistresses, or prostitutes won a ready acceptance by the army. To Sherman, the thousands that made up the majority were, understandably, an unwanted responsibility.

According to Confederate cavalry officer J. P. Austin:

When the crowd became too burdensome, the Federals would take up their bridges at the crossing of some river and leave their poor, deluded followers on the opposite bank, to ponder over the mutability of human plans and to cast a longing look at the receding forms of their supposed deliverers.

Conyngham affirms that at least one riverbank along the route to the sea was indeed host to such a scene:

The poor affrighted darkies crowded around the Jordan of their simple faith. But it proved to them a Red Sea, for Wheeler's cavalry charged on them, driving them pellmell into the waters, and mothers and children, old and young, perished alike.

Wheeler's men were to deny they harmed anyone, claiming that what they really did was to take the blacks into custody and return them "to the owners from whom they had been stolen."

Whatever happened at this time, there is no doubt that hundreds of black refugees abandoned by the Federals did perish, mainly from hunger, exposure, and sickness. In a scattering of lonely places amid Georgia's woods and swamps, says Conyngham, many a huddled group "shook off their shackles forever."

8

THE SACK OF A GREAT PLANTATION

ESPECIALLY ATTRACTIVE *to the marauding Federals were the great plantations owned by the rich. One of these was on the Ogeechee River near Louisville, about a hundred miles northwest of Savannah. Its mistress, identified only as Nora H——, explains that she and her elderly husband, Judge H——, actually spent most of their time in Macon, where they had another fine home, but were on the plantation during the days of Sherman's march:*

About the 24th of November we heard that Sherman's army were in possession of Milledgeville and were on their way to Savannah, burning and destroying everything in their course.... A few days afterward ... Kilpatrick's cavalry ... passed us, coming no nearer than six miles, and when they had passed we hoped the main army would do the same.

We thought it best, however, to take such precaution to conceal our stock so as to prevent them from being found if they should make us a visit, and stockades were built in the dense swamp of the Ogeechee—impenetrable, as we thought, to anyone not acquainted with the surroundings.

For several days squads of cavalry—Wheeler's command—would pass and tell us where Sherman's army were and of the depredations they were committing, and warn us to prepare for the worst, as they were showing no mercy; and on Sunday, the 28th of November, we heard that the destroyers were encamped just above our upper plantation, about four miles from our home.

That night the heavens looked as if they were on fire from the glare ... of burning houses, and early Monday morning a Negro man came from the upper plantation and told us they were crossing the river and that some of them were at Louisville, about two miles off; also that they were searching the houses, breaking open the stores and setting fire to them, and killing all the stock they could find.

He proposed to hide a number of hams we had hanging up in the smokehouse . . . and we gladly accepted the proposition. He accordingly dug down about two feet, laid planks at the bottom of the excavation and placed the hams on them, covering them up securely and putting syrup barrels over the place.

I told the cook to prepare enough food to last us several days, as we would not be able to have anything cooked while the Yankees were on the place. We also gave the Negroes a month's rations, thinking they would be better able to keep it than we would.

That morning Mrs. S——, the overseer's wife, and myself had gone into the woods and buried my valuables. Judge H—— was in the swamp at the time, having the stock put in the stockade and turning the fattening hogs out in the swamp, thinking they would be less liable to be killed running at large.

He had his watch with him. When he came back to the house, I got the watch from him and gave it to Mrs. S—— with the request

Federal foragers on a Georgia plantation

that she would hide it in some safe place.

About noon, just as we were ready to sit down to dinner, a little Negro boy came running in, half breathless from fright.

"Marster," he cried, "dey's coming down de lane."

"Who is coming?" asked his master.

"Two white mans wid blue coats on," the little Negro answered.

We left the dining room and looked out. Instead of "two white men with blue coats," we saw about a dozen at the Negro houses, talking to the Negroes. My husband went out, and two of them came up and spoke very politely to him, asking if he could let them have something to eat. They said they wanted some flour and were willing to pay for what they got.

They looked around the pantry and smokehouse, and one of them said, "You had better have those provisions carried into your house. Some of our men are not very particular to ask for what they want."

Another offered to take down some pieces of meat that were hanging up in the smokehouse and bring them into the house for me. I began to think they were not so bad after all, but I soon had reason to change my mind.

We hardly got the meat inside the house before hundreds of the bluecoats could be seen everywhere. One man came up to me and asked if I could tell him how long since the last Rebs passed the place. I made no reply to him, whereupon he cursed me and demanded to know why I did not answer his question.

"Don't you know that Southern women know no such persons as 'Rebs'?" another soldier observed.

"Then," said the first, "will you please tell me, madam, how long since the last Confederate soldiers passed here?"

I told him General Wheeler's men had been passing for several days, and that some of them had passed that morning. "I suppose," I added, "that they are waiting for you down in the swamp." And I hoped in my heart that they would give them a warm reception.

In our fright we had forgotten our dinner, and when we went back into the dining room everything was gone. Not a morsel of anything to eat was left. The dishes were all gone, and even the table cloth was taken. They no doubt were very much delighted to find a nice dinner already prepared for them—a large turkey, a ham, and various other things nicely cooked. We were too much frightened to feel hungry then.

As we were outside the picket line, we were not molested during the night. The army regulations were very strict, requiring all to be in camp before dark. . . .

That night . . . about 9 o'clock we heard a slight knocking on the window.

"Who is that?" asked my husband.

"A friend," was the answer. "I am a Confederate soldier."

Upon opening the door, a young Confederate officer came in. . . . He had been hiding in the woods all day and he came to ask us if we could direct him to a safe place in which to conceal himself until the enemy passed by. Judge H—— directed him to a place [in the woods] in which he thought he might hide without much danger of being discovered. The young man accordingly provided himself with some water and set out, having avoided letting the overseer or any of the Negroes know of his visit.

Early Tuesday morning the Yankees began to come in from every quarter. One could not look in any direction without seeing them. They searched every place. One of them loudly declared that he had heard we had a Confederate officer concealed in the house and that he was determined to find him. The intruders thereupon looked into closets, trunks, boxes, and every conceivable place.

One man came in and said, "I know you have got a Rebel officer hidden away in here somewhere. He was seen to come in here last night."

He accordingly began to search the bureau drawers and even opened the clock and looked into that.

"Sir," I said . . . just as he was about leaving the room, "there is one place in the room you have not looked into."

"Where is that?" he asked.

I pointed to a small pillbox on the mantel and asked him if the Confederate soldier might not be hidden in that. He turned away with a curse upon all Rebel women.

About noon some of the men insisted that my husband should go down to the swamp with them to show them where some syrup was hidden. He called a Negro man who had assisted in hiding it and told him to go, but the Yankees insisted that he should go himself. He told them he was old and feeble and not able to walk so far. One of them thereupon went and brought a mule and put him on it, and three of them started with him to the swamp. I felt very uneasy about him, but was assured by some of the soldiers that no harm would be done him.

While my husband was absent the destroyers set fire to the gin house, in which were stored over two hundred bales of cotton and several bales of kersey, which we had hidden between the bales of cotton. The granary, in which were several hundred bushels of wheat, was also set on fire.

The Negroes went out and begged for the cloth, saying that it was to make their winter clothes. The cruel destroyers refused to let the Negroes have a single piece. They told them they knew it was to make clothes for the Rebs.

One man, who had been particularly insulting, came up to me and laughed harshly.

"Well, madam," he said sneeringly, "how do you like the looks of our little fire. We have seen a great many such within the last few weeks."

I had grown desperate, and told him I didn't care—that I was thankful not a lock of that cotton would ever feed a Yankee factory or clothe a Yankee soldier's back.

He turned with an oath and left me, but after a few minutes came back, having discovered that my home was in the city of Macon and that I had heard nothing from there in some time, and told me, with a chuckle, that the army had passed through Macon, had sacked it and then burned it to the ground.

A rough-looking Western man was standing by, and he interrupted him.

"Madam," he asked, "have you friends in Macon?"

I told him I had a home and a brother there.

He then turned to the miscreant and looked him squarely in the eyes.

"Why," he demanded, "do you lie so to this lady? You know we did not touch Macon, but passed it by. God knows she will have enough to bear before this army leaves here, without being made the target of lies.

"I am glad you have a home outside of Sherman's track," he continued, addressing me, "for Heaven knows you will need it before many days pass. You will have nothing left here."

Just then I saw my husband coming up on a bareback mule

with a Yankee soldier on each side of him holding him on. He was brought up to the piazza, lifted from the mule, and brought into the house. They took him into a small room, and I followed. He turned to me and requested me to give the men his watch.

"Why?" I asked. "They have no business with your watch."

"Give it to them," he repeated with a gasp, "and let them go. I am almost dead."

Mrs. S—— was standing by, and I told her to get the watch. She, without thinking, asked me if I meant Judge H——'s watch, and I answered yes.

Of course, the Yankees inferred from her remark that she knew where other valuables were concealed, and they made her yield up everything.

I got my husband to his room as soon as possible, and found that he was very faint, as I thought, from fatigue. Imagine my horror, therefore, when he revived sufficiently to talk, to hear that the fiends had taken him to the swamp and hanged him.

He said he suspected no harm until he got about two miles from the house, when they stopped and, taking him from the mule, said, "Now, old man, you have got to tell us where your gold is hidden."

He told them he had no gold. . . . They cursed him and told him that story would not do. . . . He repeated . . . he had no gold.

They then took him to a tree that bent over the path, tied a rope around his neck, threw it over a projecting limb, and drew him up until his feet were off the ground. He did not quite lose consciousness when they let him down and said, "Now, where is your gold?"

He told them the same story, whereupon one of them cried, "We will make you tell another story before we are done with you. So pull him up again, boys!"

They raised him up again, and that time, he said, he felt as if he were suffocating. They again lowered him to the ground and cried out fiercely, "Now tell us where that gold is or we will kill you, and your wife will never know what has become of you."

"I have told you the truth. I have no gold," he again repeated, adding, "I am an old man, and at your mercy. If you want to kill me, you have the power to do it, but I cannot die with a lie on my lips. I have no gold. I have a gold watch at the house, but nothing else."

One of them, who seemed to be the leader, said, "Swing the old Rebel up again! Next time we will get the truth from him."

They then lifted him up and let him fall with more force than before. He heard a sound as of water rushing through his head, and then a blindness came over him, and a dry, choking sensation was felt in his throat as he lost consciousness.

The next thing he remembered he was some distance from the place where he was hanged, lying with his head down the hill near a stream of water, and one of the men was bathing his face and another rubbing his hands. For some time he was unable to speak. Then he heard one of them say, "We liked to have carried that game too far."

When he was able to sit up they placed him upon the mule and brought him to the house to get his watch.

When Mrs. S—— went to get Judge H——'s watch . . . the plunderers compelled her to guide them to the place where everything of value that we had was concealed, and she came to me when she returned to the house and, with trembling lips, said that she hoped I would not blame her. . . .

"I couldn't help it!" she cried. "They threatened to kill me if I did not tell. They said they had hanged Judge H—— until he was nearly dead, and they would do the same to me if I did not show them where everything was concealed. . . ."

Poor woman! I did not blame her. . . .

Oh, the horror of that night! None but God will ever know what I suffered. There my husband lay with scorching fever, his tongue parched and swollen and his throat dry and sore. He begged for water, and there was not a drop to be had. The Yankees had cut all the well ropes and stolen the buckets, and there was no water nearer than half a mile.

Just before daylight one of the Negro men offered to go to the spring for some water, but there was not a bucket or a tub to be found. Everything had been carried off. He at last found a small tin bucket that some of the Negroes had used for carrying their dinner to the field, and brought that full—about half a gallon.

The next morning, Wednesday, a rough-looking man from Iowa came to the window and asked me if he could be of any service to me. . . . I told the stranger that we had no water and nothing to eat. . . . He then left, and in about an hour returned with a wooden pail. . . .

The good Samaritan then took from his pocket two envelopes, one containing about two tablespoonfuls of parched coffee and the other about the same quantity of brown sugar.... I never appreciated a cup of coffee more than I did that one....

By the time Judge H—— had finished drinking his coffee, which he relished very much, and had bathed his face, the Yankees began to pour in from every direction. Everywhere one looked they could be seen. They were so thick in my room I could scarcely turn around. They took everything they could find.

One took the clock and started out with it. I begged him to leave it, and to my surprise he did. But in a few minutes another came and carried it off and threw it in the horse lot, where it was found by some of the Negroes and taken care of.

Not far from the house there were about a dozen banks of potatoes that the plunderers began to carry away by the bagful. They would come into the house, take any article of clothing they could find, tie a string around one end of it and make a receptacle to carry off potatoes.

My Western friend, the good Samaritan who gave me the coffee, came to the door and said, "Give me a basket and I will bring in some of those potatoes before they are all taken, for you will need them."

I fortunately had a basket in the room and gave it to him. He brought in about three bushels and put them under the bed on the floor. All the time he was bringing in the potatoes the soldiers were jeering him and calling him "Old Secesh." He paid no attention to their taunts....

Seeing Judge H—— in bed, some of the worst of the rabble insisted upon making him get up, saying they knew he had gold hidden in the bed and was only feigning sickness to keep it from being found. Two of them came to the bed and were about to pull him out when I implored them to let him alone, telling them how he had been treated, and declaring that he was not able to get up.

At last I cried out, "Is there no one in this crowd of men who will protect this sick man and prevent his being killed?"

One young man, about eighteen years old, from New York—Colton, I afterwards learned, was his name—stepped forward bravely.

"I will do my best, madam, to protect you," he said. "I have no bayonet on my gun . . . and they know I have no authority to act as guard, but I will stay by you and do all I can to protect you."

He took his stand near the bed and declared that the first man that touched either my husband or myself would do it at the risk of his life.

Just then a mean, cadaverous-looking man that had been very insulting in the morning rode up to the door and threatened to set fire to the house. He got off the mule he was riding and came in and began to curse and swear, declaring that he would pull the "old Rebel" out of the bed anyway.

I thought of my husband's being a Mason, and appealed to the crowd to know if there were any Masons in the room.

"No," the newcomer thundered with a horrible oath, "we have none of those animals with us. We left them at home. They are rather inconvenient to take along."

"My major is a Mason," young Colton whispered, "and if I can get anyone to stay with you . . . I will bring him." He then said, turning to his comrades, "Can I find a man who will protect this lady and her sick husband until I come back?"

The Iowa soldier whom I have mentioned before came in from the yard and offered to stand guard. "I will do it . . . but my gun is at my tent."

Colton then handed him his gun, advising him to use it and knock down the first man that dared to touch my husband or myself. He then left, and in a few minutes returned with an officer whom he introduced as Colonel Winkler of Wisconsin, who was the officer of the day. . . .

I was astonished to see the room and house cleared of Yankees almost in an instant. No one remained but Colonel Winkler and young Colton . . . and in a short time Colonel Winkler sent Colton to procure a guard, and we were subjected to no more insult. . . .

Colonel Winkler . . . seemed to regret very much the treatment we had received and said if any of the men could be identified they should be severely punished. He then sent to the camp and got coffee, sugar, rice, beef, flour, and other articles—enough to last several days. . . .

Wednesday night, for the first time since Sunday night, I lay down and slept. But my slumbers were not happy, as Judge H—— was still suffering from the effects of the inhuman treatment he had received. His nose would bleed, and bloody water would ooze from his ears. His eyes were bloodshot and pained him greatly.

Occasionally he would spit up blood, and his tongue was swollen. . . .

Early Friday morning we rejoiced to hear that the Yankees were preparing to leave. They were busy getting their army trains ready to move on. . . .

Everything was enveloped in a dense fog that morning. Nothing could be seen fifty yards off. In starting their trains, therefore, they . . . floundered about in the fog . . . and were going back the same way they came. About 10 o'clock, however, they got righted and . . . resumed their "grand march to the sea."

. . . Late that afternoon the guards were withdrawn, and the last of the Yankee army disappeared.

Our secreted Confederate officer came walking up just after dark Friday night. He had concealed himself during the four days in a cavity at the root of a large pine tree, almost entirely hidden by the small roots. . . . He had kept closely hidden during the day and rested himself at night by changing his position and walking around a little. . . .

The rear of the army encamped that night about four or five miles from us. We could see the glare of fires and knew from our own experience that the work of destruction was going on. . . .

Saturday morning we looked out upon a scene of desolation and ruin. We could hardly believe it was our home. One week before, it was one of the most beautiful places in the state. Now it was a vast wreck. Gin houses, packing screws, granary—all lay in ashes. Not a fence was to be seen for miles. The corn crop had not been gathered [prior to Sherman's coming] and the army had turned their stock into the fields and destroyed what they had not carried off. Burning cotton and grain filled the air with smoke, and even the sun seemed to hide its face from so gloomy a picture.

The poor Negroes had fared no better than we had. Their *friends* had stolen everything from them as well as from us. Their master had given them a month's rations, thinking they would be able to save it, but, alas, they had provisions, clothing, and everything taken from them. . . .

"Marster," they asked piteously, "what we all gwine to do now? . . ."

"I can't tell," he answered sadly. "It looks as if we would all have to starve together. . . ."

. . . One of the Negro women . . . was sitting on her doorsteps swaying her body back and forth . . . and making a mournful noise, a kind of moaning. . . . As we approached her, she raised her head.

"Marster," she said . . . "what kind of folks dese here Yankees? Dey won't even let de dead rest in de grave. . . . You know my chile what I bury last week? Dey take 'em up and left 'em on top of de groun for de hog to root. . . ."

Her story was true. We found that the vandals had gone to the graveyard and, seeing a new-made grave, had dug down into it and taken up the little coffin containing the dead baby, no doubt supposing treasure had been buried there. When they discovered their mistake, they left it above ground, as the poor mother expressed it, "for the hog to root."

We soon discovered that almost everything we had hidden had been found, and either carried off or wantonly destroyed. All around the grove were carcasses of cows, sheep, and hogs, some with only the hindquarters gone, and the rest left to spoil. . . .

The question of getting anything to eat was a very serious one. The stores were all burned, not one being left within thirty-five miles. The mills were all destroyed, or partially so, railroads were torn up, bridges broken. . . . There seemed to be nothing left to live on during the winter.

Oh! The first of December, 1864, is indelibly impressed upon my mind. We had more than a hundred Negroes to feed and clothe, and to all appearances there was nothing to do it with. We almost wished all had gone with the army, as there seemed nothing but starvation left for those who remained.

On Monday morning we saw in the distance coming towards the house a small covered wagon such as is used by the poorer class of people in the piney woods for carrying their produce to market. Walking by the side of it was a tall, thin man in his shirtsleeves and rough straw hat. He came up to the house, and Judge H—— recognized in him a man whom he had formerly known and befriended.

"Judge," he said, "when my wife heard that the Yankees had been here and destroyed all you had, she said, 'Mr. A——, we can't let Judge H—— suffer for something to eat while we have anything ourselves. Don't you remember how he helped us when we were first married? He gave us a cow and a calf and a pig and provisions to last us until we could get started. As long as I have anything to eat I will divide with him.' So she made me fix up the wagon and bring you something."

He then began to unpack that little wagon. There was meat, meal, flour, lard, butter, chickens, and various other things, enough to keep the wolf from the door for some time to come. Tears of gratitude came into our eyes, and we could not express our thanks.

Mr. A—— seemed perfectly happy to be able to give us this timely relief.

"Don't thank us, Judge," he said over and over again. "We are only paying our just debts."

Before the day was over, three more of those little covered wagons came up to our door on the same errand of love, and deposited their freight as expressions of gratitude to one who had befriended them in their early married life—as they expressed it, "helped them to get a start in life."

Verily, it was as "bread cast upon the waters to be gathered up after many days."

It was very gratifving to Judge H—— and dispelled the gloom and almost-despair that was settling down on his spirits. He seemed to take courage from that moment and believe that the God whom he served would not forsake him, but would provide some way for him to live and feed those dependent upon him.

9

CLOSING UPON SAVANNAH

BY DECEMBER 1, 1864, *Sherman's march, now two weeks old, had become the most dramatic and suspenseful episode of the war. Speculation about its outcome extended as far as Europe. England looked on with a particular intensity, for, as a voracious consumer of cotton, her sympathies were with the South. She had contributed large quantities of arms and other supplies to the Confederate effort.*

The London Times *said of the march:*

That it is a most momentous enterprise cannot be denied; but it is exactly one of those enterprises which are judged by the event. It may either make Sherman the most famous general of the North, or it may prove the ruin of his reputation, his army, and even his cause together.

To the British Army and Navy Gazette, *Sherman was a source of open concern:*

It is clear that, so long as he roams about with his army inside the Confederate States, he is more deadly than twenty Grants, and that he must be destroyed if Richmond or *anything* is to be saved.

The North was still apprehensive about Sherman's safety, though the newspapers encouraged their readers to look "for glorious events" to be shaped by "the lost army."

Southern papers continued to insist that Sherman was not only retreating but was in serious trouble. As expressed by the Richmond Whig*:*

Where is he now? We leave it to the Yankee papers to guess, supplying them only with the information that he has not found sweet potatoes very abundant in Georgia and that hog and hominy have not been served up for the entertainment of his bedeviled troops.

This kind of journalism brought no comfort to the people who lived in Sherman's path. Some condemned it roundly.

As related by the Union's Major Nichols:

I encountered an original character, an old man whom I will not name, but call him W.... A shrewd old fellow, with a comical build, he was evidently born to be fat and funny—as he was. I first saw him sitting by a huge fire our men had kindled out of a pile of pitch-pine timber, originally cut for railroad ties. His face was grave as a Quaker's but his eyes and the lower portion of his torso laughed most infectuously. He seemed to comprehend the war question perfectly, and expressed his opinions with a quaint volubility which kept his auditors in a roar of merriment....

"They say you are retreating, but it is the strangest sort of retreat I ever saw. Why, dog bite them, the newspapers have been lying in this way all along. They allers are whipping the Federal armies, and they allers fall back after the battle is over. It was that idee that first opened my eyes.... I allers told 'em it was a damned humbug, and now by God I know it, for here you are, right on old W.'s place—hogs, potatoes, corn, and fences all gone. I don't find any fault. I expected it all."

"Jeff Davis and the rest," he continued, "talk about splitting the Union.... Splitting the Union! Why ... the State of Georgia is being split right through from end to end...."

... Then, with a deep sigh and an expression of woeful resignation, he added: "It'll take the help of Divine Providence, a heap of rain, and a deal of elbow-grease to fix things up again."

In Sherman's words:

On the 3d of December I entered Millen [some seventy miles northwest of Savannah] with the Seventeenth Corps ... and there paused one day to communicate with all parts of the army.... The whole army was in good position and in good condition. We had largely subsisted on the country; our wagons were full of forage and provisions; but as we approached the seacoast the country became more sandy and barren, and food became more scarce. Still, with little or no loss we had traveled two-thirds of our distance, and I concluded to push on for Savannah.... [First] I caused the fine depot at Millen to be destroyed, and other damage done....

Major Nichols recorded in his diary that the burning of the depot was "a

Destruction of Millen Junction

brilliant spectacle" to which the men in the ranks were drawn with fascination. Nearby, however, was a less attractive sight, one "which fevered the blood of our brave boys."

It was the hideous prison-pen [now empty] used by the enemy for the confinement of Federal soldiers who had become prisoners of war. A space of ground about three hundred feet square, inclosed by a stockade, without any covering whatsoever, was the hole where thousands of our brave soldiers have been confined for months past, exposed to heavy dews, biting frosts, and pelting rains, without so much as a board or tent to protect them after the Rebels had stolen their clothing. Some of them had adopted the wretched alternative of digging holes in the ground, into which they crept at times. What wonder that we found the evidence that seven hundred and fifty men had died there!

Sherman departed Millen with the knowledge that somewhere in his front was a new Confederate force, but one whose numbers, he was certain, "could not exceed ten thousand men."

On the 5th of December I reached Ogeechee Church, about fifty miles from Savannah, and found there fresh earthworks which had been thrown up by [General Lafayette] McLaws' division; but he must have seen that both his flanks were being turned, and prudently retreated . . . without a fight.

All the columns then pursued leisurely their march toward

Savannah, corn and forage becoming more and more scarce, but rice fields beginning to occur along the Savannah and Ogeechee Rivers, which proved a good substitute, both as food and forage.

The weather was fine, the roads good, and everything seemed to favor us. Never do I recall a more agreeable sensation than the sight of our camps by night, lit up by the fires of fragrant pine knots.

On one such night, says an unnamed correspondent:

Sitting before his tent in the glow of a campfire . . . General Sherman let his cigar go out to listen to an air that a distant band was playing. The musicians ceased at last. The general turned to one of his officers: "Send an orderly to ask that band to play that tune again."

A little while, and the band received the word. The tune was "The Blue Juniata," with exquisite variations. The band played it again, even more beautifully than before. Again it ceased; and then, off to the right, nearly a quarter of a mile away, the voices of some soldiers took it up. . . .

The band, and still another band, played a low accompaniment. Camp after camp began singing. The music of "The Blue Juniata" became, for a few minutes, the oratorio of half an army.

Again in Sherman's words:

The trains were all in good order, and the men seemed to march their fifteen miles a day as though it were nothing. No enemy opposed us, and we could only occasionally hear the faint reverberation of a gun to our left-rear, where we knew that General Kilpatrick was skirmishing with Wheeler's cavalry, which persistently followed him. But the infantry columns . . . met with no opposition whatsoever. McLaws' division was falling back before us, and we occasionally picked up a few of his men as prisoners. . . .

On the 8th, as I rode along, I found the column turned out of the main road, marching through the fields. Close by, in the corner of a fence, was a group of men standing around a handsome young officer whose foot had been blown to pieces by a torpedo [i.e., a mine] planted in the road. He was waiting for a surgeon to amputate his leg, and told me that he was riding along . . . when a torpedo trodden on by his horse had exploded,

Lafayette McLaws

killing the horse and literally blowing . . . the flesh from one of his legs.

I saw the terrible wound, and made full inquiry into the facts. There had been no resistance at this point, nothing to give warning of danger. . . . This was not war, but murder, and it made me very angry. I immediately ordered a lot of rebel prisoners to be brought from the provost guard, armed with picks and spades, and made them march in close order along the road, so as to explode their own torpedoes, or to discover them and dig them up. They begged hard, but I reiterated the order, and could hardly help laughing at their stepping so gingerly along the road, where it was supposed sunken torpedoes might explode at each step; but they found no other torpedoes. . . .

That night we reached Pooler's Station, eight miles from Savannah, and during the next two days, December 9th and 10th, the several corps reached the defenses of Savannah. . . .

Savannah was located on a kind of peninsula extending eastward into the Atlantic, this strip of land lying between the Savannah River on the north and the Ogeechee on the south. The city fronted on the mouthwaters of the Savannah, with the Ogeechee's mouthwaters being about a dozen miles down the coast.

Sherman deployed his army from north to south across the peninsula, his left flank on the Savannah and his right flank on the Ogeechee.

Wishing to reconnoiter the Confederate lines in person, the general walked through a railroad cut that led directly toward the city:

About eight hundred yards off were a rebel parapet and battery. I could see the cannoneers preparing to fire, and cautioned the officers near me to scatter, as we would likely attract a shot. Very soon I saw the white puff of smoke, and, watching close, caught sight of the ball as it rose in its flight, and, finding it coming pretty straight, I stepped a short distance to one side, but noticed a Negro very near me in the act of crossing the track. . . .

Someone called to him to look out; but, before the poor fellow understood his danger, the ball—a thirty-two-pound round shot—struck the ground and rose in its first ricochet, caught the

William J. Hardee

Negro under the right jaw and literally carried away his head, scattering blood and brains about. A soldier close by spread an overcoat over the body, and we all concluded to get out of that railroad cut. . . .

As soon as it was demonstrated that Savannah was well fortified, with a good garrison commanded by General William J. Hardee, a competent soldier, I saw that the first step was to open communication with our fleet, supposed to be waiting for us with supplies and clothing at Ossabaw Sound [on the seacoast at the mouth of the Ogeechee, about a dozen miles below Savannah].

Situated on the south bank of the Ogeechee, barring Sherman's access to Ossabaw Sound, was Fort McAllister. It held fewer than 250 men, but they were determined to give a good account of themselves. Sherman ordered a division of Oliver Howard's command, that under General William B. Hazen, to cross the river, march down the south bank, and make an attack. Sherman himself remained on the north bank, taking a position at a rice mill where he could not only observe the fort but could also look down the Ogeechee for signs of the Union navy.

It was December 13, and Major Nichols wrote in his diary:

Rice mill on Ogeechee River used as observation post by Sherman

During the greater part of today the General gazed anxiously toward the sea, watching for the appearance of the fleet. About the middle of the afternoon he descried a light column of smoke creeping lazily along over the flat marshes, and soon the spars of a steamer were visible, and then the flag of our Union floated out.

What a thrilling, joyful sight! How the blood bounded when, answering [our] signal ... the brave tars ... recognized us and knew that our General was here with his army!

The sun was now fast going down behind a grove of water oaks, and as his last rays gilded the earth, all eyes once more turned toward the Rebel fort. Suddenly white puffs of smoke shot out from the thick woods surrounding the line of works. Hazen was closing in. ... A warning answer came from the enemy in the roar of heavy artillery. ...

General Sherman walked nervously to and fro, turning quickly now and then from viewing the scene of conflict to observe the sun sinking slowly behind the treetops. No longer willing to bear the suspense, he said: "Signal General Hazen that he must carry the fort by assault—tonight, if possible."

The little flag waved and fluttered in the evening air, and the answer came: "I am ready, and will assault at once."

The words had hardly passed when from out the encircling woods there came a long line of blue coats and bright bayonets, and the dear old flag was there, waving proudly in the breeze. Then the fort seemed alive with flame—quick, thick jets of fire shooting out from all its sides, while the white smoke ... covered the place and then rolled away. ...

The line of blue moved steadily on; too slowly, as it seemed to us, for we exclaimed, "Why don't they dash forward?" But their measured step was unfaltering.

Now the flag goes down, but the line does not halt. A moment longer and the banner gleams again in the front. We, the lookers-on, clutched one another's arms convulsively, and scarcely breathed in the eager intensity of our gaze.

Sherman stood watching with anxious air, awaiting the decisive moment. Then the enemy's fire redoubled in rapidity and violence. The darting streams of fire alone told the position of the fort. The line of blue entered the enshrouding folds of smoke. The flag was at last dimly seen, and then it went out of sight altogether.

"They have been repulsed!" said one of the group of officers who was watching the fight.

"No, by Heaven!" said another. "There is not a man in retreat—not a straggler in all the glorious line!"

The firing ceased. The wind lifted the smoke. Crowds of men were visible on the parapets, fiercely fighting—but our flag was planted there.

There were a few scattering musket shots, and then the sounds of battle ceased. Then the bombproofs and parapets were alive with crowding swarms of our gallant men, who fired their pieces in the air as a *feu de joie*. Victory! The fort was won.

Then all of us who witnessed the strife . . . grasped each the other's hand, embraced, and were glad; and some of us found the water in our eyes.

Having gained the key that opened the river to the fleet, Sherman exclaimed to General Howard, in the language of the black man he met at Howell Cobb's plantation, "This nigger will have no sleep this night!"

Newsman David Conyngham says that Sherman's features were "lighted up with joy."

Turning to one of his aides, he remarked, "Have a boat ready for me; I must go over there," pointing to the fort, which was now crowned with half a dozen battle flags, looking glorious with the golden light of the setting sun sparkling with a strange halo around them.

Sherman explains that he and General Howard went first to Hazen's headquarters, a house about a mile upriver from the fort:

General Hazen was there with his staff, in the act of getting supper. He invited us to join them. . . . Of course, I congratulated Hazen most heartily on his brilliant success. . . .

The fort had been taken at a cost to Hazen of about 135 men killed or wounded; the Confederates lost about 35. Present at Hazen's headquarters as a prisoner was the fort's commander, Major George W. Anderson, and he accepted an invitation to join the supper party.

Sherman goes on:

After supper we all walked down to the fort . . . held by a regiment of Hazen's troops, and the sentinel cautioned us to be very careful, as the ground outside the fort was full of torpedoes.

Indeed, while we were there, a torpedo exploded, tearing to pieces a poor fellow who was hunting for a dead comrade.

Inside the fort lay the dead as they had fallen, and they could hardly be distinguished from their living comrades, sleeping soundly side by side in the pale moonlight.

In the river, close by the fort, was a good yawl tied to a stake.... The commanding officer... manned the boat with a good crew of his men, and, with General Howard, I entered and pulled downstream [in search of the naval vessel seen from the rice mill]....

About six miles below McAllister we saw her light, and soon were hailed by the vessel at anchor. Pulling alongside, we announced ourselves, and were received with great warmth and enthusiasm on deck by half a dozen naval officers.... All sorts of questions were made and answered.... From these officers I... learned that General Grant was still besieging Petersburg and Richmond, and that matters and things generally remained pretty much the same as when we had left Atlanta. All thoughts seemed to have turned to us in Georgia, cut off from all communication from our friends.

Thus it was that Sherman himself made the first contact between his army and the navy. While down the river he wrote several hasty dispatches, including one to Grant in Virginia and one to the War Department in Washington. He also asked the commander of the fleet, Admiral John A. Dahlgren, to hasten delivery of the supplies he needed to press his investment of Savannah.

In a day or two, numerous steamers were pushing up the Ogeechee. Adjutant Hedley says they were greeted with "tremendous enthusiasm."

Soldiers and sailors who had never seen each other before grasped hands as if they were own brothers. Now supplies were distributed in lavish profusion.... Here, too, heavy mails were received, and the boys made happy by the receipt of letters from home in answer to those written from Atlanta....

David Conyngham calls Sherman's capture of Fort McAllister and the union with the navy "the consummation of his great and noble project."

It was the fulfillment of his covenant with his troops, when he told them he would lead them to a new base; and with the nation to which he had sent his last message [before launching the

Sherman's men hailing the Federal fleet

march] not to be uneasy about him, he would take care of himself. . . .

The results of our campaign were more glorious than the most sanguine could anticipate. We had passed through in our march over forty of the wealthiest counties of Central Georgia; occupied over two hundred depots, county seats, and villages; captured about fifteen thousand Negroes . . . about ten thousand head of cattle, horses, and mules; destroyed nearly two hundred miles of railroad; burned all the gins, cotton mills, and government property throughout the country; also about fifty millions worth of cotton and Confederate bonds and currency, besides supporting our army . . . on the country.

Sherman stated in his official report of the march:

I estimate the damage done to the State of Georgia and its military resources at one hundred million dollars, at least twenty millions of which has inured to our advantage, and the remainder is simple waste and destruction. This may seem a hard species of warfare, but it brings the sad realities of war home to those who have been directly or indirectly instrumental in involving us in its attendant calamities.

Sherman admitted that his foragers sometimes abused their victims, but added that "on the whole they have supplied the wants of the army with as little violence as could be expected." Murder and rape, as a matter of fact, were almost unknown.

Even as Sherman's troops were rejoicing over their mail from the North, the people of that region were rejoicing too. First to get the big news from Georgia were the city dwellers, many of whom took to the streets in the brisk December weather shouting, "Sherman has reached Savannah! Sherman has reached Savannah!" Some danced and sang, while from the church towers came a prolonged clanging of bells. The word flew from the cities to the towns, hamlets, and farms. Self-appointed couriers raced about the countryside on horseback and in carriages. Field hands cheered with frosty breath and threw their mittens into the air, and many a family knelt for thanksgiving prayers before the broad kitchen hearth, faces joyous in the firelight.

After three years and eight months of civil war, the foundations of the Confederacy were crumbling. The ascendancy of the Union seemed assured at last.

10

A CHRISTMAS GIFT FOR LINCOLN

WITH THE FALL *of Fort McAllister, Sherman considered Savannah to be as good as gained. Not that the city's defenses were weak. Many of the trenches and gun emplacements were not only abatised—that is, protected by tangles of felled trees—but also had flooded rice fields in their front. The Confederate garrison, however, numbered only about 10,000 men.*

With artillery and musket fire crashing on both sides, Sherman tightened his great river-to-river semicircle. His right, or southern flank, was at Fort McAllister on the Ogeechee, and his left, or northern flank, was on Hutchinson's Island in the Savannah. His left was the closer to the city.

Relates David Conyngham:

There were some four or five mills on Hutchinson's Island, which were busily employed for the benefit of *le grande armée* [i.e., Sherman's army], and particularly for the support of the Negroes, who were quartered here, living on rice. This is a low, swampy, miserable rice island, four miles long and one broad.... The shore around is low and marshy, liberally colonized by alligators.

Only the upriver, or western portion of the island was occupied by the Federals. The downriver portion extended past the northern flank of the defenses about Savannah. Conyngham goes on to explain that a Union officer was sent on a reconnaissance down the island "in order to view the rear of the enemy's works."

He struck upon a colony of escaped Negroes, who hailed him as the savages did Captain Cook.... They showered blessings, sweet potatoes, and rice indiscriminately upon him. They sang hymns, danced, and capered, and could scarcely believe their senses when told that they were free. I am afraid that the idea of freedom was a very vague one to most of them. Their perception of it was something about changing places with their masters.

General Sherman had intimated to military commanders that the first one that would enter Savannah should be military governor. This helped to wake up the troops wonderfully. Men would build little platforms and bridges on logs, advancing them every night, or crawl along trees, until they approached within pistol range of the enemy, and pick them off from their guns.

On the 17th December, General Sherman addressed a note to Lieutenant General W. J. Hardee, demanding a surrender of Savannah and all it contained.... He informed Hardee that he had the city closely invested, and that there was no chance of its holding out. Hardee replied ... to the effect that he ... could hold out as long as he chose.

Actually, Hardee had no intention of making a determined stand. He was planning to take his little army northward across the Savannah River into South Carolina.

As explained by Hardee's chief of artillery, Colonel Charles C. Jones, Jr.:

The evacuation of Savannah having been resolved upon, and it being impossible by means of the few steamboats and river craft at command to convey the garrison, artillery, and requisite stores with convenience and safety to Screven's Ferry [on the Carolina bank], orders were issued for the immediate construction of suitable pontoon bridges.

The line of retreat selected by the engineers ... involved the location of a pontoon bridge extending from the foot of West Broad Street to Hutchinson's Island, a distance of about a thousand feet, a roadway across that island in the direction of Pennyworth Island, a second pontoon bridge across the Middle River, another roadway across Pennyworth Island, and a third pontoon bridge across Back River, the further end of which should rest upon the rice field on the Carolina shore....

All available rice-field flats were collected. These were [towed by steamboats and] swung into position with the tide, lashed end to end ... and were kept in their places by [railroad] car wheels, the only anchors which could be procured. Above ... was a flooring of plank obtained from the city wharves.

Hardee's troops evacuating Savannah

At eight o'clock on the evening of the 17th the first pontoon bridge, spanning the Savannah River from the foot of West Broad Street to Hutchinson's Island was completed, and by half past eight o'clock P.M. on Monday the 19th the remaining bridges were finished and the route was in readiness for the retreat. . . .

The utmost activity prevailed in [Sherman's] army of investment. Arrangements were being rapidly consummated for the contemplated bombardment [of the city] and for a combined and powerful assault upon the Confederate lines. Strong works for the heavy guns were constructed at commanding points, and field guns were masked, in some instances, within one hundred and fifty yards of our entrenchments. Light bridges and fascines [i.e., bundles of sticks and straw] were accumulated with which to span the deepest portions of the inundated fields and fill the ditches and canals. . . . General Sherman . . . [was busy also] with plans for interrupting the only line of retreat open to the Confederates. . . .

The pontoon bridges having been completed and the line of retreat perfected, carefully digested orders were promulgated by General Hardee for the evacuation. . . . A more liberal expenditure of ammunition was sanctioned, and the fire of our batteries increased at every available point until the shades of night on the

20th settled upon the contending lines. . . .

Our troops were quietly withdrawn in the order and at the hours indicated in the circular issued by Lieutenant General Hardee. There was no confusion, and all movements were executed promptly and in silence. Abandoned guns were spiked, their carriages disabled, and all ammunition destroyed so far as this could be done without attracting the attention of the enemy. . . . To conceal our operations, occasional firing was maintained until the latest moment. . . . In order to deaden the sound [of the march], rice straw was thickly strewn over the pontoon bridges.

As the army moved out, Commodore Josiah Tattnall, commander of Savannah's fleet, began destroying his vessels. One was sunk, others set afire. Two or three gunboats, still in the process of construction in the city's navy yard, were ignited in their stocks. A temporary survivor among the active boats was the ironclad Savannah, *engaged in removing stores to the Carolina shore.*

Colonel Jones continues:

By three o'clock on the morning of the 21st the rear guard of the Confederate army had crossed over to Hutchinson's Island. . . . Engineer troops shortly afterwards detached the flats, cutting holes in them and setting them adrift. . . . During its march over the pontoon bridges, across the rice fields, and [to] the high ground in South Carolina . . . the retiring Confederate army en-

Confederates burning the Savannah navy yard

countered no opposition at the hands of the Federals.

But Union General John W. Geary, commander of the division entrenched on the riverbank just above Savannah, at least suspected what had happened. During lulls in the enemy's covering fire, he had cocked his ear in the dark and had picked up some of the noises made by the enemy's wagons on the pontoon bridges. He received also a visual indication as the fires on Commodore Tattnall's vessels began to grow.

Geary, according to David Conyngham,

advanced his pickets, who, meeting no opposition, pushed still farther, crawled through the abatis, floundered through dikes and ditches, scaled the first line of works, and found it deserted. General Geary pushed on his division. . . .

Says Geary himself:

Just outside of the city limits . . . I met the mayor of Savannah and a delegation from the board of aldermen, bearing a flag of truce. From them I received, in the name of my commanding general, the surrender of the city. . . . My entire division entered the city of Savannah at early dawn, and before the sun first gilded the morning clouds our National colors, side by side with those of my own division, were unfurled from the dome of the Exchange

View in the city during the occupation

and over the U.S. Customs House.

[Colonel Henry A.] Barnum's brigade, which led in entering the city, was at once ordered to patrol it, reduce it to order and quiet, and prevent any pillaging or lawlessness on the part either of soldiers or citizens. My orders on the subject were very strict, and within a few hours this city, in which I had found a lawless mob of low whites and Negroes pillaging and setting fire to property, was reduced to order....

Two regiments... were sent down to Fort Jackson [on the city's seaward side], and early in the morning had possession of it and all the intermediate and surrounding works. The iron-plated ram *Savannah,* which lay in the river below the city, threw a few shells at these two regiments as they flung the Stars and Stripes to the breeze from the walls of Fort Jackson. All the other gunboats of the enemy had been... burned to the water's edge.

Geary's division was joined by additional regiments from outside the city as the day wore on. They marched in with flags flying and bands playing, and with many of the men whooping and shouting. In general, however, the order established by Geary was maintained, much to the surprise and gratification of the citizens, the majority of whom watched from indoors.

"The poor classes," David Conyngham noted, "were grouped around, apparently well pleased with the change, for they had nothing to lose, and had suffered much during the war."

That night, the newsman goes on to say,

the *Savannah,* after kicking up a rumpus all day and sailing up and down in mock defiance of our light guns, was blown up by her commander, who sent his crew on shore [on the Carolina side] and fired the magazine. First came a flash of light; then, as if from the crater of a volcano, an immense volume of flame shot up, illumining the heavens for miles; then came the fearful report, and the rebel ram *Savannah* was no more. The concussion was fearful, rocking the city and the vessels at anchor [these being the city's commercial vessels, which hadn't been included in Commodore Tattnall's destruction order].

Sherman entered Savannah the next morning, December 22:

I... rode down Bull Street to the custom house, from the roof of which we had an extensive view over the city, the river, and the vast extent of marsh and rice fields on the South Carolina side.

Sherman's Savannah headquarters

The navy yard and the wreck of the ironclad ram *Savannah* were still smouldering, but all else looked quiet enough. . . .

I was disappointed that Hardee had escaped with his army, but on the whole we had reason to be content with the substantial fruits of victory.

Establishing his headquarters in a large, conveniently located house, Sherman sent the following telegram to President Lincoln:

I beg to present you as a Christmas gift the city of Savannah, with one hundred and fifty heavy guns and plenty of ammunition, also about twenty-five thousand bales of cotton.

"This message," Sherman explains, "actually reached him on Christmas Eve, was extensively published in the newspapers, and made many a household unusually happy on that festive day."

It was only about a week earlier that the North had received word of another Union victory in the South. In mid-December General George Thomas, detached by Sherman to counter John Hood's invasion of Tennessee, had crushed Hood at Nashville. This victory was necessary to make Sherman's complete.

Lincoln replied to Sherman:

Many, many thanks for your Christmas gift—the capture of Savannah.

When you were about leaving Atlanta for the Atlantic Coast, I was anxious, if not fearful; but feeling that you were the better judge, and remembering that "nothing risked, nothing gained," I did not interfere. Now, the undertaking being a success, the honor is all yours; for I believe none of us went further than to acquiesce. And taking the work of General Thomas into account, as it should be taken, it is indeed a great success. . . .

But what next? I suppose it will be safe if I leave General Grant and yourself to decide.

Grant's earliest idea, submitted to Sherman as soon as he reached the coast, had been for him to bring his army to Virginia by sea. But Sherman had won Grant over to his own plan, having written:

With Savannah in our possession . . . we can punish South Carolina as she deserves, and as thousands of people in Georgia hope we will do [South Carolina being in bad favor for having led the ill-faring secession movement]. I do sincerely believe that the whole United States, North and South, would rejoice to have this army turned loose on South Carolina, to devastate that state in the manner we have done in Georgia, and it would have a direct and immediate bearing on your campaign in Virginia.

Sherman made no apology for his seemingly vengeful attitude. The South had only to surrender, he reiterated, and all his acts against her would cease.

With Grant still stalled before Lee's lines at Richmond and Petersburg, the siege being all of six months old, Sherman seemed all the more successful, and his stock soared. Congress tendered him its thanks, and there was talk of making him at least Grant's equal in the army's command structure, perhaps even his superior. Sherman was pleased with the resolution of thanks, but stated firmly: "I will accept no commission that would tend to create a rivalry with Grant."

Sherman called Grant "a great general," adding in his bluff way: "He stood by me when I was crazy, and I stood by him when he was drunk. And now, by thunder, we stand by each other!"

As for Savannah, it became both an army and a navy base, the navy bringing in supplies from the North. Sherman's aide, Major Nichols, reported in his diary that "hundreds of vessels" were scattered over the surface of the river:

Ships are unloading at the piers; steamboats are surging painfully against the tide; rafts and rowboats are filled with curious soldiers who are enjoying the novel spectacle of a seaport for the first time.

The city's historical connections fascinated many of the Yankees. David Conyngham took a particular interest in its role during the Revolutionary War:

It fell into the hands of the English in 1778, but was recovered in 1783. Though the old mounds and ditches and forts of Revolutionary times are now obliterated, new ones have sprung up in their places to excite the curiosity of other men and other times.

Sherman had known the city during his days as a young lieutenant, and was pleased to see again its "large yards, ornamented with shrubbery and flowers," and the streets and parks that were lined with willow-leaf live oaks, which he considered to be "the handsomest shade trees" he had ever ridden beneath.

"It was estimated," Sherman explains,

that there were about twenty thousand inhabitants in Savannah, all of whom had participated more or less in the war and had no special claims to our favor, but . . . I concluded to give them the option to remain or to join their friends in Charleston or Augusta, and so announced in general orders.

The mayor . . . was completely "subjugated," and, after consulting with him I authorized him to assemble his City Council to take charge generally of the interests of the people; but warned all who remained that they must be strictly subordinate to the military law and to the interests of the General Government. . . .

The great bulk of the inhabitants chose to remain in Savannah, generally behaved with propriety; and good social relations at once arose between them and the army. . . .

As the division of Major General John W. Geary, of the Twentieth Corps, was the first to enter Savannah, that officer was appointed to command the place, or to act as a sort of governor. He very soon established a good police [and] maintained admirable order. . . .

The guard-mountings and parades, as well as the greater reviews, became the daily resort of the ladies, to hear the music of our excellent bands. Schools were opened, and the churches every Sunday were well filled with most devout and respectful congregations. Stores were reopened, and markets for provisions, meat, wood, etc., were established, so that each family, regardless of race, color, or opinion, could procure all the necessaries and even luxuries of life, provided they had money. Of course, many families were actually destitute of this, and to these were issued stores from our own stock of supplies.

The women, particularly the younger ones, grew in their cordiality toward the army. "Each little knot of soldiers," says Adjutant Hedley, "made acquaintance with fair ones, glad to entertain and be entertained with cards, dance, and song."

There were, of course, notable exceptions—women who, for example, stepped off the pavement and walked in the street rather than pass under a Union flag flying from an upper window.

Sherman had little patience with these diehards, particularly since he knew they had much to do with prolonging the war. In the face of almost certain defeat, they were urging the men at the front to keep fighting.

While on the street one day, Sherman was accosted by a woman who said, "General, you may conquer, but you can't subjugate us."

He snapped back, "I don't want to subjugate you; I mean to kill you, the whole of you, if you don't stop this rebellion!"

About this same time, Sherman wrote in a private letter:

I do not think a human being could feel more kindly toward an enemy than I do to the people of the South, and I only pray that I may live to see the day when they and their children will thank me as one who labored to secure and maintain a government worthy the land we have inherited.

Major Nichols avers that the children of Savannah, at least, were already on the warmest of terms with Sherman:

His headquarters and private room became the playground of hosts of little ones, upon whom the door was never closed, no matter what business was pending.

During the earliest days of the occupation, Sherman encountered a curious situation. Almost everywhere he rode he saw buildings flying the British flag. That nation's consul seemed to have offices in profusion.

According to an unnamed newspaper correspondent:

General Sherman soon ascertained that these flags were on buildings where cotton had been stored away, and at once ordered it to be seized.

Soon after that, while the general was busily engaged at his headquarters, a pompous gentleman hastened in and inquired if he was General Sherman.

Having received an affirmative reply, the pompous gentleman remarked that when he left his residence the United States troops were engaged in removing his cotton from it, where it was protected by the British flag.

"Stop, sir!" said General Sherman. "Not *your* cotton, but *my* cotton—my cotton in the name of the United States Government. I have noticed a great many British flags here, all protecting cotton. I have seized all of it in the name of my government."

"But, sir," said the consul indignantly, "there is scarcely any cotton in Savannah that does not belong to me."

"There is not a pound of cotton here, sir, that does not belong to *me,* for the United States," responded Sherman.

"Well, sir," said the consul, swelling himself up with the dignity of his office and reddening in the face, "my government shall hear of this. I shall report your conduct to my government."

"Ah! Pray, who are you, sir?"

"Consul to Her British Majesty."

"Oh, indeed!" responded the general. "I hope you *will* report me to your government. You will please say for me that I have been fighting the English Government all the way from the Ohio River to Vicksburg, and thence to this point. At every step I have encountered British arms and British goods of every description. And now, sir, I find you claiming all the cotton. I intend to call on *my* government to order me to Nassau at once."

[The capital of England's Bahama Islands, Nassau was a port much used by vessels whose object was to run the Union navy's blockade of the Southern coast, the means by which England gained cotton in exchange for supplies that helped support the Confederacy.]

"What do you propose to do there?" asked the consul, somewhat taken aback.

"I will," replied the general, "take with me a quantity of picks and shovels, and throw that cursed sand hill into the sea, sir. You may tell *that* to your government.... Good day, sir!"

It is needless to add that General Sherman was not again troubled by officious representatives of Her Majesty's Government.

On December 28 a Union soldier wrote in his diary:

Last night a rebel blockade runner came into port, not having heard that the city had changed hands, with a cargo of tea, coffee, sugar, and bacon. This morning when they saw the Stars and Stripes floating over town they realized the situation and surrendered as gracefully as possible.

Sherman, who intended to save Savannah's cotton for disposal by the United States Treasury Department, defended it not only against the British but also against speculators who hastened down from the North.

"You have come to the wrong place, gentlemen," he said. And they disappeared when he threatened them with arrest.

Sherman had a strong dislike for men whose chief interest in the war was to make money. He himself was never tempted to use his position as a means toward any gain other than his salary. His patriotism, Major Nichols noted in his diary, was "as pure as the faith of a child."

He has given himself and all that he has to the national cause. Personal considerations, I am sure, have never influenced him. . . . It is impossible to discern any selfish or unworthy motive, either in his words or deeds. I do not believe it possible for a man more absolutely to subordinate himself and his personal interests to the great cause than he.

Sherman's elation over the capture of Savannah was marred by a private tragedy. He learned that the baby son who had fallen sick two months earlier had died, as it was feared he would.

"All spoke of him as so bright and fair," Sherman wrote his wife, "that I hoped he would be spared us to fill the great void in our hearts left by Willy."

Sherman believed that Willy would have understood the significance of the march, and in the same letter he said: "Oh, that Willy were living. How his eyes would brighten and his bosom swell with honest pride. . . ."

The last evening of the year 1864 found Sherman alone in the room of his headquarters that was his own, a quiet and reflective mood upon him. From nearby rooms came laughter and the clink of glasses as the officers of his staff made toasts to 1865, and the street outside rang with the celebrations of the enlisted men.

Sherman picked up his pen and began a letter to his brother John. He wished, he said, he could slip away from his responsibilities and see more of his family. The children, he lamented, were growing up almost strangers to him.

I have now lost Willy and the baby without even seeing him, and were it not for General Grant's confidence in me I should insist upon a little rest. As it is, I must go on.

The guest of honor at a New Year's Day banquet, Sherman heard his officers compare him to Hannibal and Caesar. He drew a laugh and a round of applause by responding that these generals were only "small potatoes," as they had never seen such wonders as the New York Herald *nor had a photograph taken.*

Sherman, incidentally, did not like the photographs taken of him, claiming they made him look stern and forbidding when he was really an amiable man who smiled often.

Though now famous both at home and abroad, Sherman was not overly impressed with himself. The fame had not really been sought. From the start he had viewed each new task as a weightier duty rather than as another step in a great career. When he learned that the North was beginning to regard him as presidential timber, his reaction was characteristic: "If forced to choose between the penitentiary and the White House for four years, I would say the penitentiary, thank you."

Sherman was well aware that fame was at best an uncertain thing. Before leaving Atlanta to begin the march, he had written Ellen: "Long before this war is over, much as you hear me praised now, you may hear me cursed and insulted."

Even as he began the year 1865 as master of Savannah, a shadow fell. His old friend Henry Halleck wrote him from his headquarters in Washington:

While almost everyone is praising your great march . . . there is a certain class having now great influence with the President . . . who are decidedly disposed to make a point against you—I mean in regard to "Inevitable Sambo." They say you have manifested an almost *criminal* dislike of the Negro, and that you are not willing to carry out the wishes of the Government in regard to him, but repulse him with contempt.

They say you might have brought with you to Savannah more than 50,000, thus stripping Georgia of that number of laborers, and opening a road by which as many more could have escaped from their masters; but that, instead of this, you drove them from your ranks. . . .

To those who know you as I do, such accusation will pass as the idle winds, for we presume that you discouraged the Negroes from following you because you had not the means of supporting them, and feared they might seriously embarrass your march. But there are others, and among them some in high authority, who think—or pretend to think—otherwise, and they are decidedly disposed to make a point against you.

Sherman replied:

If it be insisted that I shall so conduct my operations that the Negro alone is consulted . . . I shall be defeated, and then where will be Sambo? Don't military success imply the safety of Sambo, and vice versa?

By this time Sherman had come to accept the death of slavery as the proper outcome of the war. But he was convinced that the former slave "must pass through a probationary state before he is qualified for utter and complete freedom."

He said further to Halleck:

The South deserves all she has got for her injustice to the Negro, but that is no reason why we should go to the other extreme. I do, and will do, the best I can for the Negroes, and feel sure that the problem is solving itself slowly and naturally. It needs nothing more than our fostering care.

One of the Washington officials who was "making a point" against Sherman was Secretary of War Edwin M. Stanton, and on January 11 he

Edwin M. Stanton

stepped from a revenue cutter to a Savannah pier to pay Sherman a visit. Stanton's interest in the Southern black, according to Sherman,

was not of pure humanity, but of *politics.* The Negro question was beginning to loom up among the political eventualities of the day, and many foresaw that not only would the slaves secure their freedom, but that they would also have *votes.* . . .

Mr. Stanton seemed desirous of coming into contact with the Negroes to confer with them, and he asked me to arrange an interview for him. I accordingly sent out and invited the most intelligent of the Negroes, mostly Baptist and Methodist preachers, to come to my rooms to meet the Secretary of War. Twenty responded. . . .

Each . . . gave his name and partial history, and then selected Garrison Frazier as their spokesman.

Stanton began by asking Frazier whether he and his associates understood President Lincoln's Emancipation Proclamation. To the Secretary's surprise, Frazier gave a completely correct view of the proclamation, and in an erudite manner. There followed a general discussion of topics related to black interests, with Frazier continuing to make intelligent and perceptive comments.

"Up to this time I was present," says Sherman, "and on Mr. Stanton's intimating that he wanted to ask some questions affecting me, I withdrew."

But Sherman was offended:

It certainly was a strange fact that the great War Secretary should have catechized Negroes concerning the character of a general who had commanded a hundred thousand men in battle, had captured cities, conducted sixty-five thousand men successfully across four hundred miles of hostile territory, and had just brought . . . thousands of freedmen to a place of security; but because I had not loaded down my army by other hundreds of thousands of poor Negroes I was construed . . . as hostile to the black race.

While Sherman paced the hallway outside the closed door, Stanton asked Frazier, "What is the feeling of the colored people in regard to General Sherman? Do they regard his sentiments and actions as friendly to their rights and interests, or otherwise?"

Frazier answered:

We looked upon General Sherman, prior to his arrival, as a

man in the Providence of God especially set apart to accomplish this work, and we unanimously feel inexpressible gratitude to him, looking upon him as a man that should be honored for the faithful performance of his duty.

Some of us called on him immediately upon his arrival, and it is probable that he did not meet the Secretary of War with more courtesy than he did us. His conduct and deportment toward us characterized him as a friend and a gentleman.

We have confidence in General Sherman, and think that whatever concerns us could not be in better hands.

Stanton had no choice but to alter his opinion of Sherman's dealings with Georgia's black population. Again in Sherman's words:

He asked me to draft an order on the subject, in accordance with my own views, that would meet the pressing necessities of the case, and I did so. We went over this order . . . very carefully. The Secretary made some verbal modifications. When it was approved by him in all its details, I published it, and it went into operation at once.

It provided fully for the enlistment of colored troops, and gave the freedmen certain possessory rights to land . . . but we did not undertake to give fee-simple title; and all that was designed by these special field orders was to make temporary provisions for the freedmen and their families during the rest of the war, or until Congress should take action. . . .

I saw a good deal of the Secretary socially during the time of his visit to Savannah. He kept his quarters on the revenue cutter . . . but he came very often to my quarters. . . . Though appearing robust and strong, he complained a good deal of internal pains. . . . He professed to have come from Washington purposely for rest and recreation, and he spoke unreservedly of the bickerings and jealousies at the national capital. . . .

He said that the price of everything had so risen in comparison with the depreciated money that there was danger of national bankruptcy, and he appealed to me, as a soldier and patriot, to hurry up matters so as to bring the war to a close. He . . . promised to go north without delay, so as to hurry back to me the supplies I had called for as indispensable for the prosecution of the next stage of the campaign.

I was quite impatient to get off myself, for city life had become dull and tame, and we were all anxious to get into the pine woods again, free from the importunities of rebel women asking for protection, and of the civilians from the North who were coming to Savannah for ... all sorts of profit.

About this time, some Northerners arrived whose purpose was not profit. They came on vessels laden with food for Savannah's needy. This was a paradoxical development. Sympathetic Northerners began helping Georgia during the very days when Sherman was preparing to devastate South Carolina.

On board one of the mercy vessels from the North was Charles Carleton Coffin, a correspondent for the Boston Journal. *He relates:*

The people of Savannah generally were ready to live once more in the Union. The fire of Secession had died out.... At a meeting of the citizens, resolutions expressive of gratitude for the charity bestowed by Boston, New York, and Philadelphia were passed, also of a desire for future fellowship and amity....

Society in the South, and especially in Savannah, had undergone a great change. The extremes of social life were very wide apart before the war. They were no nearer the night before Sherman marched into the city. But the morning after, there was a convulsion, an upheaval, a shaking up and a settling down of all the discordant elements. The tread of that army of the West, as it moved in solid column through the streets, was like a moral earthquake, overturning aristocratic pride, privilege, and power.

Old houses, with foundations laid deep and strong in the centuries, fortified by wealth, name, and influence, went down beneath the shock. The general disruption of the former relations of master and slave, and forced submission to the Union arms, produced a common level....

On the night before Sherman entered the place, there were citizens who could enumerate their wealth by millions; at sunrise the next morning they were worth scarcely a dime. Their property had been in cotton, Negroes, houses, land, Confederate bonds and currency, railroad and bank stocks.

Government had seized their cotton; the Negroes had possession of their lands ... [and] had become freedmen; their houses were occupied by troops; Confederate bonds were waste paper; their railroads were destroyed, their banks insolvent. They had not only lost wealth, but they had lost their cause.

Up in Richmond, Virginia, a clerk in the Confederacy's war offices wrote in his diary: "Men are silent, and some dejected. It is unquestionably the darkest period we have yet experienced."

All of this was ample proof Sherman was correct in his conviction that he could accomplish more by attacking the South's material resources than by concentrating upon her armies. Though his methods seemed grossly cruel, they were saving lives on both sides.

Sherman was aware that future generations the world over, having an imperfect conception of his aims, were almost certain to regard him as a ruthless vandal. He shrugged at this knowledge, pausing only to ponder the curious fact that a general who destroyed property was invariably looked upon as a greater brute than one who fought terrible battles.

11

THE COLUMNS PIVOT NORTHWARD

ACCORDING TO *Major Nichols, Sherman's troops had been in Savannah for three and a half weeks, maintaining "the most perfect order," when they got the word they were waiting for:*

It was thoroughly understood by all the intelligent veterans who composed the legions of Sherman that, so long as Lee and his forces stood defiant at the Rebel capital, Richmond was the real objective of our campaign. How and when we were to reach that point [about 500 miles to the north] were the questions discussed throughout the camp; but our men said that while "Uncle Billy" had the matter in his hands, it was sure to go right.

The new expedition had already been determined in the mind of our chief before we saw Savannah. . . . The capture of Savannah was but a pivot upon which he swung his army; this campaign was but a part of the *grand idea.* The 15th of January [1865] saw the troops actually set in motion for the new campaign, and it was soon known that South Carolina was to be the next field of operations.

On January 18 Sherman turned control of Savannah over to General John G. Foster, who commanded the Union's Department of the South—i.e., the beachheads on the coast—from Hilton Head, in lower South Carolina, where a landing had been made as early as 1861. Foster chose to remain at his headquarters at Hilton Head, occupying the city with a division which had just reached him by ship from Grant's command in Virginia.

Sherman says that he issued his first general orders for the march northward on January 19.

The army remained substantially the same as during the

march from Atlanta, with the exception of a few changes in the commanders of brigades and divisions, the addition of some men who had joined from furlough, and the loss of others from the expiration of their term of service....

Of course, I gave out with some ostentation... that we were going [northeast] to Charleston or [northwest] to Augusta; but I had long before made up my mind to waste no time on either, further than to play off on their fears, thus to retain for their protection a force of the enemy which would otherwise concentrate in our front and make the passage of some of the great rivers that crossed our route more difficult and bloody.

Sherman's plan for launching the march was for the greater part of the army, including the entire left wing and the cavalry, to make its movement from Savannah by land, crossing the Savannah River into South Carolina, most of the units aiming first for Robertsville, some forty miles to the north. Earlier, however, one corps of the right wing had been sent from Savannah by water, steaming down the river toward the sea.

Adjutant Hedley made this trip in the wooden gunboat Winona*:*

Of course there were no accommodations below except for the ordinary ship's crew, and the soldiers were disposed on deck.... There was an unusually heavy sea, and... the crazy old *Winona* pitched about at a terrible rate. Most of the men were dreadfully seasick; and, without strength to hold on to anything, they tumbled from one side of the vessel to the other... being so thumped and pounded that many of them were sore with bruises for days afterward....

Sometime after dark, Hilton Head was reached and anchor cast, but the vessel continued to roll wildly all night, making sleep impossible to the sore and weary landsmen. In the morning the *Winona* steamed into Beaufort [about thirty-five miles northeast of Savannah] and the men disembarked, thanking God they had escaped from an experience compared with which plain soldiering was heavenly happiness.

Beaufort was a beautiful little town, extremely southernish in every aspect. The houses, all of wood, were low, covering considerable ground and encompassed on all sides with spacious verandas. The fortifications were garrisoned by Foster's corps, all Negroes, well clothed, well armed, and in a high state of discipline. Large numbers of freedmen were in the vicinity, cultivating abandoned plantations.

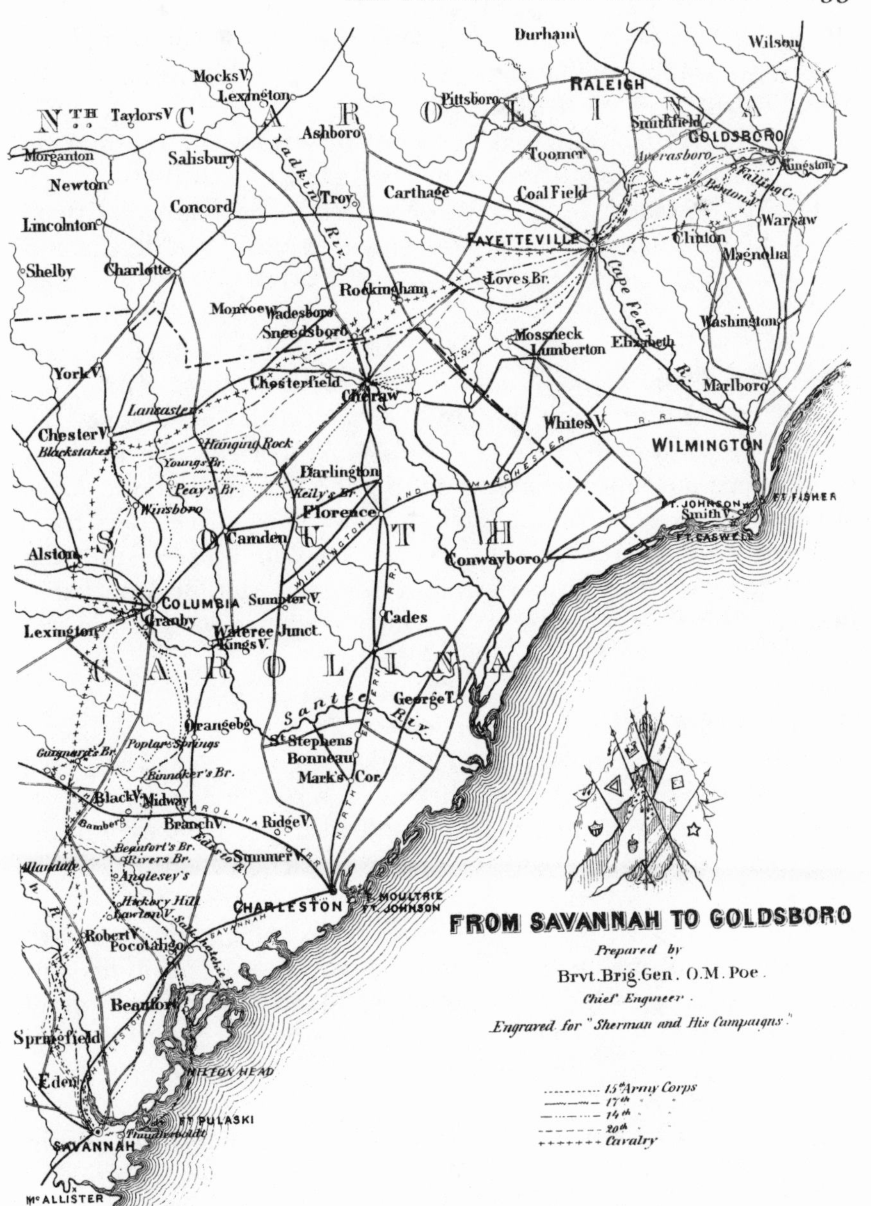
FROM SAVANNAH TO GOLDSBORO
Prepared by
Brvt. Brig. Gen. O.M. Poe.
Chief Engineer.
Engraved for "Sherman and His Campaigns."
15th Army Corps
17th
14th
20th
Cavalry
NTH CAROLINA
SOUTH CAROLINA
Durham
Wilson
Raleigh
Mocks V.
Lexington
Pittsboro
Taylors V.
Ashboro
Smithfield
Goldsboro
Morganton
Salisbury
Toomer
Averasboro
Kingston
Newton
Troy
Carthage
Coal Field
Concord
Lincolnton
Fayetteville
Clinton
Warsaw
Magnolia
Shelby
Charlotte
Loves Br.
Rockingham
Monroe
Wadesboro
Sneedsboro
Mossneck
Lumberton
Elizabeth
Washington
York V.
Chesterfield
Cheraw
Marlboro
Lancaster
Whites V.
Chester V.
Blackstakes
Hanging Rock
Wilmington
Youngs Br.
Darlington
Peay's Br.
Kelly's Br.
Ft. Johnson
Ft. Fisher
Winsboro
Florence
Smith V.
Ft. Caswell
Camden
Alston
Conwayboro
Columbia
Granby
Sumpter V.
Cades
Lexington
Wateree Junct.
Kings V.
Santee Riv.
George T.
Orangebg.
St. Stephens
Bonneau
Poplar Springs
Mark's Cor.
Binnaker's Br.
Black V.
Midway
Bamberg
Branch V.
Ridge V.
Beaufort's Br.
Rivers Br.
Summer V.
Allandale
Anglesey's
Charleston
Ft. Moultrie
Ft. Johnson
Hickory Hill
Lawton V.
Robert V.
Pocotaligo
Beaufort
Springfield
Hilton Head
Eden
Ft. Pulaski
Savannah
McAllister

In the harbor lay ships displaying the flags of almost all nations, and among them . . . were several captured blockade runners . . . evidences of "British neutrality."

. . . The troops marched out of Beaufort, and after making five miles, ran against the enemy. He was driven without much difficulty, however; and, after penetrating the country fifteen miles, the command halted at Pocotaligo, near the Charleston and Savannah Railroad. . . .

With another unit that left Savannah by boat, but on a quieter day, was a soldier from Minnesota, Alonzo L. Brown, who wrote in his diary:

There was fun when the boys began to draw water over the side of the ship with their kettles to make coffee. The first got good river water and their coffee was good, but the last ones were not so fortunate, and after having made their coffee their faces expressed . . . surprise and disgust. . . . They inquired of the first ones if their coffee was all right and were considerably puzzled at first to discover the difference, which was that we were in salt water.

Sherman himself left Savannah on January 21:

With my entire headquarters, officers, clerks, orderlies, etc., with wagons and horses, I embarked on a steamer for Beaufort, South Carolina, touching at Hilton Head to see General Foster. The weather was rainy and bad, but we reached Beaufort safely on the 23d. . . .

All the country between Beaufort and Pocotaligo was low alluvial land, cut up by an infinite number of salt-water sloughs and fresh-water creeks, easily susceptible of defense by a small force; and why the enemy had allowed us to make a lodgment at Pocotaligo so easily I did not understand, unless it resulted from fear or ignorance.

It seemed to me that the terrible energy they had displayed in the earlier stages of the war was beginning to yield to the slower but more certain industry and discipline of our Northern men. It was to me manifest that the soldiers and people of the South entertained an undue fear of our Western men, and . . . had invented such ghostlike stories of our prowess in Georgia that they were scared by their own inventions. Still, this was a power, and I intended to utilize it.

Somehow our men had got the idea that South Carolina was the cause of all our troubles. Her people were the first to fire on Fort Sumter, had been in a great hurry to precipitate the country into civil war; and therefore on them should fall the scourge of war in its worst form.

Taunting messages had also come to us, when in Georgia, to the effect that when we should reach South Carolina we would find a people less passive, who would fight us to the bitter end, daring us to come over, etc. . . .

Personally I had many friends in Charleston, to whom I would gladly have extended protection and mercy, but they were beyond my personal reach, and I would not restrain the army [among other South Carolinians] lest its vigor and energy should be impaired. . . .

General Foster's Department of the South had been enlarged to embrace the coast of North Carolina. . . . General A. H. Terry held Fort Fisher [near Wilmington]. . . . He had about eight

Pierre G. T. Beauregard

thousand men. General [John M.] Schofield was also known to be en route from Nashville for North Carolina with the entire Twenty-third Corps, so that I had every reason to be satisfied I would receive additional strength as we progressed northward. . . .

General W. J. Hardee commanded the Confederate forces in Charleston. . . . It was also known that General [Pierre G. T.] Beauregard had come from the direction of Tennessee and had assumed the general command of all the troops designed to resist our progress.

The heavy winter rains had begun early in January, rendering the roads execrable, and the Savannah River became so swollen that it filled its many channels, overflowing the vast extent of rice fields that lay on the east bank. This flood delayed our departure two weeks; for it swept away our pontoon bridge at Savannah, and came near drowning John E. Smith's division of the Fifteenth Corps. . . .

The utmost activity prevailed at all points, but it was manifest we could not get off much before the 1st day of February; so I determined to go in person to Pocotaligo, and there act as though we were bound for Charleston. On the 24th of January I started from Beaufort with a part of my staff, leaving the rest to follow at leisure, rode . . . to a plantation not far from Pocotaligo. . . .

There we found a house with a majestic avenue of live oaks whose limbs had been cut away by the troops for firewood, and desolation marked one of those splendid South Carolina estates where the proprietors formerly had dispensed a hospitality that distinguished the old regime of that proud state.

I slept on the floor of the house, but the night was so bitter cold that I got up by the fire several times, and when it burned low I rekindled it with an old mantel clock and the wreck of a bedstead which stood in a corner of the room—the only act of vandalism that I recall done by myself personally during the war. . . .

We . . . rested quietly about Pocotaligo, collecting stores and making final preparations, until the 1st of February, when I learned that the cavalry and two divisions of the Twentieth Corps were fairly across the river. . . .

An officer who was present at the crossing says that each regiment gave three cheers as it entered South Carolina:

The men seemed to realize that at last they had set foot on the state which had done more than all others to bring upon the country the horrors of civil war. In the narrow road leading from the ferry on the South Carolina side torpedoes had been planted, so that several of our men were killed or wounded by treading upon them. This was unfortunate for that section of the state.

As these first units raided and burned their way toward Robertsville, which was about twenty miles west of Pocotaligo, the rest of the army completed the crossing. Sherman was now able to issue orders for a general advance:

The actual strength of the army ... was at the time sixty thousand and seventy-nine men, and sixty-eight guns. The trains were made up of about twenty-five hundred wagons, with six mules to each wagon, and about six hundred ambulances, with two horses each. The contents of the wagons embraced an ample supply of ammunition ... forage for about seven days, and provisions for twenty days, mostly of bread, sugar, coffee, and salt, depending largely for fresh meat on beeves driven on the hoof and such cattle, hogs, and poultry as we expected to gather along our line of march.

Major Nichols reported in his diary:

General Sherman has reduced the army to its simplest and most effective fighting and marching conditions, rejecting as superfluities all that is not essential to its health, or that may clog its movements.

In all these personal sacrifices General Sherman demands nothing of his soldiers which he does not himself share. His staff is smaller than that of any brigade commander in the army. He has fewer servants and horses than the military regulations allow. His baggage is reduced to the smallest possible limit. . . .

When we left Atlanta we thought the army had been stripped to the lowest possible point, but our experiences thus far prove that we can go several steps lower, and that a man may have but little and still be contented, if not comfortable. Farther than this, we discover how unnecessary, if not enervating, are the conventionalities and luxuries of city life.

Again in Sherman's words:

To resist or delay our progress north, General Wheeler had

Wade Hampton

his division of cavalry (reduced to the size of a brigade by his hard and persistent fighting ever since the beginning of the Atlanta campaign); and General Wade Hampton had been dispatched from the Army of Virginia to his native state of South Carolina, with a great flourish of trumpets and extraordinary powers to raise men, money, and horses, with which "to stay the progress of the invader," and "to punish us for our insolent attempt to invade the glorious state of South Carolina." He was supposed at the time to have, at and near Columbia [the state capital], two small divisions of cavalry commanded by himself and General [William] Butler.

Of course, I had a species of contempt for these scattered and inconsiderable forces, knew that they could hardly delay us an hour; and the only serious question that occurred to me was, would General Lee sit down in Richmond (besieged by General Grant), and permit us, almost unopposed, to pass through the states of South Carolina and North Carolina, cutting off and consuming the very supplies on which he depended to feed his army in Virginia, or would he make an effort to escape from General Grant and endeavor to catch us inland somewhere between Columbia and Raleigh?

Even as Sherman pondered this question, General Lee was replying in the following manner to a letter he had just received from the Governor of South Carolina, A. G. Magrath:

I . . . regret exceedingly to learn the present condition of affairs in the South. I infer from your letter that you consider me able to send an army to arrest the march of General Sherman. If such was the case I should not have waited for your application, for I lament as much as you do his past success, and see the injury that may result from his further progress. . . .

According to your statement of General Sherman's force, it would require this whole army to oppose him. It is now confronted by General Grant with a far superior army. If it was transferred to South Carolina, I do not believe General Grant would remain idle on the James River. It would be as easy for him to move his army south as for General Sherman to advance north. You can judge whether the condition of affairs would be benefited by the concentration of two large Federal armies in South Carolina. . . .

Sherman sums up the resistance, excluding Lee, that he might expect to encounter:

I knew full well . . . that the broken fragments of Hood's army, which had escaped from Tennessee, were being hurried rapidly across Georgia, by Augusta, to make junction in my front. Estimating them at the maximum twenty-five thousand men, and Hardee's, Wheeler's, and Hampton's forces at fifteen thousand, made forty thousand; which, if handled with spirit and energy, would constitute a formidable force and might make the passage of such rivers as the Santee and Cape Fear a difficult undertaking.

As during Sherman's march from Atlanta, however, the Confederates were uncertain of his intentions. They did not know where to concentrate.

Though he was aware of this advantage, Sherman took "all possible precautions."

I . . . arranged with Admiral Dahlgren and General Foster to watch our progress inland by all the means possible, and to provide for us points of security along the coast. . . .

Still, it was extremely desirable in *one march* to reach Goldsboro in the state of North Carolina, distant four hundred and twenty-five miles, a point of great convenience for ulterior operations, by reason of the two railroads which meet there, coming from the seacoast at Wilmington and New Bern. [New Bern had been taken by a Union amphibious force in 1862, and Wilmington was about to be assailed.] Before leaving Savannah I had sent to New Bern Colonel W. W. Wright, of the engineers, with orders to look to these railroads, to collect rolling stock, and to have the roads repaired out as far as possible in six weeks—the time estimated as necessary for us to march that distance.

The question of supplies remained still the one of vital importance, and I reasoned that we might safely rely on the country for a considerable quantity of forage and provisions, and that, if the worst came to the worst, we could live several months on the mules and horses of our trains.

Sherman regarded this campaign as the one that would decide the war. Later in his life he was to realize, with a certain surprise, that he was to be remembered chiefly for his march to the sea:

I considered this march as a means to an end, and not as an essential act of war. Still . . . the march to the sea was generally regarded as something extraordinary . . . something out of the usual order of events; whereas, in fact, I simply moved from Atlanta to Savannah, as one step in the direction of Richmond. . . .

Were I to express my measure of the relative importance of the march to the sea, and of that from Savannah northward, I would place the former at one and the latter at ten, or the maximum.

12

VENGEANCE UNLIMITED

THERE CAN BE no denial of the assertion [explains Union newsman David Conyngham] that the feeling among the troops was one of extreme bitterness towards the people of the state of South Carolina. . . . Threatening words were heard from soldiers who prided themselves on "conservatism in house-burning" while in Georgia, and officers openly confessed their fears that the coming campaign would be a wicked one.

Just or unjust as this feeling was towards the country people of South Carolina, it was universal. I first saw its fruits at Purysburg, where two or three piles of blackened brick and an acre or so of dying embers marked the site of an old Revolutionary town—and this before the column had fairly got its "hand in."

. . . If a house was empty, this was *prima facie* evidence that the owners were rebels [and not Union sympathizers, for the latter often opted against flight], and all was sure to be consigned to the flames. If they remained at home, it was taken for granted that *everyone* in South Carolina was a rebel, and the chances were the place was consumed. . . .

The pine forests were fired, the resin factories were fired, the public buildings . . . were fired. The middle of the finest day looked black and gloomy, for a dense smoke arose on all sides, clouding the very heavens. At night the tall pine trees seemed so many huge pillars of fire. . . .

Vandalism of this kind, though not encouraged, was seldom punished. . . .

I was standing on the piazza of a plantation house, watching the burning dwellings around. The owner turns to me with an exultant look and says:

"There, I knew it would be so. I told the damned fools it would come to that, but they only laughed at me. There is Jennings' mills on fire. Well, serves him right; he was always preaching secession, the damned scoundrel. I hope they will hang him! Then, there is Milken's house in a blaze, too; and there is Harrison's following. . . . I told them it would be so, but the fools laughed at me and called me a Yankee. Well, now they know who was the fool. . . ."

Major Nichols wrote in his diary:

South Carolina has commenced to pay an instalment, long overdue, on her debt to justice and humanity. With the help of God, we will have principal and interest before we leave her borders. . . . Little did she dream that the hated flag would again wave over her soil; but . . . a thousand Union banners are floating in the breeze, and the ground trembles beneath the tramp of thousands of brave Northmen who know their mission and will perform it to the end.

Conyngham says that "foragers and bummers heralded the advance of the army, eating up the country like so many locusts."

Fancy a ragged man, blackened by the smoke of many a pine-knot fire, mounted on a scraggy mule without a saddle, with a gun, a knapsack, a butcher knife, and a plug hat, stealing his way through the pine forests far out on the flanks of a column, keen on the scent of rebels, or bacon, or silver spoons, or corn, or anything valuable, and you have him in your mind. Think of how you would admire him if you were a lone woman with a family of small children, far from help, when he blandly inquired where you kept your valuables. . . . There are hundreds of these mounted men with the column, and they go everywhere.

But the campaign involved more than burning, foraging, and stealing. Minnesota diarist Alonzo Brown, who marched from Pocotaligo with the right wing, gives this account of the first few days as he saw them:

February 1st. . . . Our march today was through a low, wet, timbered country for fifteen miles. . . . We came up with rebel cavalry at 3:00 o'clock P.M. Our skirmishers drove them back. The trees they had felled across the road were removed, when we went on, going into camp at dark in a large cottonfield. We had one man killed today, but not of our regiment. Country level, covered with small pines.

February 2d. . . . We marched at 8:00 A.M. Weather warm and

foggy. We hear cannonading away to our left. Probably the Fourteenth and Twentieth Corps of the left wing. We marched twelve miles today over very bad roads.

February 3d.... Our brigade leads today. We marched six miles to crossing of Duck Creek. Our regiment was sent to drive the rebels from the other side of the stream. We deployed four companies as skirmishers, reserves of two companies each, one in center and one on either flank....

The regiment waded the creek. Water three feet deep. The rebels left without ceremony. Our boys and those of the Sixty-third Illinois charged through the stream, and as they came back they captured an alligator, seven feet long, lying torpid in the mud, which they pulled ashore and into camp. He could scarcely move, but when poked would strike viciously with his tail....

We moved on a short distance and went into camp on a big plantation where "old massa runned away, and missus stayed to home," or rather the overseer's wife did. She was a Yankee woman, and a true blue Union woman at that, and she was overjoyed to see us.

Among "old massa's" papers we found a requisition from Wheeler for a large quantity of corn. [The Confederates, too, lived off the country, with Wheeler and his horsemen telling the South Carolinians, "Shell out; you started this muss!"] He had just served it when our brigade ran him off, and he did not get that corn.... A new factor had entered... and that corn went into United States wagons. There was about one thousand bushels of it, and then we "done took ole massa's" bacon, chickens, turkeys, ducks, and sweet potatoes—all good forage for Uncle Billy's boys and teams....

Sherman's aide Major Nichols found this same day, February 3, particularly interesting because it "afforded opportunities to talk with the people."

Three very queer specimens of white women were at the corner of the road as our column wound around to cross Jackson's Creek at Barker's Mills. The day was cold and windy, and now and then the rain would fall in torrents, to be thirstily absorbed by the sandy soil, except here and there in the roadway, where it stood in huge puddles.... It was a wild day, and a dreary place for three lone women.

Supposing that they had been burned out of house and home

by the soldiers, I asked the old woman—the other two were not more than sixteen—if I could be of any service to them.

"Anan?" was the reply.

"Can I help you in any way?"

"Oh, no. We jist cum out h'yar to see the soldiers go by. Never seed so many men in all my life. We live back here off the road a spell."

"How do you make a living?"

"We spin, and make cloth, and do our own farming."

I noticed that they were standing in the cold mud with their bare limbs and feet exposed, and asked them where were their shoes."

"We ain't got none. . . ."

All this time the two girls were peering out at us from beneath the long hoods covering their faces, so that we could only see their eyes. There was a simplicity and bashfulness in this action which was not only odd but really charming. . . .

I asked the old lady, who proved to be their mother, if they were frightened.

"Lor' bless you, sir, no. They are a little backward, that's all. They never seed so much company, sir, before today."

"I should think not," I replied. "If you don't look out, some of these blue-eyed Yankees will marry them and elope."

She nodded her head with satisfaction and said, "May be."

I left them standing in the cold rain, gazing with curious, wondering eyes upon the long column of troops as it wound along the road and crossed the swollen river.

Alonzo Brown continues his day-by-day report:

February 4th. . . . We marched at 6:00 A.M. Rain falling and roads muddy. . . . Country rich, level, and wet. Pine and oak. The forage details are having fine times, but they have to keep a sharp lookout for rebel cavalry. We camped within three miles of the . . . Salkehatchie River. . . . Distance marched, ten miles.

February 5th. . . . We reached the Salkehatchie last night and found the bridge gone. Today is Sunday. We had reveille at 4 A.M., and marching at six we crossed the Salkehatchie swamp and river, passing over twenty-four bridges [some left undestroyed by the Confederates, and others constructed by the Union pioneers], and camped in the timber, one mile beyond the crossing. . . .

The divisions of Generals Giles A. Smith and Joe Mower of the

Joseph A. Mower

Seventeenth Corps crossed below. . . . The stream at that point was fully three miles wide, and as the enemy was fortified on the opposite shore, those troops encountered severe opposition. The deep water of the stream and swamps being full of cypress trees and tangled underbrush, our forces advanced very slowly and with the greatest difficulty, some of the troops being in the water three hours before they emerged on solid ground. General Wager Swayne . . . of the Forty-third Ohio, lost a leg in crossing the swamp. He was sent back to Pocotaligo.

February 6th. . . . Left camp at 6:00 A.M. The roads are good. The plantations are large and the forage is abundant. Our advance is skirmishing with and driving the enemy. . . . Camped at 3:00 P.M. It rained in the evening. It was our melancholy duty to bury the remains of John Smith of Company K of our regiment here on a lonely hillside. He died of dysentery. Distance marched, nine miles.

Sherman's expeditious passage of the flooded Salkehatchie River and arrival on better ground astonished the Confederates, who were sure he would bog down. General Joseph E. Johnston, at this time in Lincolnton, North Carolina, still without an active command after his replacement by Hood at Atlanta, was later to say:

When I learned that Sherman's army was marching through

the Salk swamps, making its own corduroy roads at the rate of a dozen miles a day and more, and bringing its artillery and wagons with it, I made up my mind that there had been no such army in existence since the days of Julius Caesar.

A Confederate enlisted man serving in South Carolina wrote home: "i hev conkludid that the dam fulishness uv trying to lick sherman had better be stoped." Mail captured by the Federals revealed many other soldiers to be despondent about the war's outcome.

Captured militiamen often proved to be old men. General William Hazen, the hero of Fort McAllister, says of one such group:

I did not turn these old gentlemen over to the provost guard but gave them some tents near my headquarters. In the evening they all came over to my campfire and entertained me with an account of their novel war experiences. Each man had some peculiar and personal malady, an account of which figured largely in the conversation. In the morning I had a handsome walking stick cut for each, gave them a good breakfast, and let them go. They thanked me pleasantly for the entertainment, liked the walking sticks, and did not see the joke.

By the end of the first week in February the right wing of the army, with which Sherman was traveling, was nearing Midway, one of the stations on the railroad that ran in a northwesterly direction from Charleston to Augusta. Sherman gave orders for the columns to hasten forward.

"I expected severe resistance at this railroad, for its loss would sever all the communications of the enemy in Charleston with those in Augusta."

The march was made during a rainstorm in the early hours of February 7. Sherman tells of something that happened to General Oliver Howard, the right wing's top commander:

He was with the Seventeenth Corps, marching straight for Midway, and when about five miles distant he began to deploy the leading division so as to be ready for battle. Sitting on his horse by the roadside, while the deployment was making, he saw a man coming down the road [from Midway], riding as hard as he could, and as he approached he recognized him as one of his own foragers, mounted on a white horse, with a rope bridle and a blanket for a saddle.

As he came near he called out, "Hurry up, general. We have got the railroad!"

A skirmish in the swamps

So, while we, the generals, were proceeding deliberately to prepare for a serious battle, a parcel of our foragers, in search of plunder, had got ahead and actually captured the South Carolina Railroad, a line of vital importance to the rebel government.

As soon as we struck the railroad, details of men were set to work to tear up the rails, to burn the ties, and twist the bars. This was a most important railroad, and I proposed to destroy it completely for fifty miles, partly to prevent a possibility of its restoration and partly to utilize the time necessary for General Slocum to get up [with the army's left wing].

Included among the left wing's targets was the town of Barnwell, some twenty miles west of Midway. Living at Barnwell's edge on a plantation called The Oaks was Mrs. A. P. Aldrich, who relates:

Early in the morning of the 5th of February we heard the anticipated sounds like a death-knell, the bombarding of the fortifications on the Salkehatchie, three miles below our town.... What mirth that structure, a mere molehill, must have created in the great Union army....

The first detachment that entered the town was Kilpatrick's cavalry.... It was a party of this cavalry who, crossing the beautiful little stream which separates our place ... from the town, came dashing up the avenue as if they were afraid some of their comrades might outstrip them and secure the booty they hoped to grasp.

As I stood upon the piazza and looked at these first bluecoats approaching, I will not deny that my heart sank within me, and I felt like falling, for I remembered the horrible accounts we had for months been listening to of the brutal treatment of the army to the women of Georgia in their march from Atlanta to Savannah. The courage of which I had always felt myself possessed, I confess, forsook me then and I prayed God to protect me and my little ones from the invaders.

The first soldiers who rushed into the house seemed only intent on searching for food, and when the safe [i.e., food cabinet] was opened to them, ate like hungry wolves. So soon, however, as they were satisfied, their tramp through the house began. By this time they were pouring in at every door, and without asking to have bureaus and wardrobes opened, broke with their bayonets every lock, tearing out the contents, in hunting for gold, silver, and jewels, all of which had been sent off weeks before....

Finding nothing to satisfy their cupidity so far, they began turning over mattresses, tearing open featherbeds, and scattering the contents in the wildest confusion....

Unfortunately a few bottles of whiskey had been overlooked in the wine closet.... This prize they were not long in finding, which seemed soon to infuriate and rouse all their evil passions, so that the work of destruction began in earnest. Tables were knocked over, lamps with their contents thrown over carpets and mattings, furniture of all sorts broken, a guitar and violin smashed. The piano escaped in the general wreck....

Provisions as much as they wanted were carried off. The policy of the first comers seemed to be not to ruin or destroy any food, but to leave all they did not require for those that were to come after.

The infantry soon appeared and were ... days ... passing through in detachments. During that time their tents were pitched all around us, and our park lit up by their campfires, and our yard and home filled with hundreds of rude soldiers. When one swarm departed, another more hungry for spoil would file in. And so we lived for days and nights, with guns and bayonets flashing in our faces and the coarse language of this mass of ruffians sounding in our ears. . . .

Almost the last division that composed that "left wing" was an Indiana regiment commanded by General Hunter—so his soldiers, or "boys," as he called them, addressed him. [This was Morton C. Hunter, an acting brigadier.]

My youngest son . . . came by on his way to Virginia a short time after the Federal army left Savannah, to bid me good-bye, and when about to leave said: "Mother, when the army comes, as surely it will, always try to get a general officer to make headquarters in the house or at the gate, and you will be protected."

Remembering this, when I found the new arrivals pitching their tents by the front gate I sent at once to ask protection, and in reply was assured that I should be safe from intrusion. Very soon, however, the soldiers began to walk into the library and help themselves to books and papers as they liked.

After a while the General himself came . . . into the piazza, and with only a nod of his head to me, seated himself. His face I will never forget. It was that of a fiend. Several of his officers joined him. . . . They were courtly, elegant gentlemen; two especially, Captain [Americus] Whedon and the surgeon. . . .

They came to the library door and said most respectfully, "Good morning, madam."

A few moments after, one of the privates walked in and took an armful of books from the bookcase. I thought this did not look much like protection, and . . . I stepped to the door and said:

"General, I understood you to say my house should be protected," pointing to a man with a second supply of books.

With a sardonic smile, he replied: "The boys are all fond of reading. I guess they will not hurt the books."

Of course, I never saw them again.

The surgeon, a tall, fine-looking man with one of the most magnetic faces I ever saw, knocked at the front door that evening, the first one of that army who had observed such etiquette. When I invited him to come in, he took off his cap and stood before me.

"Mrs. Aldrich," he said, "we have learned that you have a fine piano, and, having along with us a good performer, we would be glad to enjoy his music, if you do not object."

"Sir, I have no power to refuse," I replied.

He bowed his head sorrowfully.

"I beg your pardon," he said, bowing, "but no foot shall enter your house tonight that can offend you. I will see to that."

He went on to say that the German musician should tune the instrument and leave it in beautiful order.

As this had not been done during the war, I was quite willing to receive this remuneration for the pleasure conferred on this courteous gentleman, and told him he was welcome to use the piano. . . .

The next morning Captain Whedon, who made the most exquisite toilet I had seen for a long time, and wore the most immaculate linen, looking quite like a Frenchman, a sunny face with bright blue eyes and a winning manner, soon made friends with the children. He came when I was walking in the yard with two of them, and after saying, "Good morning," asked me to let him take the children to his tent for breakfast. . . .

Whether or not any of our groceries had found their way to this particular tent, of course we could not tell. . . . This was the last good breakfast the little ones got for many a day. . . .

In the afternoon of that same day the news was brought me that the stables were on fire. Alongside of them was the corn house, containing all the corn not consumed by the army. . . .

I ran out to the General's tent and found him seated outside, surrounded by his staff. They arose, with cap in hand, most respectfully. He kept his seat, his hat pulled over his eyes. . . . I implored him to come with me and have the fire extinguished.

"Madam, I have very little control over the boys," he replied. "You must remember we are in South Carolina now. We entered this state with 'gloves off.'"

He then looked like a hyena gloating over his victim.

"For heaven sake, General, come and save my corn house. Surely you do not intend to destroy our last provisions and leave us to perish? Do come!"

At last he reluctantly arose and slowly followed me. I hurried on, looking back and begging him to quicken his pace or it would be too late.

When he got in speaking distance, he called out: "Boys, put out that fire!"

A dozen or more "boys" leaped the fence and soon extinguished it.

I turned to him and said that did not look as if he had lost control over them.

He approached nearer to me and said, "Madam, this is war—the war which you women helped to bring on yourselves."

"Yes," I said, "but we did not expect to deal with barbarians. . . ."

"You women can soon stop this thing," he rejoined, "by bringing your husbands and sons out of the army to protect you."

. . . When I told him we could not bring them from their post of duty if we would, and we would not if we could, he laughed a laugh that rang in my ears long after, and said: "Madam, the end will soon come when we have finished our work in this state!"

As he struck his tents and moved off, the corn house I had tried so hard to save was discovered in flames.

The woman's home, however, was spared. Barnwell, the town nearby, was not so fortunate, the Yankees bragging later that they changed its name from Barnwell to Burnwell.

Mrs. Aldrich laments:

All the public buildings were destroyed. The fine brick courthouse which cost the state between $12,000 and $15,000, with most of the stores, laid level with the ground, and many private residences with only the chimneys standing like grim sentinels; the Masonic Hall in ashes. I had always believed that the archives, jewels, and sacred emblems of the Order were so reverenced by Masons everywhere, whether belonging to friend or foe, that those wearing the Blue would guard the temple of their brothers in Gray. Not so, however. Nothing in South Carolina was held sacred. All fell under the heel of the oppressor alike.

As town after town shared Barnwell's fate, and as farms and plantations also suffered in ever growing numbers, more than a few Federals began to have at least momentary misgivings about their role as avengers.

It is grievous [Major Nichols confessed in his diary] to see a beautiful woman, highly cultured and refined, standing in the gateway of her dismantled home, perhaps with an infant in her arms, while she calls upon some passing officers to protect her home from further pillage.

Sherman, whose idea of punishing South Carolina was to take with a free hand the supplies he needed, to destroy as much public property as possible, and, for extra measure, to burn private homes that had been abandoned, regretted the pillaging of occupied homes and urged his generals to try to control it. But he paid little attention to the complaints of the victimized people.

"I allege that those who struck the first blow and made war inevitable ought not in fairness to reproach us for the natural consequences."

Union newsman David Conyngham often did what he could to help unfortunate citizens. He gives an example:

I came up to a retired plantation house, just set on fire. The soldiers were rushing off on every side with their pillage. An old lady and her two grandchildren were in the yard, alarmed and helpless. The flames and smoke were shooting through the windows. The old lady rushed from one [man] to another, beseeching them at least to save her furniture. They only enjoyed the whole thing, including her distress.

I turned to them and said, "Boys, look at that poor, crazy woman and those helpless children. You all have mothers, some of you children. Think of them, and any of you that are men will follow me."

They did follow me, and soon a thousand dollars' worth of splendid furniture was rescued from the burning house. I was near losing my life in saving a photograph of her husband, which hung over the mantel-tree in one of the rooms on fire.

Conyngham's compassion extended even to South Carolina's dog population:

I must say that few bloodhounds were allowed to live, except some peculiar one that took the fancy of an officer. As for the general run of these animals, they were relentlessly shot down, the men simply remarking, "Here goes to spoil that 'ere dog's scent for Union prisoners or niggers." And a bullet did for the poor brute.

As we came near deserted houses, it was pitiful to see the poor, half-starved cur go up to the men with a most melancholy countenance, as much as to say, "I have seen better days but am now starving. Just let me go along, and I will be a good, dutiful dog."

Sometimes he gets a kick or a bullet for his confidence. At other times he is not noticed as he strives hard to look as if he belonged to someone. . . . He will follow an officer who calls him, wag his tail as if it would twist off, appear most grateful, and would fain follow him to the end of the earth if allowed. . . . He lives well on the offal of the camp, and if anyone gives him protection he is all right.

"In every instance," Conyngham goes on to say,

the Negroes have proved our friends, giving us valuable information relative to the enemy's movements; also acting as scouts and spies, informing us where the enemy had concealed their cattle, and the like. The poor, despised Negroes look upon our arrival as fulfilling the millennium—the days of "jubilon."

As during the march from Atlanta to the sea, thousands of blacks of all ages fell in behind the Union columns, some on foot, some astride mules, and some in horse-drawn wagons and carriages. They had with them, as one officer noted, "all their earthly goods, and many goods which were not theirs."

Moving some miles ahead of the Union columns were processions of a different nature. As explained by native South Carolinian William Gilmore Simms, one of the era's best-known novelists:

Daily did long trains of fugitives line the roads, with wives and children, and horses and stock and cattle, seeking refuge from the pursuers. Long lines of wagons covered the highways. Half-naked

Refugees and their servants moving ahead of Sherman's columns.

people cowered from the winter under bush tents in the thickets, under the eaves of houses, under the railroad sheds, and in old cars left . . . along the route. All these repeated the same story of suffering, violence, poverty, and nakedness. Habitation after habitation, village after village—one sending up its signal flames to the other, presaging for it the same fate—lighted the winter and midnight sky with crimson horrors.

Though General Sherman was a talkative man, he made a practice of keeping his ultimate plans to himself, revealing even to those near him only as much as he had to. With the army now about a hundred miles north of Savannah, Major Nichols wrote:

The heads of column of the different corps are all pointed northward, and it would seem as if the first grand movement of the Georgia campaign was to be repeated now. Then we threatened Macon and Augusta, and captured Milledgeville, the state capital. Now . . . we are . . . demonstrating upon both Charleston and Augusta. Shall we continue the parallel, and advance upon Columbia, South Carolina's capital? A few days will tell the story.

Meanwhile the people of Charleston and Augusta are in great fear. Their newspapers are filled with frantic appeals to the citizens to resist the invader, and all sorts of preparations have been made for our reception. All the while we are perfectly sure that one or both cities are . . . within our power, even if we do not choose to go and take possession. . . .

It is useless to conjecture what will be the next move. I think the army is altogether indifferent about the matter. It has such an abiding faith in General Sherman that it will go wherever he leads. "Leads" is the proper word, for he is always on the skirmish line, frequently pitching his camp there. He never rests contented with the reports of others; he must see the condition of affairs for himself, and so is generally to be found in the front.

With all of his columns having reached, or having at least neared the South Carolina Railroad, and with the heads of various units resting at intervals along this northwesterly line from Charleston to Augusta, Sherman prepared to press his advance northward. The next barrier was the South Fork of the Edisto River. Sherman made his personal approach to the river at Binnaker's Bridge. A mile beyond this crossing was a planta-

tion where Mrs. "H.J.B." was staying with her sister-in-law, Mrs. "Dr. S."

Mrs. H.J.B. relates:

All day long we had been expecting the enemy, waiting his dreaded approach in fear and trembling.... I had run from the enemy once before, being one of the many unfortunates whom his rain of shot and shell had forced to leave Atlanta, but now I was literally at my "row's end." I could go no further.

For the time being I had found a safe and pleasant refuge in the family of my sister-in-law.... We were both the wives of Confederate soldiers.... The house... was justly considered... one of the largest and finest in that section of the country....

The bridge across the Edisto at this point had been destroyed... for the purpose of obstructing the passage of the enemy.... The bridge gone, it seemed almost impossible that they could effect a crossing, as all the swamps in the vicinity were overflowed, and even the construction of a pontoon bridge seemed for the time impossible....

Somehow the impression had gotten abroad, doubtless by his own adroit maneuvering, that Sherman, with the full strength of his forces, was bearing upon Augusta, and had left merely a raiding party behind him to complete the destruction of the railroad.... Very little apprehension was at first entertained of their intention or desire to cross the river at this point, where but a

Crossing the South Edisto

mere handful of our men guarded it. For two or three days [these men] had kept up a slow kind of desultory firing, occasionally "picking off" a stray bluecoat as he carelessly exposed himself upon the river's bank.

However, on Tuesday afternoon [February 9] just before sundown, one of our colonel's aides came rushing up to the house to inform us that it was Sherman himself, with his [Seventeenth Corps] . . . in camp on the opposite side of the river, and worse than all, they were on the point of effecting a crossing. . . .

Previous to this startling announcement we had about come to the conclusion that we would try to get away if we could. 'Tis true that Sherman had made official announcement that if we would remain in our homes they would not be destroyed, neither would we be molested so long as we remained passive. But with the full details of the many deeds of brutality enacted by his men, of which helpless women and children were the victims, while "hoping against hope," we yet awaited the inevitable with sinking hearts.

We knew now that it was impossible for us to get away. Time was too short. Besides the weather was bitterly cold, and the roads wet and almost impassable in many places. Some of our children, too, were sick, and we dreaded the exposure for them.

No sooner was the information given us by the soldier than our friends hastened at once to their homes to hide their mules, horses, and other stocks in the hammocks and swamps, and the masculine portion of them—old men, boys nearly grown, and a few soldiers home on sick leave—to conceal themselves wherever they could. . . .

The sun was just sinking as our men [i.e., the detachment guarding the river crossing] began their retreat. Poor fellows! How sad and forlorn they looked as they filed slowly by the gate. I stood upon the piazza and watched them with tears rushing down my cheeks. . . .

My heart was in a perfect agony of suspense over the future fate of my sister-in-law, myself, and our young and helpless children, yet there was not a cord within it but ached keenly as I gazed upon this forlorn band of worn and defeated heroes who had nobly born the brunt of a hundred battles and must yet retreat ignominiously before the advancing hosts of the enemy and leave the helpless women and children. I could well imagine their feelings, as with bowed heads, tattered clothing, and pinched hungry-looking faces, they passed with slow, monotonous tramp, tramp, tramp along the road. . . .

With their departure every remnant of assistance and protection seemed snatched away from us, and I dreaded, beyond the power of pen to describe, what I knew we had to encounter, for my sister-in-law was a timid young creature and I knew she and the children would look to me for everything. I prayed fervently to God to give me courage to meet the foe with firmness, and that I might never forget that I was a true Southern soldier's wife. . . .

As I saw the rear of the small body of men passing the gate I ran out to them and entreated them to tell me how long it would be before the Yankees came.

An officer answered at once, hurriedly and excitedly: "For God's sake, madam, go back to the house, unless you want your head taken off by a sharpshooter! They are right up the lane, not a half mile away. Do you not hear the firing?"

I was not long in getting back to the house. . . . I went into my sister-in-law's bedroom [on the first floor, across a hallway from the parlor] and found her terribly excited.

"Janie," I said, "let us go into the parlor and meet them there."

She demurred at first, but finally consented in fear and trembling, and we went, followed by the poor, frightened children, who were too young, thank God, to take in fully the situation.

After sitting a while before the fire my sister-in-law became dreadfully nervous and begged that we should go back to the room we had just quitted. She was afraid, she said, that we would be shot at through the windows . . . for the sound of firing up the lane was gradually growing nearer. I tried to pacify her, but in vain, and finally we went back to the bedroom.

There I took up a book, pretending to read, in order to show her, as I hoped, that I was not afraid. But I couldn't distinguish one word from another. The whole page was a blur before my eyes. [As darkness fell and the shooting ended,] I grew nervous and restless myself. . . . I began to grow anxious for them to come. Anything to end the dreadful suspense.

Arising, I went to one of the windows to reconnoiter. The night was bitterly cold and the moon was shining clearly and brightly. . . . While I stood there I saw a man, whom I rightly guessed by his musket and uniform to be a Yankee soldier, enter the yard by a side gate and move slowly and cautiously towards the rear of the house, followed by another, and still another. They were sent in advance to see if the way was clear, I was sure, and in a little while, apparently well assured of this fact, they retreated to a small strip of woodland in plain sight of the house.

But a few moments elapsed after this preliminary inspection until the whole army came in upon us in overwhelming numbers. The lawn, the yards, the halls, every room in the house—not excepting the one bedroom we had reserved for ourselves—were soon filled with the struggling, cursing mass of bluecoats.

For a time Pandemonium reigned supreme. . . . Their first object seemed plunder. Closets, bureaus, and trunks were violently opened and ruthlessly rifled of their contents. Nothing seemed sacred from their vile touch—pictures, old letters, locks of hair, pressed flowers, and other hallowed mementoes of the dead were scattered about and trampled upon as worthless objects.

You could hear their clothes crackle and snap as they moved about, for . . . they had waded through the swamps up to their waists, and every garment was frozen stiff; and when their work of plunder was finished their next desire seemed to be to get to the fires to warm and dry themselves. And, pushing and jostling and swearing, they crowded us away from even the one fireplace and stood there turning themselves around before the cheerful blaze as they could find room to do so, the ice as it melted running in pools of water from their clothing, and the smoke and steam arising therefrom making the close atmosphere almost unendurable.

Out in the yard and all around the plantation we could hear the work of destruction going on—cows lowing, pigs squealing, lambs bleating, turkeys, geese, chickens, and ducks squawking.

Very soon the officers in command arrived. I heard their tones of authority [through the open bedroom door] as they came into the hall. I also heard one of them ask if the house was occupied, and our home servant . . . replied:

"Yes, sir; and the ladies want to see you a few moments in the parlor."

We had instructed her to say this, as we desired to ask for a guard to protect us as soon as the officers came. I listened anxiously for the answer, and all too soon it came, falling upon us with brutal, stunning force.

"The ladies, the devil! If it hadn't been for them encouraging and egging on the men to fight, the war would have been squelched years ago."

For a few moments I felt completely dazed by this speech. Were these the men from whom we were to ask mercy and protection? I tried to move across the hall to the door of the parlor, which had just closed behind them, but for the moment I seemed rooted to the spot. Making a mighty effort I recovered my composure and my courage at the same time and turned and spoke to my trembling young sister-in-law.

"Come, Janie, let us go now and get through with this hateful business as speedily as possible."

"No, no, I cannot!" she said, bursting into tears and looking at me so pitifully that I saw it would be a cruelty to force her. There was then no other alternative for me than to "face the music" alone.

As I entered the parlor two of the officers who were sitting in front of the fire arose at once and politely greeted me. I was sure neither of these could have been the speaker of the language I had heard from the hall.

I told . . . them that we had understood General Sherman had promised protection to all those who remained in their homes, and we expected that protection, and if we did not get it right away we would not need it when we did get it, for the men were at that very moment plundering the house and laying violent hands upon everything worth appropriating.

No sooner had the words been uttered than both turned at once and, going into the hall, each caught hold of the first soldier that came in his way and gave them orders to clear the house immediately, and to keep guard until relieved. In a few moments we were alone and unmolested. But, alas, our home was bare, our larder especially so. . . .

Very soon [a] general and his staff arrived. . . . The officers began crowding into every room where there was a fire to warm themselves. I left my room at once and went again into the parlor, as I wished particularly to see General Sherman, although I was uncertain as to whether or not he had yet arrived.

The room was completely filled the second time, and I did not meet with the ready politeness and attention the two officers had at first shown me.

As I made my way to the fireplace my attention was at once attracted to one of the officers who sat in the corner with a map open on his knee. From the pictures I had from time to time seen of him I knew at once that this was General Sherman. But I determined to feign ignorance so long as I could.

The map proved to be a complete diagram of all the farms, roads, and rivers in [our] county. As I advanced towards him he raised his head at once, and without any preliminaries whatever, asked abruptly, "Whose farm is this, madam?"

"Dr. S.'s, sir," I replied at once. . . .

"I want nothing but the truth, remember," said Sherman, again as abruptly and as offensively as before.

"Unlike yourself," I answered hotly, "I am incapable of anything else, sir."

A slight flush of annoyance gathered upon his face for a moment. . . .

"Are you a rebel soldier's wife, madam?" he questioned again.

"I?"

"Yes, you."

"Am"—I said the word slowly and then paused to look into General Sherman's face with the most innocent stare imaginable.

"Well?" he questioned impatiently.

"I am the"—I go on, then another pause—"wife"—I again pause—"of"—pause—*"a Confederate soldier, and glory in the thought"*-the last words being rolled out with a volume and an intensity that surprised even myself.

At this moment the book [of maps] was shut up with a vicious snap, and the back of the hero of the March to the Sea was politely turned upon me.

"I say, my little man," exclaimed one of the officers present at this juncture, as he patted my little nephew Willie upon the head, "did you ever see so many Yanks before?"

"Oh, yes, sir," the child answered. . . .

"Where?"

"In Atlanta."

"Are you from Atlanta, madam?" the man turned to ask of me.

"Yes," I answered. "I am one of those whom Sherman's shells drove from the dismantled city. He has made some of us women wade through seas of pain and suffering, I can tell you. But as much as we have suffered from his cruelty, there isn't one of us who would exchange places with him in the next world for all the wealth and stores he has allowed his men to steal from we poor, downtrodden 'rebels,' as he terms us. By-the-by, how long before he will be here? I am nearly dying with curiosity to see him. I hear he is the very handsomest man in the army."

As these words escaped me, a broad smile went the rounds of the officers, and Sherman himself, who without doubt saw through my feigned ignorance, turned at once and said sharply:

"I don't think your presence is further needed here, madam. You may retire."

And, putting on his hat, he himself walked towards the door.

"Thank you, kindly, for the permission," I said with broad sarcasm as he passed me.

A moment later the door closed upon his retreating form, and that was the first and last time my eyes ever rested upon General William Tecumseh Sherman.

Sherman rose early the next morning and rode westward about fifteen miles to Blackville:

I conferred with Generals Slocum and Kilpatrick [of the left wing] . . . and . . . made orders for the next movement north to Columbia, the right wing to strike Orangeburg en route. Kilpatrick [with his cavalry] was ordered to demonstrate strongly toward Aiken, to keep up the delusion that we might turn toward Augusta; but he was notified that Columbia was the next objective, and that he should cover the left flank against Wheeler, who hung around it. I wanted to reach Columbia before any part of Hood's army could possibly get there. Some of them were reported as having reached Augusta. . . .

Sherman rejoined the army's right wing, accompanying it on its march to Orangeburg. Approaching the town with the head of the Seventeenth Corps on February 12, he was one of the first men to cross a repaired bridge over the North Edisto and make the entry. Orders were given for the destruction of public property only, but soon a good part of the town was in flames.

Again in Sherman's words:

I . . . visited a large hospital, on a hill near the railroad depot, which was occupied by the orphan children who had been removed from the asylum in Charleston. We gave them protection and . . . provisions. The railroad and depot were destroyed. General [F. P.] Blair was ordered to break up this railroad forward to the point where it crossed the Santee. . . .

On the morning of the 13th I . . . joined the Fifteenth Corps . . . and moved straight for Columbia. . . . Orders were sent to all of the columns to turn for Columbia, where it was supposed the enemy had concentrated all the men they could from Charleston, Augusta, and even from Virginia.

That night I was with the Fifteenth Corps, twenty-one miles from Columbia, where my aide, Colonel [J. C.] Audenried, picked up a rebel officer on the road, who, supposing him to be of the same service with himself, answered all his questions frankly, and revealed the truth that there was nothing in Columbia except Hampton's cavalry.

The march into Blackville, South Carolina

The fact was that General Hardee, in Charleston, took it for granted that we were after Charleston. The rebel troops in Augusta supposed they were our objective. So they abandoned poor Columbia to the care of Hampton's cavalry, which was confused by the rumors that poured in on it, so that both Beauregard and Wade Hampton, who were in Columbia, seem to have lost their heads.

13

THE BURNING OF COLUMBIA

AMONG THE CIVILIANS *in Columbia at this time was the author, William Gilmore Simms. He says that "daily accessions of fugitives, bringing with them their valuables and provisions, made ample report of the progress of the Federal army."*

Columbia was naturally held to be one of the most secure places of refuge. It was never doubted that this capital city, which contained so many of the manufactures of the Confederate Government, the Treasury, etc., would be defended with . . . concentrated vigor . . . especially, too, as upon the several railroads connected with the city the army of Lee and the safety of Richmond were absolutely dependent.

Young women of family were sent in large numbers to the city . . . [which] seemed to promise a degree of security not to be hoped for in any obscure rural abode. The city was accordingly doubled in population.

And here also was to be found an accumulation of wealth, in plate, jewels, pictures, books, manufactures of art and virtu, not to be estimated—not, perhaps, to be paralleled in any other town of the Confederacy. In many instances, the accumulations were those of a hundred years—of successive generations—in the hands of the oldest families of the South.

A large proportion of the wealth of Charleston had been stored in the capital city, and the owners of these treasures, in many instances, were unable to effect any farther remove. If apprehensive of the dangers, they could only fold their hands and, hoping against hope, pray for escape from a peril to which they could oppose no farther vigilance or effort.

Still the lurking belief with most persons who apprehended the approach of the Federal army encouraged the faith that, as the city was wholly defenseless, in the event of a summons, it would be surrendered upon the usual terms, and that these would necessarily insure the safety of noncombatants and protect their property.

But, in truth, there was no small portion of the inhabitants who denied or doubted, almost to the last moment, that Sherman contemplated any serious demonstration upon the city. They assumed—and this idea was tacitly encouraged, if not believed, by the authorities, military and civil—that the movement on Columbia was but a feint....

Simms goes on to explain that all speculation about Sherman's intentions ended on Tuesday, February 14, 1865, when the Federal army reached a point about twelve miles below the city:

Here the Confederate troops, consisting of the mounted men of Hampton, Wheeler, Butler, etc., made stubborn head against Sherman.... This skirmishing continued throughout Wednesday, but failed to arrest his progress; and as the Federal cannon continued momently to sound more heavily upon our ears, we were but too certainly assured of the hopelessness of the struggle. The odds of force against the Confederates were too vast....

On this same day, Simms continues, the city was placed under martial law, with General E. M. Law holding the top authority:

With characteristic energy, the officer executed his trusts... in the maintenance of order. This, with some few exceptions, was surprisingly maintained. There was some riotous conduct.... Some highway robberies were committed, and several stores broken open and robbed. But, beyond these, there were but few instances of crime and insubordination.

Terrible, meanwhile, was the press, the shock, the rush, the hurry, the universal confusion—such as might naturally be looked for in the circumstance of a city from which thousands were preparing to fly without previous preparations for flight—burdened with pale and trembling women, their children and portable chattels—trunks and jewels, family Bibles, and the *lares familiares* [servants].

The railroad depot for Charlotte was crowded with anxious waiters upon the train—with a wilderness of luggage—millions, perhaps, in value—much of which was left finally and lost.... These scenes of struggle were in constant performance.

The citizens fared badly. The Governments of the State and of the Confederacy absorbed all the modes of conveyance. Transportation about the city could not be had, save by a rich or favored few. No love could persuade where money failed to convince, and SELF, growing bloated in its dimensions, stared from every hurrying aspect as you traversed the excited and crowded streets.

Shortly the sound of musketry, in addition to that of cannonry, could be heard in the city. By this time, according to a woman identified simply as Mrs. "E.L.L.," people who were staying at home were busy "burying valuables underground and in every conceivable place."

My sister raised one or two boards of our storeroom floor and, with some difficulty, the clay soil being as hard as rock, dug a hole in which she hid away some bottles of brandy.... She sewed up one bottle in our mattress.

Says another resident, Mrs. S. A. Crittenden:

I had dressed a day or two before for any emergency.... I had taken an apron of strong Scotch gingham, doubled it up and run casings in it, and into these casings stowed away important papers belonging to my husband, some money, and a few articles of jewelry. This I wore as a bustle....

On February 16 the Federals arrived in force on the south bank of the Congaree River, just across from the city. The diarist from Minnesota, Alonzo Brown, felt that the army must have impressed the Confederates as looking like "a great war picture on canvas."

The blue uniforms, glistening arms, fluttering banners, and shining brass guns of the artillery, with the many regiments of cavalry and the long train of army wagons with their white covers, taken all together, made up a scene that can probably never be forgotten by the people of Columbia who witnessed it.

Sherman himself was present:

Riding down to the river bank, I saw the wreck of the large bridge which had been burned by the enemy, with its many stone piers still standing.... Across the Congaree River lay the city of Columbia, in plain, easy view. I could see the unfinished State House, a handsome granite structure, and the... railroad depot.... Occasionally a few citizens or cavalry could be seen running across the streets, and quite a number of Negroes were seemingly busy in carrying off bags of grain or meal which were piled up near the . . . depot.

Captain [Francis] De Gress had a section of his twenty-pound Parrott guns unlimbered, firing into the town. I asked him what he was firing for. He said he could see some rebel cavalry occasionally at the intersections of the streets, and he had an idea that there was a large force of infantry concealed on the opposite bank, lying low, in case we should attempt to cross over directly into town.

The shellfire caused great consternation among Columbia's citizens, but, according to William Gilmore Simms, the damage "was comparatively slight."

The new capitol building was struck five times, but suffered little or no injury. Numerous shells fell into the inhabited portions of the city, yet we heard of only two persons killed—one in the hospital square, and another near the South Carolina Railroad Depot. The venerable Mr. S. J. Wagner, from Charleston, an aged citizen of near eighty, narrowly escaped with his life, a shell bursting at his feet. His face was excoriated by the fragments . . . but . . . the hurts were slight. . . .

Adds Mrs. Crittenden:

I was promenading the front piazza, listening to the dull boom of cannonry as it came borne on the western breeze from across the river, feeling all the horrors of the situation, when my attention was attracted to a ragged little darkey—one of the institutions of all Southern cities—as he went whistling quite unconcernedly on the opposite side of the street.

Suddenly a bombshell came hurtling through the air, struck a limb just over his head, shivering it into a thousand pieces. Like lightning the little Arab rolled himself into an inconceivably small black ball, crouching against the fence, with scarcely anything visible but the whites of his eyes, which he turned in amazement towards the shattered limb.

For one brief moment he lay there. Then springing up he exclaimed . . . "Fore God, I thought he had me!" and fled like the wind.

According to the Union adjutant, Fenwick Hedley, the Yankees crowding the south bank of the Congaree recognized Columbia as being the hotbed of the Rebellion, the birthplace of nullification, out of which came secession as a legitimate fruit; and they looked upon its occupation as a triumph even more significant than the capture of Richmond itself.

But for the moment the army was frustrated. The Congaree, which flowed in a southeasterly direction, was wide and swift. It could not be crossed without great risk. Just northwest of the city (to the army's left), however, was the juncture of the two rivers that made up the Congaree, the Saluda and the Broad, which were less fierce. Both had to be crossed to gain access to the city. The effort was begun on Thursday, February 16, at the Saluda Factory, which stood on the very bank of the river.

Among the officers present was Major Nichols:

When I visited the factory our skirmishers occupied the windows facing the river and were exchanging shots with the Rebels, who lay concealed among the bushes and timber on the other side. This circumstance, however, did not hinder the operatives, all of whom were women, from hurrying through the building, tearing the cloth from the looms and filling bags with bales of yarn, to be "toted" home, as they phrased it.

It must not be imagined that these Southern factory operatives are of the same class with the lively and intelligent workers of New England. I remember that while reading descriptions of the Saluda Factory and discussing the probabilities of finding it in our line of march through South Carolina, many of our officers drew fanciful sketches of pretty, bright-eyed damsels, neatly clad, with a wealth of flowing ringlets and engaging manners. Such factory girls were visible in the great mills of Lowell, and the enthusiastic Northerners doomed to fight on Southern soil were excusable for drawing mental pictures of them.

But when we came to see the reality at Saluda Factory, sensations of disgust and mirthfulness struggled for the mastery—disgust at the repulsive figures whom we encountered, and amusement at the chopfallen air of the gallant young staff officers who were eager to pay their court to beauty and virtue.

It would be difficult to find elsewhere than at this place a collection of two hundred and fifty women so unkempt, frowzy, ragged, dirty, and altogether ignorant and wretched. Some of them were chewing tobacco; others, more elegant in their tastes, smoked. Another set indulged in the practice of "dipping" [using snuff]. Sights like this soon put to flight our rosy ideals.

The residences of these people accorded with their personal appearance. Dirty wooden shanties, built on the river bank a few hundred feet above the factory, were the places called homes—homes where doors hung shabbily by a single hinge, or were destitute of panels; where rotten steps led to foul and close passageways, filled with broken crockery, dirty pots and pans, and other accumulations of rubbish; where stagnant pools of water bred disease; where half a dozen persons occupied the same bed chamber; where old women and ragged children lolled lazily in the sunshine; where even the gaunt fowls that went disconsolately about the premises partook of the prevailing character of misery and dirt. . . .

The factory is a large stone building, filled with machinery for the manufacture of yarn and the variety of coarse cotton cloth known as Osnaburgs. The looms were dirty and rusty; the spindles were worn out by misuse; the spools appeared conscious that they had fulfilled their mission; the engine was out of joint and dirty. . . .

As I left the premises and rode away down the glen, I passed a group of the degraded and unfortunate women . . . toiling up the hill with back-loads of plunder. Some of our soldiers were helping them to carry their cloth and yarn.

At the same time, other soldiers were setting the factory afire. Some of the women laid down their plunder and turned to watch. David Conyngham says it was sad to see them "weeping and wringing their hands in agony, as they saw . . . their only means of support in flames."

Major Nichols, still writing on February 16, goes on to explain:

After sharp skirmishing, we managed to get a few men across the river in boats. I never saw more spirited, determined fighting than that of those few hundred brave fellows. Usually our foragers have the advance, but in this instance the skirmishers had all the fun to themselves.

Gaining the shelter of a rail fence thirty yards from the river, they formed a line, and at a given signal clambered over, and with inspiring cries ran across the open field for the woods, in which the Rebels were posted, and out of which the well-aimed shots of our soldiers instantly drove them.

In two hours from that moment a pontoon had been stretched

across the stream, and a division had driven the Rebels across the peninsula to Broad River, which it is necessary to bridge before we can enter Columbia. . . .

General [John A.] Logan promises he will have a brigade across Broad River and bridge the stream before morning.

Logan was in a jubilant mood. He is credited with inventing a ditty:

Hail Columbia, happy land;
If I don't burn you, I'll be damned!

Whether of Logan's invention or not, the ditty was chanted widely among the men of his proud Fifteenth Corps.

Many of the Federals had acquired an additional reason for hating the city. On the banks of the Saluda they had come upon the remains of another prisoner of war camp. Sherman describes it as being a set of "mud hovels and holes in the ground which our prisoners had made to shelter themselves from the winter's cold and the summer's heat."

But it wasn't Sherman's intention to devastate Columbia. It is true he had issued orders for the destruction of "the public buildings, railroad property, manufacturing and machine shops," but he had ordered the sparing of "libraries, asylums, and private dwellings."

That night, with hundreds of Union bivouac fires in sight on the peninsula between the Saluda and Broad rivers, and with the sound of band music, song, and laughter drifting across the water toward the city, the Confederates lost their last degree of hope.

"At a late hour," says William Gilmore Simms,

the Governor, with his suite and a large train of officials, departed. The Confederate army began its evacuation. . . . After all the depletion, the city contained, according to our estimate, at least twenty thousand inhabitants, the larger proportion being females and children and Negroes. . . .

The inhabitants were startled at daylight on Friday morning by a heavy explosion. This was the South Carolina Railroad Depot. It was accidentally blown up. Broken open by a band of plunderers, among whom were many females and Negroes, their reckless greed precipitated their fate. This building had been made the receptacle of supplies from sundry quarters, and was crowded with stores of merchants and planters, trunks of treasure, innumerable wares and goods of fugitives—all of great value.

It appears that, among its contents, were some kegs of powder. The plunderers paid, and suddenly, the penalties of their crime. Using their lights freely and hurriedly, the better to *pick,* they fired a train of powder leading to the kegs. The explosion followed, and the number of persons destroyed is variously estimated from seventeen to fifty....

At an early hour on Friday, the commissary and quartermaster stores were thrown wide, the contents cast out into the streets and given to the people. The Negroes especially loaded themselves with plunder.... Wheeler's cavalry also shared largely of this plunder, and several of them might be seen bearing off huge bales upon their saddles.

Mrs. "E.L.L." takes up:

In trepidation and haste we dressed ourselves and children, and waited in great anxiety the further development. Breakfast was served, but we were too much disturbed to partake of it. Then, too, the enemy sent their shells again, reminding us of their proximity. One falling in the yard where my sister was staying, just across the street, made us start from our seats and run out, eagerly inquiring where to seek protection for our little ones.

No place was to be found, so we nerved ourselves and prayed for strength to meet our fate. While standing on the porch to see, if possible, someone who would or could tell us what to expect, General Beauregard and staff, with heads bowed as if in great sorrow, rode slowly and sadly past.

Bareheaded women rushed out of their doors, asking what was the matter, and entreating him not to leave them. After riding on apace, he sent one of his aides back to inform us that they were retreating....

"What? Leave us?" was the agonized cry which burst from every lip. "Leave us in the hands of the dreaded foe? Then God have mercy upon us poor, helpless, deserted women!"

Union General Logan's men were still working on their pontoon bridge across Broad River. One of Logan's brigades, that of Colonel George A. Stone, had already crossed the river in boats and on rafts and were engaging some lingering units of Wheeler's cavalry as they made their way toward the city.

Among the Federals on the peninsula who were awaiting the comple-

tion of Logan's bridge was David Conyngham, who relates that

the high bluff on the margin [of the river] was crowded with officers and men. There was General Sherman, now pacing up and down in the midst of the group . . . with an unlit cigar in his mouth . . . now and then abruptly halting to speak to some of the generals around him. Again he would sit down, whittle a stick, and soon nervously start up to resume his walk. . . .

Sitting on a log . . . was Howard, reading a newspaper and occasionally stopping to answer a question of Sherman's or make a comment on some passage. Howard always looks the same—the kind, courteous general, the Christian soldier.

Another of the group was Frank P. Blair, with his strongly marked features, indicative alike of talent, energy, and ability.

John A. Logan, too, was there, with his dark, almost bronzed countenance, the fiery, commanding eye, the true type of the dashing general.

Not least was General Hazen, the hero of McAllister, with his frank, expressive features and finely moulded head, betokening the warm-hearted gentleman, the soldier of mind and brains.

These, with several other generals, with a host of gay officers and orderlies in the background, formed a group worthy the pencil of a Rubens or Vandyke.

Colonel Stone's brigade was now advancing on Columbia, and . . . he met the mayor . . . and three members of the city council, coming out in a carriage to surrender the town. . . .

As soon as the pontoon was laid, General Sherman, accompanied by several other generals, their staffs and orderlies, forming a brilliant cavalcade, rode into the city amidst a scene of the most enthusiastic excitement. Ladies crowded the windows and balconies, waving banners and handkerchiefs. They were the wives and sisters of the few proscribed Union people of Columbia. . . .

Negroes were grouped along the streets, cheering, singing, and dancing in the wild exuberance of their newborn freedom. Perhaps the most flattering compliment paid to us was by a Negro, whom, with upturned features and clasped hands, I heard exclaim, "At last! At last! Our saviours!"

Many of the black people swarmed around Sherman's horse and reached for his hand, which he gave them freely. Other blacks, and even some of the whites, were busy presenting the Yankees with buckets of liquor they had pilfered, which increased the general joy.

Conyngham goes on to say that

Ringing cheers and shouts echoed far and wide, mingled with the martial music of the bands as they played "Hail Columbia," "Yankee Doodle," and other national airs.

In the words of one of the white spectators, a woman of Confederate sympathies:

I counted twelve bands of music pass by playing at full blast, and yet they were at such a distance from each other that the music of the one had died away before that of another reached my ears. They were a strong, healthy, well-fed looking set of men. . . . When I looked upon these and contrasted them with the pallid, hungry, ill-clad men I had been associated with for so long, and thought of the thin garments, tattered blankets, and scanty rations of the few men I had seen leave Columbia a few hours before, and reflected on the unequal struggle that for nearly four years had been going on, the proud tears rained down from my eyes as I prayed God to make me worthy to be the countrywoman of such heroes.

"Near the market square," Sherman discloses,

we found Stone's brigade halted, with arms stacked, and a large detail of his men, along with some citizens, engaged with an old fire-engine, trying to put out the fire in a long pile of burning cotton bales, which I was told had been fired by the rebel cavalry on withdrawing from the city that morning. . . . To avoid this row of burning cotton bales, I had to ride my horse on the sidewalk.

In the market square had collected a large crowd of whites and blacks, among whom was the mayor of the city, Dr. [T. J.] Goodwyn, quite a respectable old gentleman, who was extremely anxious to protect the interests of the citizens. He was on foot, and I on horseback, and . . . I told him then not to be uneasy, that we did not intend to stay long, and had no purpose to injure the private citizens or private property.

About this same time, according to Major Nichols,

the General was met by some of our prisoners, who had escaped before . . . our approach took place, and had been secreted in the town by the Negroes. . . . [Never] have I seen his face beam with such exultation and kindly greeting as when he took these poor fellows by the hand and welcomed them home—home to the army, to protection, to the arms of their brave comrades, to the dear old flag which had gone out of sight many months ago upon some well-remembered battlefield.

One of these men was Samuel H. M. Byers, adjutant of the Fifth Iowa Infantry, who had been captured fifteen months earlier while fighting under Sherman at Chattanooga. During his confinement Byers had managed to keep track of the general's work, and had written a song he called "Sherman's March to the Sea," which the Columbia Prison glee club sang not only for fellow inmates but also for visiting Confederate women.

Byers now handed a beautifully penned copy of the song to Sherman, which the general simply slipped into his pocket. Later, when he found time to turn his attention to the gift, he was to be so pleased with the stirring words and lively melody that he would attach Byers to his staff. The song was destined to become a great success in the North, and was to be sung for generations. (See Appendix for text of song.)

Sherman's orders for the troops to respect private property made an exception of their foraging for food and other necessities, and these activities were already leading to abuses. The guards being placed along the streets were unable to maintain a proper order. In some cases, the guards were joining in the abuses.

States the Southern author William Gilmore Simms:

Stores were broken open . . . and gold, silver, jewels, and liquors eagerly sought. . . . And woe to him who carried a watch with a gold chain pendant, or who wore a choice hat, or overcoat, or boots or shoes. He was stripped in the twinkling of an eye. . . . Purses shared the same fate; nor was the Confederate currency repudiated.

It was the confiscation of watches, Simms points out, that was the most common offense:

A frequent mode of operating was by first asking you the hour. If thoughtless enough to reply, producing the watch . . . it was quietly taken. . . . And if you hinted any dislike of the proceeding, a grasp was taken of your collar and the muzzle of a revolver put to your ear.

Adjutant Hedley reveals that Sherman was not altogether unaware that these things were going on:

It was a sight for a painter, the smile which overspread his features as his eyes fell upon one of his "bummers," who was just crossing the street in front of his horse's head. The fellow was far gone in liquor, his gait being wonderfully irregular. He wore a handsome silk dressing-gown reaching nearly to his feet, and outside of it were buckled his accoutrements. He carried his musket at a loose "shoulder shift." In place of his military head-gear, he wore a shiny "plug" hat, tilted well back, and around his neck were strung a number of epaulettes, evidently part of the stock of some military furnishing store. A moment after, he was in the clutches of the provost guard.

When Alonzo Brown's regiment entered the city in mid-afternoon, Brown noted that it was teeming with "drunken soldiers and drunken Negroes" and that "many long faces gazed from the windows."

Most of the citizens, however, had become cautiously optimistic. Considering that there were about 30,000 Yankees in and about the city, the pillaging was moderate and there seemed no threat of a general conflagration. It is true that the cotton ignited by the Confederates was still burning and giving off sparks in the wind; and that the embers of two railroad depots were doing the same (the one having been blown up accidentally and the other having been fired, along with the cotton, during the Confederate retreat); and that the inmates of the city's prison, entering into the spirit of things, tried twice to set the building afire. But the Yankees had started only a few fires, and none had spread. One of the estates burned in the suburbs was that of General Wade Hampton.

Adjutant Hedley tells of a bit of Yankee mischief:

A jolly party met in the old senate chamber, where, thirty-three years before, the legislature of South Carolina proclaimed its hostility to the Federal Union. A mock senate was organized, and a vote of censure was passed against John C. Calhoun, the great nullificationist, whose States' Rights doctrines had found their logical sequence in the existing wicked and unhappy rebellion. His marble bust, a conspicuous ornament of the hall, was

Yankees taking possession of Columbia's old state house

made the target for inkstands and spittoons. The secession ordinance was repealed. "John Brown" was then sung with great enthusiasm, and the senate adjourned. . . .

Sherman established his headquarters at the home of Blanton Duncan, located on a side street about seven blocks from the center of town. The general recounts that late in the afternoon

the mayor, Dr. Goodwyn, came to my quarters . . . and remarked that there was a lady in Columbia who professed to be a special friend of mine. On giving her name, I could not recall it, but inquired as to her maiden or family name. He answered Poyas. It so happened that, when I was a lieutenant at Fort Moultrie in 1842–1846 I used very often to visit a family of that name on the east branch of Cooper River, about forty miles from Fort Moultrie, and to hunt with the son, Mr. James Poyas, an elegant young fellow and a fine sportsman. His father, mother, and several sisters composed the family, and were extremely hospitable.

One of the ladies was very fond of painting in water colors, which was one of my weaknesses, and on one occasion I had presented her with a volume treating of water colors. Of course, I was glad to renew the acquaintance, and proposed to Dr. Goodwyn that we should walk to her house and visit this lady, which we did.

The house stood . . . in a large lot, was of frame, with a high porch, which was reached by a set of steps outside. Entering this yard, I noticed ducks and chickens, and a general air of peace and comfort that was really pleasant to behold at that time of universal desolation.

The lady in question met us at the head of the steps and invited us into a parlor which was perfectly neat and well furnished. After inquiring about her father, mother, sisters, and especially her brother James, my special friend, I could not help saying that I was pleased to notice that our men had not handled her house and premises as roughly as was their wont.

"I owe it to you, general," she answered.

"Not at all. I did not know you were here till a few minutes ago."

She reiterated that she was indeed indebted to me for the perfect safety of her house and property, and added, "You remember, when you were at our house on Cooper River in 1845 you gave me a book."

And she handed me the book in question, on the flyleaf of which was written: "To Miss Poyas, with the compliments of W. T. Sherman, First-lieutenant, Third Artillery."

She then explained that, as our army approached Columbia, there was a doubt in her mind whether the terrible Sherman who was devastating the land were W. T. Sherman or T. W. Sherman, both known to be generals in the Northern army. But, on the supposition that he was her old acquaintance, when Wade Hampton's cavalry drew out of the city, calling out that the Yankees were coming, she armed herself with this book and awaited the crisis.

Soon the shouts about the market house announced that the Yankees had come. Very soon men were seen running up and down the streets. A parcel of them poured over the fence, began to chase the chickens and ducks, and to enter her house. She observed one large man, with full beard, who exercised some authority, and to him she appealed in the name of his general.

"What do you know of Uncle Billy?"

"Why," she said, "when he was a young man he used to be our friend in Charleston, and here is a book he gave me."

The officer or soldier took the book, looked at the inscription, and, turning to his fellows, said: "Boys, that's so. That's Uncle Billy's writing, for I have seen it often before."

He at once commanded the party to stop pillaging, and left a man in charge of the house to protect her until the regular provost guard should be established.

I then asked her if the regular guard or sentinel had been as good to her.

She assured me that he was a very nice young man, that he had been telling her all about his family in Iowa, and that at that very instant of time he was in another room minding the baby. . . .

I made her a long social visit. . . .

Sherman was acquainted with one or two other women in Columbia. Earlier in the day he had received a note from the superioress of the city's convent explaining that she had been a teacher at the convent in Brown County, Ohio, at the time his daughter Minnie was a pupil there. Would he provide her buildings special protection? Though the superioress was known to be an ardent secessionist, Sherman had sent an officer to tell her that not only the convent but the entire city, except for war-related property, was safe from destruction.

To Mayor Goodwyn, Sherman explained that he had put off destroying the doomed buildings until the wind subsided enough to reduce the danger of a general fire.

His day having been long, busy, and tiring, Sherman returned to the Duncan house at sunset and lay down on his bed to rest.

David Conyngham takes up:

I spent the evening in the capitol looking over the archives and libraries. Part of Colonel Stone's brigade . . . was on duty there.

Towards night, crowds of our escaped prisoners, soldiers, and Negroes intoxicated with their new-born liberty, which they looked upon as a license to do as they pleased, were parading the streets in groups.

As soon as night set in, there ensued a sad scene indeed. The suburbs were first set on fire—some assert by the burning cotton which the rebels had piled along the streets.

It was windy, so the first fires may have originated in this way. But arsonists were busy at an early hour. Says Mrs. S. A. Crittenden:

We stood in the observatory and saw these fires—these tokens of a nation's shame and sin—kindle, one by one, along the horizon's verge. Soon they flashed out of the darkness nearer and nearer, rose higher and higher, spread wider and wider. . . .

Again in Conyngham's words:

I trust I shall never witness such a scene again—drunken soldiers rushing from house to house, emptying them of their valuables and firing them; Negroes carrying off piles of booty . . . and exulting like so many demons; officers and men revelling on the wines and liquors until the burning houses buried them in their drunken orgies. . . .

The frequent shots on every side told that some victim had fallen. Shrieks, groans, and cries of distress resounded from every side. . . .

A troop of cavalry . . . were left to patrol the streets, but I did not once see them interfering with the groups that rushed about to fire and pillage the houses.

True, Generals Sherman, Howard, and others were out giving instructions for putting out a fire in one place, while a hundred fires were lighting all around them. How much better would it have been had they brought in a division or brigade of sober troops and cleared out the town, even with steel and bullet. . . .

While the streets were crowded with . . . groups of demons from all the corps in the army, hundreds of noble-minded officers and civilians were exposing their own lives to save the lives and property of the citizens.

By this time, according to Mrs. "E.L.L.," the scene was "as bright as day."

The whole town was turned into a fearful bedlam. . . . The

Columbia in flames

men decked themselves with artificial flowers from the milliner's stores and danced in the streets. Musical instruments were dragged about and strummed upon, the cruel laughter and mocking jeers of the brutes called soldiers heightening the demoniacal scene.

Conyngham explains that the streets were also crowded "with helpless women and children, some in their night clothes." He saw "agonized and affrighted mothers" rushing around in search of children who were lost.

Invalids had to be dragged from their beds, and lay exposed to the flames and smoke that swept the streets, or to the cold of the open air in back yards. . . .

In the hospitals were some hundreds of rebel wounded. The agony and terror of the poor, helpless fellows while the fire raged around them were fearful; but, fortunately, the buildings did not catch fire.

Many of the private homes that escaped the fire were vandalized. "In several instances," says William Gilmore Simms,

parlors, articles of crockery, and even beds, were used by the soldiers as if they were water closets [i.e., toilets]. In one case, a party used vessels in this way, then put them on the bed, fired at them and smashed them to pieces, emptying the filthy contents over the bedding.

At the convent, prayer had been the order of the night since the first fires sprang up. In the words of one of the schoolgirls:

How many hours we remained upon our knees, poor affrighted creatures, I can't tell. But I do remember how we were suddenly brought to our feet by the awful cry, "The convent is on fire!"

Simultaneously with this cry came a fearful crash, and the chapel doors gave way before the battering rams of some of the fiends, and rapidly the sacred home was filled with soldiery. . . .

Good Father Lawrence collected us all in the lower hall, preparatory to marching us in some order to the Catholic Church, at that time beyond the falling houses and fierce flames.

A few friends and myself ran into the basement room where the trunks were kept, and with the strength of despair succeeded in smashing the ends of our trunks and drawing forth a few caskets of jewels and silver. . . .

Having no wrap, I threw over me a huge velvet cloak.... The Misses H., Miss C., and myself were among the last to leave the convent. And we were hurried off by the soldiers pouring down upon us, saying, "Don't you know everyone has gone with the Catholic priest? What are you girls doing here?"

"Trying to save a few things from you!" I said. And on we went to join our companions.

A sorrow-stricken cortege we were.... The priest with uplifted crucifix headed the procession. Behind him followed the nuns... their pallid faces, black habit, and dignified bearing lit up by the flames on either side through which we had to pass.... Behind the nuns came the schoolgirls, some of them little things, clinging to their older companions in terror, lest they might be torn away....

The crowd in the street did not interrupt us, as we had been furnished a guard....

Some of the Confederate cavalrymen who had been among the last soldiers to leave Columbia were at this time occupying an elevation only about a mile to the north. The scene, according to Major J. P. Austin, was "terrible to witness."

By 12 o'clock the city was one great sea of fire. From the position we occupied, the frightful conflagration seemed like the eruption of an hundred volcanoes, sending forth their lurid glare and lighting the horizon for miles around. Wreaths of flame shot upward and mingled with the clouds.

It seemed to Austin and his comrades that the Yankees had become "demons of fire." And to the people of the city, many of the Yankees were nothing less.

"While the flames were at their highest and most extensively raging," says William Gilmore Simms,

groups might be seen at the several corners of the streets, drinking, roaring, revelling, while the fiddle and accordian were playing their popular airs among them....

Ladies were hustled from their chambers, their ornaments plucked from their persons, their bundles from their hands.... Men and women bearing off their trunks were seized... [and] in a moment the trunk burst asunder with the stroke of axe or gun butt, the contents laid bare, rifled of all the objects of desire, and the residue sacrificed to the fire.

You might see the ruined owner, standing woebegone, aghast, gazing at his tumbling dwelling, his scattered property, with a dumb agony on his face.... Others you might hear, as we did, with wild blasphemies assailing the justice of Heaven, or invoking, with lifted and clenched hands, the fiery wrath of the avenger. But the soldiers plundered and drank, the fiery work raged, and the moon sailed over all....

People near the Market Hall in the center of town noted that the dial of the great clock in the tower became suddenly illuminated from within. Simms says that at 1:00 A.M. it struck the hour:

It was its own last hour which it sounded.... In less than five minutes after, its spire went down with a crash ... sending up ... great billowy showers of glowing fiery embers.

Throughout the whole of this terrible scene the soldiers continued their search after spoil. The houses were severally and soon gutted of their contents. Hundreds of iron safes, warranted "impenetrable to fire and the burglar," it was soon satisfactorily demonstrated were not "Yankee proof." They were split open and robbed, yielding, in some cases, very largely of Confederate money and bonds, if not of gold and silver.

Jewelry and plate in abundance was found. Men could be seen staggering off with huge waiters, vases, candelabra—to say nothing of cups, goblets, and smaller vessels, all of solid silver. Clothes and shoes, when new, were appropriated....

In the household where Mrs. "E.L.L." and her family awaited the Yankee onslaught, some members had grown "suddenly stout."

Two or three suits were added to the children's clothing as well as the grown persons', and hoopskirts provided receptacles for valuables of all kinds. My sisters were weighted down with jewelry and gold, not to speak of shoes and other articles of dress. One, naturally very slight, with a large shawl thrown around her ... appeared to weigh two hundred pounds. In spite of all this they escaped the ordeal of being searched, to which many others were subjected.

Mrs. E.L.L. herself was in bed when the soldiers arrived, having that very night become a mother. Her room was not molested, though the rest of the house was ransacked, and the threat of fire from groups outside was constant. One of her sisters, the woman explains, appealed to a Yankee captain for protection:

He promised to save the house, and he kept his word, fighting hard with every new party that set [a] fire, and succeeding in extinguishing the flames.

Mrs. E.L.L. goes on to say that her sisters displayed such courage in facing the Yankees that "some of them said they knew where to come, after the war, for wives—Southern women were so plucky."

"It was not always, however," adds Simms, "that our women were able to preserve their coolness and firmness."

We have quite an amusing story of a luckless wife who was confronted by a stalwart soldier with a horrid oath and a cocked revolver at her head.

"Your watch, your money, you damned rebel bitch!"

The horrid oaths, the sudden demand, fierce look, and rapid action so terrified her that she cried out, "Oh, my God! I have no watch, no money, except what's tied round my waist!"

We need not say how deftly the Bowie Knife was applied to loose the stays of the lady. She was then taught, for the first time in her life, that the stays were wrongly placed. They should have been upon her tongue.

Again becoming serious, Simms states that one elderly man

on beholding some too familiar approach to one of his daughters bade the man stand off at the peril of his life; saying that while he submitted to be robbed of property, he would sacrifice life without reserve—his own and that of the assailant—before his child's honor should be abused.

Mr. James G. Gibbes . . . pistol in hand, and . . . with the assistance of a Yankee officer, rescued two young women from the clutches of as many ruffians.

The author goes on to explain that the soldiers were "generally forbearing" in regard to sexual advances toward white women, but that a lot of black women were not so fortunate:

The poor Negroes were terribly victimized by their assailants, many of them . . . being left in a condition little short of death. Regiments, in successive *relays,* subjected scores of these poor women to the torture of their embraces. . . .

Simms claims that he knew of at least two women who were murdered, "one of them being thrust, when half dead, head down into a mud puddle, and there held until she was suffocated."

Mrs. S. A. Crittenden, who had been watching the progress of the fires from her home's observatory since early evening, was safe until about 2:00 A.M. Then:

I took a little bird in its cage, which I could not bear to leave to the flames, in one hand, and my little child's hand in the other, and walked out from under our burning roof into the cold and pitiless street. Hundreds, nay thousands, were there before me. . . .

The terrified lowing of cattle, the frenzied flight of pigeons circling high above their blazing cotes, the ribald jests and brutal assaults of our drunken conquerors . . . made up a picture whose counterpart can be found only in the regions of the eternally lost.

The people whom Mrs. Crittenden and her child joined in the streets were, like herself, looking for safety from the flames.

"These families," Simms relates,

moved in long procession, the aged sire or grandsire first—a sad, worn, and tottering man, walking steadily on, with rigid, set features and tearless eyes—too much stricken, too much stunned, for any ordinary shows of suffering. Perhaps the aged wife hung upon one arm, while the other was supported by a daughter. And huddling close, like terrified partridges, came the young, each bearing some little bundle—all pressing forward under the lead of the sire, and he witless where to go.

The ascending fire-spouts flamed before them on every hand—shouts assailed them at every step—the drunken soldiers danced around them as they went, piercing their ears with horrid threats and imprecations. The little bundles were snatched from the grasp of their trembling bearers, torn open, and what was not appropriated was hurled into the contiguous pile of flame.

And group after group, stream after stream of fugitives thus pursued their way through the paths of flaming and howling horror, only too glad to fling themselves on the open ground, whither, in some cases, they had succeeded in conveying a featherbed or mattress. The malls, or open squares, the centers of the wide streets, like Assembly Street, were thus strewn with piles of bedding on which lay exhausted mothers—some of them with anxious physicians in attendance and girded by crouching children and infants, wild and almost idiotic with their terrors....

It was scarcely possible to advise in which direction to fly. The churches were at first sought by many several streams of population. But these were found to afford no security. The churches of God were set on flame. Again driven forth, numbers made their way into the recesses of Sidney Park, and here fancied to find security, as but few houses occupied the neighborhood, and these not sufficiently high to lead to apprehension from the flames.

But the fireballs were thrown [i.e., blown by the wind] from the heights into the deepest hollows of the park, and the wretched fugitives were forced to scatter, finding their way to other places of retreat, and finding none of them secure.

About three o'clock in the morning a shift in the wind stopped the progress of the fires, sparing sections of the town whose doom had seemed imminent. And, according to Union newsman David Conyngham, by five o'clock sober troops brought into the city had the rioters under control.

Who is to blame for the burning of Columbia is a subject that will long be disputed. I know the Negroes and escaped prisoners were infuriated, and easily incited the inebriated soldiers to join them in their work of vandalism. Governor Magrath and General Wade Hampton are partly accountable for the destruction of their city. General Beauregard, the mayor, Dr. Goodwyn, and others wanted to send a deputation as far as Orangeburg to surrender the city, and, when evacuating, to destroy all the liquors. In both of these wise views they were overruled by the Governor and Wade Hampton, the latter stating that he would defend the town from house to house.

On the other hand, I must honestly say that I saw nothing to prevent General [Charles R.] Woods, who was in command [of the Union provost guard] ... from bringing sufficient troops to clear out the place, or his superior generals, either, from putting a stop to such disgraceful scenes....

The 18th of February dawned upon a city of ruins.... The noble-looking trees that shaded the streets, the flower gardens that graced them, were blasted and withered by fire. The streets were full of rubbish, broken furniture, and groups of crouching, desponding, weeping, helpless women and children....

In one place I saw a lady richly dressed, with three pretty little children clinging to her. She was sitting on a mattress, while round her were strewn some rich paintings, works of art, and virtu. It was a picture of hopeless misery surrounded by the trappings of refined taste and wealth....

The scene of desolation the city presented... was fearful. That long street of rich stores, the fine hotels, the court-houses, the extensive convent buildings, and the old capitol, where the order of secession was passed, with its fine library and state archives, were all in one heap of unsightly ruins and rubbish. Splen-

Ruins of Columbia. Lower right: the unfinished capitol

did private residences, lovely cottages, with their beautiful gardens, and the stately rows of trees, were all withered into ashes....

Old and young moved about seemingly without a purpose. Some mournfully contemplated the piles of rubbish, the only remains of their late happy homesteads. Old men, women, and children were grouped together. Some had piles of bedding and furniture which they saved from the wreck. Others who were wealthy the night previous had not now a loaf of bread to break their fast.

Children were crying with fright and hunger; mothers were weeping; strong men, who could not help either them or themselves, sat bowed down, with their heads buried between their hands.

The yards and offices of the Lunatic Asylum were crowded with people who had fled there for protection the night previous. Its wards, too, had received new subjects, for several had gone crazy from terror, or from having lost their children or friends in the flames.

The [remaining] churches were full of people who had crowded into them for shelter. The Park was sought as a refuge, and in one corner of it the helpless nuns and their timid charges were huddled together.

Sherman says that General Howard, second-in-command to himself in the city, aided Mayor Goodwyn in doing all that was possible to find shelter for those without homes:

And by my authority he turned over to the Sisters of Charity [i.e., the nuns] the Methodist College, and to the mayor five hundred beef cattle to help feed the people. I also gave the mayor one hundred muskets, with which to arm a guard to maintain order after we should leave the neighborhood.

Sherman had some unfinished business, and the suffering he saw on all sides did not deter him from what he believed to be his correct course.

As recorded by Major Nichols on February 19:

General Sherman has given orders for the farther destruction of all public property in the city, excepting the new capitol, which will not be injured. I think the General saves this building more because it is such a beautiful work of art than for any other reason.

The arsenal... store-houses, magazines... and cotton to the amount of twenty thousand bales are today destroyed. There is not a rail upon any of the roads within twenty miles of Columbia but will be twisted into corkscrews before the sun sets....

This afternoon several loud explosions were heard in the direction of the river. I learned that, as the troops who were detailed for the purpose were depositing the shells and powder [from the arsenal] in the river, one of the former accidentally exploded, the fire communicating to other ammunition, and to a large pile of powder on the banks. The result was mournfully disastrous, for several men were killed, and twenty were wounded....

General Sherman was horrified upon hearing of the accident, and remarked that the life of one of his soldiers was of more value than all the arsenals and magazines in the South, or even the city of Columbia itself.

Sherman was now ready to resume his march northward. It was thereafter to be the conviction of most Southerners and many Northerners that the general deliberately engineered Columbia's ruin. Years later, he himself was to say: "Though I never ordered it and never wished it, I have never shed many tears over the event, because I believe it hastened what we all fought for, the end of the war."

14

FINALE AT DURHAM'S STATION

PROSPECTS *for a quick end to the war were improving momentarily. The capture of Columbia forced the evacuation of Charleston. Had the garrison remained there, it would have been cut off as Sherman continued northward. When both the city and Fort Sumter in the harbor were seized by Federals operating on the coast, another great shout of exultation arose in the North. The foremost symbol of the uprising, Sumter had been in Confederate hands for nearly four years.*

On February 22, Wilmington, North Carolina, the South's last major seaport, fell to General Terry, as Sherman anticipated. This made his task easier, for he could draw both supplies and reinforcements from that point.

Up at Richmond and Petersburg, General Grant, much encouraged and abetted by Sherman's work, was waiting only for the advent of spring and good weather to launch an all-out effort against Lee.

Desertions from the Confederate armies were growing critical, as Sherman had predicted they would. "The simple fact that a man's home has been visited by an enemy makes a soldier very, very anxious to get home to look after his family and property."

Many a returned soldier found his property ravaged and his family scattered. Some of the disconsolate men began raiding the properties of the rich slaveowners Sherman hadn't reached, the rich being the people they blamed for the terrible turn of events.

It was during these last desperate days that the Confederacy turned again to General Joseph E. Johnston:

I was residing in Lincolnton, North Carolina, in February, 1865, and on the 23d of the month received . . . a dispatch from General Lee. . . . In it he directed me to assume the command of the Army of Tennessee and all troops in the Department of South Carolina, Georgia, and Florida, and to "concentrate all available forces and drive back Sherman."

... I ... accepted the command.... This was done with a full consciousness on my part, however, that we could have no object in continuing the war than to obtain fair terms of peace; for the Southern cause must have appeared hopeless then to all intelligent and dispassionate Southern men.

Johnston soon decided that "the first serious opposition to General Sherman's progress was to be in North Carolina."

I suggested to the general-in-chief that it was important that the troops of that department should be added to my command. The suggestion was adopted, and the necessary orders given without loss of time.

Among the Union marchers, no man was happier or more optimistic at this time than Sherman's newest staff member, Samuel Byers, until lately a prisoner of war, and the composer of "Sherman's March to the Sea."

What a change it was, from the degradation, the starving, the suffering ... to the headquarters of the most brilliant general of modern times.

Sherman was marching northward ... in four columns, on as many different roads.... One day he would ride with this column, the next day with that. But whenever he appeared among the soldiers it was one loud and continued cheer for "Billy Sherman."

Here was the general whom everybody knew, and whom everybody loved.... He was, indeed, looked upon as a sort of common property, in which every man in the army had a special and particular interest.... Whenever he appeared, the knapsacks of the boys grew lighter, the step brisk, and the face bright....

It rained nearly all the time. The roads were horrid, and had to be corduroyed with poles and rails half the way. The wagons and the artillery stuck in the mire hourly, and the soldiers had to drag them out with their own hands. Every stream had to be bridged, every quagmire filled, and every mile skirmished with the enemy....

Through all this the boys tugged and fought, and amidst their tugging sang and cheered. It was the magnetism of one really great man.... Riding alongside the regiments struggling through the mud or the underbrush ... he would often speak to the nearest soldiers with some kind and encouraging word. Nor was it unusual to hear private soldiers call out to him....

At headquarters [each evening] there was little pretense and no show.... A hasty but substantial meal was enjoyed, amid conversation on almost every topic but the war. On this he was oftenest silent, preferring to keep his own judgment, hopes and fears to himself. He wrote most... of his own dispatches, leaving his staff little or nothing to do. After supper he studied his maps in the firelight, or heard the reports from the other columns for the day. He was last in bed at night, and first in the saddle in the morning.

Dinner consisted of a light lunch at twelve. All dismounted at the roadside, and an hour's rest brought us again to the saddle.

So the days passed, and the enemy was continually pushed or beaten back from each and every chosen position.

At the end of one of these days, Alonzo Brown wrote in his diary:

Some of our men who were captured while out foraging had their throats cut and a label appended to their bodies upon which was written, "Death to all foragers." In retaliation for these murders, two of the rebels whom we had taken... were immediately tied to a tree and shot.

Advance units of the army reached Cheraw, near the North Carolina border, on March 3. David Conyngham noted that it was "a pleasant-

Union horsemen driving Confederates from Cheraw, South Carolina

looking town . . . on the Great Pee Dee River."

Here we captured twenty-five pieces of artillery . . . twelve cars, one locomotive, eighteen tons of powder, several thousand bales of cotton, and a large supply of stores. . . . A few houses were on fire when we entered the town. We burned the railroad depot and buildings.

Some of the stores found in the town, explains General Henry Slocum, had been sent up from Charleston for safekeeping:

Among the stores was a large quantity of very old wine of the best quality, which had been kept in the cellars of Charleston many years, with no thought on the part of the owners that in its old age it would be drunk from tin cups by Yankee soldiers.

Sherman was still about ten miles in the rear at this time, riding at the head of another column. Coming to a branch in the road that he believed led to the town, he paused to make certain:

Seeing a Negro standing by the roadside looking at the troops passing, I inquired of him what road that was.

"Him lead to Cheraw, master!"

"Is it a good road, and how far?"

"A very good road, and eight or ten miles."

"Any guerrillas?"

"Oh, no, master. Dey is gone two days ago. You could have played cards on der coattails, dey was in sich a hurry!"

I was on my Lexington horse, who was very handsome and restive. . . . I turned my horse down the road, and the rest of the staff followed.

General [W. F.] Barry took up the questions about the road, and asked the same Negro what he was doing there.

He answered, "Dey say Massa Sherman will be along soon!"

"Why," said General Barry, "that was General Sherman you were talking to."

The poor Negro, almost in an attitude of prayer, exclaimed, "De great God! Just look at his horse!"

He ran up and trotted by my side for a mile or so, and gave me all the information he possessed, but he seemed to admire the horse more than the rider.

We reached Cheraw in a couple of hours in a drizzling rain. . . .

General Howard . . . had already ordered his pontoon bridge

to be laid across the Pee Dee . . . and Mower's division was already across, skirmishing with the enemy about two miles out. . . . I was satisfied . . . that the enemy had not divined our movements, and that consequently they were still scattered. . . .

Having thus secured the passage of the Pee Dee, I felt no uneasiness about the future, because there remained no further great impediments between us and Cape Fear River, which I felt assured was by that time in possession of our friends [who had assaulted Wilmington from the Union beachhead at Fort Fisher].

On March 4, the twenty-five Confederate cannon captured in Cheraw were used to fire a salute in honor of Abraham Lincoln's second inauguration.

"Our honored President," says Major Nichols,

would have been as glad and proud as we, could he have heard the roaring of our cannon and our shouts of joy and victory. His first inauguration was not celebrated in South Carolina . . . but the glorification over the beginning of his second term goes to make up the deficiency.

The army was now about to leave South Carolina. By this time the men had learned that not everybody in the North approved of the way they had treated the state. One lieutenant wrote home angrily:

If you hear anyone condemning us for what we have done, tell them for me and for Sherman's army that we found here the authors of all the calamities that have befallen this nation, and the men and women whose hands are red with all the innocent blood that has been shed in this war, and that their punishment is light when compared with what justice demanded.

Sherman issued orders for the men to be gentler with North Carolina. Whereas South Carolina had been the first state to secede from the Union, North Carolina had been one of the last.

But this state was only to be slightly happier than its southern neighbor to see the Yankees. It was necessary that the daily foraging be continued, which, of course, would make for the continuance of many of the same old abuses.

The foraging soldier now had a stock answer when asked by an officer how he had happened to acquire such an object as a gold watch, a fine piece of jewelry, a silver goblet, or some other treasure. "It was given to me by a lady who was grateful because I saved her house from burning."

But uppermost in the minds of nearly all the men at this time was that the great march was rolling to a conclusion.

"On the 6th of March," relates wing commander Henry Slocum, "we moved toward Fayetteville."

General Sherman had received word that Wilmington was in possession of General Terry, and had sent two messengers with letters informing Terry when he would probably be at Fayetteville.

Both messengers arrived safely at Wilmington, and on Sunday [March 12], the day after our arrival at Fayetteville, the shrill whistle of a steamboat [coming up the Cape Fear River from Wilmington] floating the Stars and Stripes announced that we were once more in communication with our own friends. As she came up, the banks of the river were lined by our soldiers, who made the welkin ring with their cheers.

On March 14, Major Nichols recorded:

Several transports arrived yesterday from Wilmington, bringing supplies for the army. They returned laden with our sick and wounded soldiers. . . .

We have also taken this opportunity to disencumber the army of the host of Negroes who have joined us day by day. . . . By order of General Sherman, all of these people have been gathered

Federals taking Fayetteville, North Carolina

together from the different corps into one camp; and now, under the direction of a competent officer, with a sufficient guard and ample supplies, they are to march to Wilmington. . . .

God help the poor creatures! They have endured exposure and suffering in pursuit of freedom, and they have attained the boon at last.

Sherman had taken up his quarters at Fayetteville's old United States Arsenal. It was, he explains,

in fine order, and had been much enlarged by the Confederate authorities, who never dreamed that an invading army would reach it from the west. And I also found in Fayetteville the widow and daughter of my first captain [of the early 1840s]. . . . Learned that her son Fred had been the ordnance officer in charge of the arsenal, and had of course fled. . . .

I then knew that my special antagonist, General Joseph E. Johnston, was back with part of his old army; that he would not be misled by feints and false reports, and would somehow compel me to exercise more caution than I had hitherto done. . . .

I was determined, however, to give him as little time for organization as possible, and accordingly crossed the Cape Fear River, with all the army, during the 13th and 14th, leaving one division as a rear guard, until the arsenal could be completely destroyed. This was deliberately and completely leveled on the 14th, when fire was applied to the wreck. Little other damage was done at Fayetteville. . . .

On the 15th of March the whole army was across Cape Fear River, and at once began its march for Goldsboro.

The next day, at Averasboro, the army's left wing, under Slocum, encountered a part of Johnston's army commanded by William Hardee, formerly of Savannah and Charleston. Hardee was compelled to fall back.

Johnston now began to concentrate his forces at Bentonville in an effort to block Sherman's march to Goldsboro, his goal ever since leaving Savannah. Johnston's army consisted of a fine array of general officers but of only about 20,000 men. Sherman's army was more than 60,000 strong and was about to be reinforced to 90,000 by troops from Wilmington.

The battle was joined on March 19. Southern cavalryman J. P. Austin says that for a time the Confederates at Bentonville fought "with the same old-time vigor." The canny Johnston, in fact, had pushed Sherman into a contest he wasn't wholly prepared for.

A glimpse of Sherman at Bentonville is given by a private soldier, Melvin Grigsby, who had been wandering around the field looking for him "so as to see how a great commander would act while a battle was in progress."

I found him and his staff in the yard in front of a farmhouse. The general was walking back and forth in the shade of some large trees. . . . He had a cigar in his mouth, and stepping up to an officer who was smoking, asked him for a light. The officer handed him his cigar. As the general lit his own cigar he seemed to be listening to the noise of the battle. Suddenly he turned, dropped the officer's cigar on the ground, and walked off puffing his own. The officer looked at him a moment then laughed, picked up the cigar and continued his smoke.

The fighting continued intermittently until March 21.

"Late in the day," relates Confederate Captain D. Augustus Dickert, the enemy made a spirited attack upon us, so much so that General McLaws sent two companies of boys, formerly of Fizer's Brigade of Georgia Militia. The boys were all between sixteen and eighteen, and a finer body of young men I never saw.

He also sent a regiment of North Carolina Militia, consisting of old men from fifty to sixty, and as these old men were coming up on line the enemy were giving us a rattling fire from their sharpshooters. The old men could not be induced to come up. . . .

The colonel, a venerable old graybeard, riding a white horse, as soon as the bullets began to pelt the pines in his front, leaped from his horse and took refuge behind a large tree. I went to him and tried every inducement to get him to move up his men on a line with us, but all he would do was to grasp me by the hand and try to jerk me down beside him.

"Lie down, young man," said he, "or by God you'll be shot to pieces. Lie down!"

The old militiaman, I saw, was too old for war, and was "not built that way."

But when I returned to the skirmish line, on which were my own brigade skirmishers, reinforced by the two boy companies, the young men were fighting with a glee and abandon I never saw equalled. I am sorry to record that several of these promising young men, who had left their homes so far behind, were killed and many wounded.

Thus ended the Battle of Bentonville. . . .

The sun of the Confederacy, notwithstanding the hopes of our generals, the determination of the troops, and the prayers of the people, was fast sinking in the west. . . . Destiny seemed to be against us. . . .

On the night of the 21st the army began its retreat. . . .

The battle had cost the Federals about 1,500 in killed, wounded, captured, and missing, while the Confederates had lost more than 2,600, with the number of captured predominating.

Johnston moved northwestward toward Raleigh. Sherman did not pursue, choosing to proceed eastward to Goldsboro for a junction with the reinforcements from the coast. There the entire army went into camp, and, as one man put it, began "receiving letters from home, getting new clothes, and taking regular doses of quinine."

When orders went out that all foragers and bummers must turn in their horses and rejoin their original regiments, some of these men chose instead to desert and to ride westward, led on by the prospect of new adventures among the pioneers and Indians.

"Thus was concluded," says Sherman, "one of the longest and most important marches ever made by an organized army in a civilized country."

Confederates fighting "with destiny against them."

The distance from Savannah to Goldsboro is four hundred and twenty-five miles, and the route traversed embraced five large navigable rivers . . . at either of which a comparatively small force, well handled, should have made the passage most difficult, if not impossible.

The country generally was in a state of nature, with innumerable swamps, with simply mud roads, nearly every mile of which had to be corduroyed. In our route we had captured Columbia, Cheraw, and Fayetteville, important cities and depots of supplies, had compelled the evacuation of Charleston . . . had utterly broken up all the railroads of South Carolina, and had consumed a vast amount of food and forage essential to the enemy for the support of his own armies.

We had in mid-winter accomplished the whole journey of four hundred and twenty-five miles in fifty days, averaging ten miles per day, allowing ten lay days [i.e., days during which the army paused in cities and other places], and had reached Goldsboro with the army in superb order, and the trains almost as fresh as when we had started from Atlanta.

Adds Major Nichols:

War means bloodshed; yet there are ways of conquering a peace without excessive destruction of human life, and it is in this light that General Sherman's grand campaign looms up in magnificent proportions, equalling the most splendid achievements of the world's greatest captains.

In a letter explaining the march to his wife, Sherman wrote:

My wants are few and easily gained, but if this fame which fills the world contributes to your happiness and pleasure, enjoy it as much as possible. Oh, that Willy could hear and see!

Sherman's army was now only about 175 miles south of Richmond, and he was ready to work in direct cooperation with Grant, who was still in his siege lines. Feeling it was necessary that he and Grant have a personal consultation, Sherman took the train to the coast and a ship north to Grant's headquarters at City Point, on the James River near the Confederate capital.

The reunion of these two friends after a separation of more than a year impressed Grant's aide, Horace Porter, as being "more like that of two schoolboys coming together after a vacation than the meeting of the chief actors in a great war tragedy."

That evening Sherman sat by Grant's campfire, and, with Mrs. Grant and a number of other officers present, related the story of the march.

Never [says Porter] were listeners more enthusiastic; never was a speaker more eloquent. The story, told as he alone could tell it, was a grand epic related with Homeric power.

During the discussion of plans on how to end the war, it was decided that the two great Union armies continue to work separately. Grant was now fully prepared to break the nine-and-a-half-month siege, and he needed no further help from Sherman other than that he keep Johnston occupied in North Carolina.

During his two-day stay at City Point, Sherman met also with President Lincoln, who was quartered aboard a vessel on the James. Sherman was delighted to find that Lincoln seemed to share his own view that the South be treated leniently once she surrendered.

Sherman was back with his army at Goldsboro by the evening of March 30:

I . . . at once addressed myself to the task of reorganization and replenishment of stores, so as to be ready to march by April 10th, the day agreed on with General Grant.

Word reached Sherman on April 6 that Grant had flanked Lee out of Richmond and Petersburg, and that the Confederates were retreating westward, with Grant in pursuit.

Sherman wired Grant:

I am delighted and amazed at the result of your move, and Lee has lost in one day the reputation of three years, and you have established a reputation for perseverance and pluck that would make Wellington jump out of his coffin.

Sherman began to press toward Raleigh and Joe Johnston on April 10, as planned.

Union General Jacob D. Cox says of the eleventh:

The day was a warm and bright spring day. The columns had halted for the usual rest at the end of each hour's march. The men were sitting or lying upon the grass on either side of the road . . . when a staff officer was seen riding from the front, galloping and gesticulating in great excitement, the men cheering and cutting strange antics as he passed. When he came nearer he was heard to shout, "Lee has surrendered!"

The soldiers screamed out their delight. They flung their hats at him as he rode. They shouted, "You're the man we've been looking for these three years!" They turned somersaults like over-excited children. They knew the long Civil War was virtually over.

Another phase of the universal rejoicing in the land was quite as well illustrated by the roadside. A Southern woman had come to the gate with her children . . . and as she caught the meaning of the wild shout she looked down upon the wondering little ones, while tears streamed down her cheeks, saying to them only, "Now father will come home."

From this time the march had military importance only as it led to the quickly approaching end. The skirmishing of advance and rear guards continued, but Johnston was only delaying Sherman's movements till he could communicate with the Confederate President.

The Federals occupied Raleigh on April 13, and the next day Johnston sent Sherman a flag of truce. His note asked for a suspension of hostilities "to stop the further effusion of blood and devastation of property" and "to enter into the needful arrangements to terminate the existing war."

As Sherman made arrangements to confer with Johnston at Durham's Station, he was in a generous mood. His enemy stood submissive before him. All he wanted now was peace. Though he was well aware the North held many people (so-called "Radical Republicans") who were crying loudly for retribution, he himself felt it was sufficient to tell the conquered people "to go and sin no more." Sherman was convinced that this leniency would be supported by President Lincoln.

The general relates:

I ordered a car and locomotive to be prepared to convey me up to Durham's at eight o'clock of the morning of April 17. Just as we were entering the car, the telegraph operator, whose office was upstairs in the depot building, ran down to me and said that he was at that instant of time receiving a most important dispatch in cipher . . . which I ought to see. I held the train for nearly half an hour, when he returned with the message translated and written out. It was from Mr. Stanton, announcing the assassination of Mr. Lincoln. . . .

Sherman's subordinate, General Cox, was to say later:

The conjuncture of events was one of the strangest that the strange current of human history has ever presented, and we puzzle our brains in the vain effort to conjecture how the destiny of the country might have been modified if that horrible murder had not been committed.

Though aware that a new wave of bitterness against the South was sweeping the North, Sherman went ahead as he had planned. He was further disposed in Johnston's favor by the general's reaction when told of Lincoln's death. Sherman noted:

The perspiration came out in large drops on his forehead, and he did not attempt to conceal his distress. He denounced the act as a disgrace to the age, and hoped I did not charge it to the Confederate Government.

The terms Sherman granted Johnston—subject to the approval of Lincoln's successor, Andrew Johnson—exceeded even Lincoln's concepts. For one thing, the Confederates were to be allowed to keep their weapons and take them home for deposit in their state arsenals. Not stopping with military considerations, Sherman took up civil matters, which were beyond his authority. He negotiated not only an end to hostilities but a treaty of

Meeting of Sherman and Johnston at Durham's Station

peace. The people of the South were to enjoy an immediate return to their rights under the Constitution. Existing state governments, upon the renouncement of their revolutionary aims, were to stay in power.

When the terms were signed on April 18, Sherman at once sent a copy to General Grant, then in Washington. Grant's aide, Horace Porter, says that the general received the document on April 21:

Perceiving that the terms covered many questions of a civil and not of a military nature, he suggested to the Secretary of War [Edwin Stanton] that the matter had better be referred at once to President Johnson and the cabinet for their action.

A cabinet meeting was called before midnight, and there was a unanimous decision that the basis of the agreement should be disapproved, and an order was issued directing General Grant to proceed in person to Sherman's headquarters and direct operations. . . .

Instead of merely recognizing that Sherman had made an honest mistake in exceeding his authority, the President and the Secretary of War characterized his conduct as akin to treason, and the Secretary denounced him in unmeasured terms.

At this General Grant grew indignant and gave free expression to his opposition to an attempt to stigmatize an officer whose acts throughout all his career gave ample contradiction to the charge that he was actuated by unworthy motives.

Grant takes up:

When I arrived I went to Sherman's headquarters, and we were at once closeted together. I showed him the instructions and orders under which I visited him. I told him that I wanted him to notify General Johnston that the terms which they had conditionally agreed upon had not been approved in Washington, and that he was authorized to offer the same terms I had given General Lee. [These terms were simple: Lee's men had been deprived of their arms and sent home on parole.]

I sent Sherman to do this himself. I did not wish the knowledge of my presence to be known to the army generally; so I left it to Sherman to negotiate the terms of the surrender solely by himself, and without the enemy knowing that I was anywhere near the field. As soon as possible I started to get away, to leave Sherman quite free and untrammelled.

At Goldsboro on my way back, I met a mail containing the latest newspapers, and I found in them indications of great excitement in the North over the terms Sherman had given Johnston [the furore having been stirred up by public statements made by Secretary Stanton]. . . .

I knew that Sherman must see these papers, and I fully realized what great indignation they would cause him, though I do not think his feelings could have been more excited than were my own. But like the true and loyal soldier that he was, he carried out the instructions I had given him, obtained the surrender of Johnston's army, and settled down in his camp about Raleigh to await final orders.

Sherman, however, had been "outraged beyond measure" by Stanton's work against him—a work that seems to have been inspired in large part by the Secretary's fear of Sherman's potential for political power in a nation unsettled by an assassination. History held no shortage of idolized generals who had seized shaky governments. It is likely that even the prospect of Sherman's making a legitimate entry into politics was unacceptable to Stanton. A Republican with radical views toward the South, the Secretary believed that the Democrats, their membership largely moderate, wanted Sherman on their ticket. With his reputation intact, Sherman would have been a hard man to beat.

As it turned out, Sherman's reputation easily rebounded from its sudden fall. His services to the nation had been far too valuable for him to be ruined by one mistake—especially since the mistake was quickly corrected. But Sherman remained bitter toward Stanton. And he also broke with his old friend Henry Halleck. The chief of staff, who in an earlier role had supported Sherman when people were calling him insane, had sided with Stanton against him, taking an equally radical stand.

Orders soon came for the encamped army to report to Washington to share the spotlight with Grant's Army of the Potomac in a grand review.

"On the other hand," laments Southern officer J. P. Austin,

the shattered remnants of the Confederate army, with their bloodstained banners trailing in the dust; footsore, weary, and broken in spirits; without money and with scarcely sufficient clothing to shield them from the scorching rays of the summer sun . . . must scatter singly, or in groups, to make their way as best they could through a devastated country, to their distant and desolate homes. God, in his infinite wisdom, had decreed against them, and they were forced to bow in humble submission to this stern and immutable decree.

As related by Union newsman David Conyngham:

Sherman's army marched through Richmond on their way home, and over the bloody battlefields on which their brother Army of the Potomac so long and nobly contended, and concentrated around Washington and Alexandria.

On the 23d of May the Grand Army of the Potomac . . . passed in review through Washington before the President and dignitaries not only of this country but of foreign nations.

[The next day] the greatest anxiety prevailed to see Sherman's army. Every door, window, and house roof were crowded with eager spectators. Arches of flowers festooned the streets and windows.

About 10 o'clock, Sherman and staff and generals appeared at the head of the column. The air echoed with cheers and shouts as the worn veterans marched up Pennsylvania Avenue, their bands playing and their shattered and torn banners floating on the breeze. . . .

The streets were strewn with flowers; garlands were woven around the horses' necks, and bouquets of the most exquisite kind presented to the general, officers, and even privates.

As they reached the stand occupied by the President and the elite of other nations . . . all rose and, in wild and grateful acclamations, welcomed our heroes home.

Immediately after the review the men broke ranks and turned their faces toward the cities, villages, and farms they had come from.

"This," says Major Nichols, "was the farewell of Sherman's army. So, too, ends the Story of the Great March."

EPILOGUE

SHERMAN WAS NOT *discharged with the volunteers, since he held a commission in the regular army, but he received a furlough. Arriving at the railroad station in his native town of Lancaster, Ohio, he was met by a brass band and several thousand cheering people, many of whom were waving small American flags. The situation called for a patriotic speech:*

I claim no special honor, only to have done a full man's share; for when one's country is in danger, the man who will not defend it and sustain it with his natural strength is no man at all. . . . I have done simply what all the boys in blue have done. I have only labored with the strength of a single man, and have used the brains I inherited and the education given by my country. . . .

The past is now with the historian, but we must still grapple with the future. In this we need a guide, and, fortunately for us all, we can trust the Constitution which has safely brought us through the gloom and danger of the past. . . . The Government of the United States and the Constitution of our fathers have proven their strength and power in time of war, and I believe our whole country will be even more brilliant in the vast and unknown future than in the past.

Sherman played an important role in the promotion of the national greatness he envisioned, his services always of a military nature. Holding politics in strong aversion, he was not tempted by the presidency, though a simple nod of acceptance would have gained it for him. Even an attempt to draft him was spurned: "If nominated I will not run; if elected I will not serve." He said he would leave politics to the professional politicians: "I have absolute faith in the vitality of this young nation, and believe it will withstand a good deal of bad doctoring."

During his days as a young officer in California, Sherman had recog-

nized the necessity of spanning the nation with rails, and immediately after the war he was given the job of protecting, and assisting with, the construction of the transcontinental railroad that had been chartered by Congress even as the war progressed.

Sherman enjoyed his visits to the Western plains. While riding past the civilian crews who were busy laying rails under the wide expanse of sky, he was often hailed as "Uncle Billy." Many of the veterans were still wearing their blue uniforms, now much mended. Sherman laughed with them over the fact that not long ago they had been associated with railroads in an altogether different way.

Though Sherman sympathized with the Indians who were being dispossessed and felt that Congress was not sufficiently responsive to their plight, he was unyielding in his efforts to subdue them. Meeting with their chiefs at Fort Laramie in 1867, he declared: "You cannot stop the locomotives any more than you can stop the sun or moon." Laments by Eastern humanitarians were parried with a question: "How are you going to settle this great continent from the Atlantic to the Pacific without doing some harm to the Indians who stand in the way?"

Sherman succeeded Grant as General of the Army in 1869, and was therefore in Washington when, on May 10, a telegram from the West brought the exciting news that a ceremonial "last spike" had been driven and that the railroad was an accomplished fact. Sherman regarded this as being as important to the nation as the reconstruction of the South, then progressing stormily toward its completion.

Sherman's relations with the South were not so bad as might have been expected. It is true that some intense bitterness existed, but it was by no means universal. For one thing, many Southerners liked Sherman's open disapproval of Federal legislation that attempted to raise the black people from slavery to first-class citizenship in one quick step. He believed that the South should be allowed some discretion in this matter.

Very soon after the war Sherman's military duties carried him through a section of Mississippi he had devastated.

Many people [he explains] met me along the road in the most friendly spirit. I spent a whole day in Jackson, where chimney stacks and broken railroads marked the presence of Sherman's army. But all sorts of people pressed to see me, and evinced their natural curiosity, nothing more.

Later he had occasion to travel through Georgia, and was greeted respectfully even in Atlanta, which he had burned. Everywhere he went, huge crowds of both whites and blacks gathered to get a look at him. From Georgia he went to Louisiana. It was Mardi Gras time, and he was given a royal welcome, being declared "a Duke of Louisiana." Some festive hours were spent with John Hood, who had fought him so bitterly at Atlanta.

The people of South Carolina were, of course, the least forgiving. But at least one person, Mrs. A. P. Aldrich, of Barnwell, whose plantation had suffered severely at the hands of Sherman's looters, and who had watched them burn the homes of many of her neighbors, came at last to regard the terrible deeds as "blessings in disguise . . . the harbingers of that perfect Union designed by the founders of this great republic."

Sherman made an unofficial foreign tour in 1871 and 1872, visiting Spain, France, Italy, Egypt, Turkey, Russia, Poland, Austria, Switzerland, Germany, and the British Isles. He was entertained by some of the world's leading royal, political, and military figures, but also found enjoyment in mingling with the people in the streets, language barriers notwithstanding. In Switzerland he spent a week with the American consul general, Samuel Byers, formerly a member of his staff and the composer of "Sherman's March to the Sea." Byers was later to marvel:

I never saw a man so run after by women in my life. When he was leaving a train at Bern a whole crowd of women, old and young, pretty and ugly, children and all, kissed him.

At veterans' reunions, Sherman was ever a popular speaker. At Columbus, Ohio, on a rainy day in 1880, he stood on a wooden platform before a large assemblage of both veterans and civilians and gave a brief impromptu talk, the first part of which was directed at the veterans. They listened with rapt attention, oblivious to the rain that pattered on their old campaign hats.

It delights my soul [he said] to look on you and see so many of the good old boys left yet. They are not afraid of rain. We have stood it many a time. . . .

We are to each other, all in all, as man and wife; and every soldier here today knows that Uncle Billy loves him as his own flesh and blood. . . .

The war is away back in the past, and you can tell what books cannot. When you talk you come down to the practical realities, just as they happened.

He was referring to remembered evils and horrors, and his next words were addressed to the youngsters in the crowd:

There is many a boy here today who looks on war as all glory, but, boys, it is all hell. You can bear this warning voice to generations yet to come.

Though Sherman qualified these statements by adding that he himself would go to war again if it was necessary, his "warning voice" was destined to keep its full strength. He would thereafter be remembered as the general who said that "war is hell."

In 1885, two years after his retirement from the army, Sherman settled in New York City. He told friends he had gone into "winter quarters" where there was "good grass and water."

In the words of Chauncey Depew, New York's famed orator, railroad magnate, lawyer, and politician:

He was at once the most distinguished and delightful figure in our metropolitan society.... He loved to be in the company of men and women... and very often he would be found at late suppers, especially theatrical suppers....

I have been with him at hundreds of public dinners, and in studying closely his mental methods and habits of speech, have come to regard him as the readiest and most original talker in the United States.

But according to another of Sherman's friends, Philadelphia journalist A. K. McClure, the general's appeal as a speaker had a limitation:

He was incapable of dissembling, and often blurted out the truth as he accepted it in a way that was not always acceptable to his hearers.

Sherman's wife Ellen shared few of his social activities, her chief interest being to work for the church. But the two were nonetheless devoted to one another, their common ground being their six children. When Ellen died in the autumn of 1888, Sherman was plunged into the deepest melancholy, and for weeks it seemed that his own health must fail. But the beginning of the year 1889 found him rallying in both health and spirits, and he soon settled into a kind of sunset content.

Explains Grant's former aide, Horace Porter, who had been acquainted with Sherman since the occupation of Atlanta:

In whatever circle he moved, he was the center; at whatever table he sat, he was the head. The nation had lifted him to the highest military rank; Congress had presented him with votes of thanks; universities and colleges had conferred on him the degree of L.L.D.; numberless home and foreign clubs and societies had made him an honorary member. There were no more public honors to bestow, and now he was receiving the courtesies and attentions of private life in a manner which gave the sweetest solace to the veteran's declining years.

At the close of the year 1890, when Sherman was nearing his seventy-first birthday, he confided to a friend that he believed he was nearing death: "I feel it coming sometimes when I get home from an entertainment or banquet, especially these winter nights. I feel death reaching out for me, as it were. I suppose I'll take cold some night and go to bed, never to get up again."

It happened very nearly as he predicted. He died of pneumonia on February 14, 1891. Among the many notables who attended his funeral was Joe Johnston, then eighty-four years old. While standing on the sidewalk in the raw weather with his head uncovered as Sherman's flag-draped coffin was carried from his house, the old Southerner was urged by a friend to put on his hat. Johnston replied, "If I were in his place and he were standing here in mine, he would not put on his hat." Johnston was to die of pneumonia a month later.

Sherman was buried in St. Louis, Missouri, beside Ellen and Willy. His passing, of course, was noted throughout the world. Had he been aware of his eulogies, none would have pleased him more than one published in a Southern newspaper, the Atlanta Constitution:

He had his faults, very serious ones, but he also had many shining virtues. He always, in his heart, really liked Southerners, and had many personal friends among them. The rebuilding of Atlanta gratified him very much, and he was a firm believer in the future greatness of this region.

When all is said that can be said, the fact looms up that this man was one of the greatest soldiers of the age. . . . He was a hard fighter, and never grew sentimental in the presence of bloodshed and death. But when the business of war was over—when he had accomplished his mission—he showed a softer side, and men and women, even among his former foes, found him a very lovable man.

APPENDIX

Sherman's March to the Sea

Composed by Adjutant Samuel H. M. Byers, Fifth Iowa Infantry. Arranged and sung by the Union prisoners of war in Columbia Prison.

1.

Our campfires shone bright on the mountain
  That frowned on the river below,
As we stood by our guns in the morning
  And eagerly watched for the foe;
When a rider came out of the darkness
  That hung over mountain and tree,
And shouted, "Boys, up and be ready!
  For Sherman will march to the sea!"

Chorus.

Then sang we a song of our chieftain
  That echoed o'er river and lea;
And the stars of our banner shone brighter
  When Sherman marched down to the sea!

2.

Then cheer upon cheer for bold Sherman
  Went up from each valley and glen,
And the bugles reechoed the music
  That came from the lips of the men;
For we knew that the stars in our banner
  More bright in their splendor would be,
And that blessings from Northland would greet us
  When Sherman marched down to the sea!

Then sang we a song, etc.

3.

Then forward, boys! Forward to battle!
 We marched on our wearisome way;
We stormed the wild hills of Resaca—
 God bless those who fell on that day!
Then Kennesaw frowned in its glory,
 Frowned down on the flag of the free;
But the East and the West bore our standard,
 And Sherman marched on to the sea!

Then sang we a song, etc.

4.

Still onward we pressed, till our banners
 Swept out from Atlanta's grim walls,
And the blood of the patriot dampened
 The soil where the traitor-flag falls;
But we paused not to weep for the fallen,
 Who slept by each river and tree,
Yet we twined them a wreath of the laurel
 As Sherman marched down to the sea!

Then sang we a song, etc.

5.

Oh, proud was our army that morning,
 That stood where the pine darkly towers,
When Sherman said, "Boys, you are weary,
 But today fair Savannah is ours!"
Then sang we a song of our chieftain
 That echoed o'er river and lea,
And the stars of our banner shone brighter
 When Sherman camped down by the sea!

BIBLIOGRAPHY

Andrews, Eliza Frances. *The War-Time Journal of a Georgia Girl.* New York: D. Appleton and Company, 1908.

Andrews, Matthew Page (ed.). *The Women of the South in War Times.* Baltimore: The Norman, Remington Co., 1924.

Angle, Paul M., and Miers, Earl Schenck. *Tragic Years: 1860-1865.* 2 vols. New York: Simon and Schuster, 1960.

Annals of the War. Philadelphia: The Times Publishing Company, 1879.

Austin, J. P. *The Blue and the Gray.* Atlanta: The Franklin Printing and Publishing Co., 1899.

Barrett, John G. *Sherman's March Through the Carolinas.* Chapel Hill, N.C.: The University of North Carolina Press, 1956.

Battles and Leaders of the Civil War. 4 vols. Robert Underwood Johnson and Clarence Clough Buel (eds.). New York: The Century Company, 1884-1888.

Bowman, S. M., and Irwin, R. B. *Sherman and His Campaigns.* New York: Charles B. Richardson, 1865.

Boynton, H. V. *Sherman's Historical Raid: The Memoirs in the Light of the Record.* Cincinnati: Wilstach, Baldwin & Co., 1875.

Brown, Alonzo L. *History of the Fourth Regiment of Minnesota Infantry Volunteers During the Great Rebellion.* St. Paul, Minn.: The Pioneer Press Company, 1892.

Carter, Samuel III. *The Siege of Atlanta, 1864.* New York: St. Martin's Press, 1973.

Catton, Bruce. *The Centennial History of the Civil War.* 3 vols. Garden City, N.Y.: Doubleday and Company, 1961-1965.

Chase, Edward. *The Memorial Life of General William Tecumseh Sherman.* Chicago: R. S. Peale & Co., 1891.

Chesnut, Mary Boykin. *A Diary from Dixie.* New York: D. Appleton and Company, 1905.

Chittenden, L. E. *Personal Reminiscences.* New York: Richmond, Croscup & Co., 1893.

Civil War Naval Chronology. Compiled by Naval History Division, Navy Department. Washington, D.C.: Government Printing Office, 1971.

Coffin, Charles Carleton. *The Boys of '61.* Boston: Estes and Lauriat, 1884.

Commager, Henry Steele. *The Blue and the Gray.* Indianapolis and New York: The Bobbs-Merrill Company, 1950.

Conyngham, David P. *Sherman's March Through the South.* New York: Sheldon and Company, 1865.

Cox, Jacob D. *Atlanta* (Campaigns of the Civil War, vol. 9). New York: Charles Scribner's Sons, 1882.

———. *The March to the Sea: Franklin and Nashville* (Campaigns of the Civil War, vol. 10). New York: Charles Scribner's Sons, 1882.

Davis, Jefferson. *The Rise and Fall of the Confederate Government.* 2 vols. Cranbury, N.J.: Thomas Yoseloff, 1958.

De Leon, T. C. *Joseph Wheeler: the Man, the Statesman, the Soldier.* Kennesaw, Ga.: Continental Book Company, 1960.

Dickert, D. Augustus. *History of Kershaw's Brigade.* Introduction to new edition by Dr. Wm. Stanley Hoole. Dayton, Ohio: Press of Morningside Bookshop, 1976. Original edition published in 1899.

Dodson, W. C. (ed.). *Campaigns of Wheeler and His Cavalry, 1862–1865.* Atlanta, Ga.: Hudgins Publishing Company, 1899.

Duyckinck, Evert A. *National History of the War for the Union.* 3 vols. New York: Johnson, Fry and Company, 1868.

Evans, Clement A. (ed.). *Confederate Military History.* 12 vols. New York: Thomas Yoseloff, 1962.

Fletcher, Thomas C. *Life and Reminiscences of Gen. Wm. T. Sherman by Distinguished Men of His Time.* Lenox Publishing Company, 1891.

Frank Leslie's Illustrated History of the Civil War. New York: Mrs. Frank Leslie, 1895.

Gay, Mary A. H. *Life in Dixie During the War.* Atlanta, Ga.: Charles P. Byrd, 1897.

Gerrish, Theodore, and Hutchinson, John S. *The Blue and the Gray.* Portland, Me.: Hoyt, Fogg & Donham, 1883.

Grant, U. S. *Personal Memoirs.* New York: Charles L. Webster & Company, 1894.

Greeley, Horace. *The American Conflict.* 2 vols. Hartford: O. D. Case & Company, 1864, 1867.

Grigsby, Melvin. *The Smoked Yank.* Sioux Falls, S.D.: Dakota Bell Publishing Co., 1888.

Guernsey, Alfred H., and Alden, Henry M. *Harper's Pictorial History of the Great Rebellion.* 2 vols. Chicago: McDonnell Bros., 1866, 1868.

Hale, Edward E. (ed.). *Stories of War Told by Soldiers.* Boston: Roberts Brothers, 1879.

Harper's Encyclopaedia of United States History. 10 vols. New York: Harper & Brothers, 1915.

Harper's Weekly: May 4, 1861, to May 13, 1865 (reissue). Shenandoah, Iowa: Living History, Inc., 1961–1965.

Headley, P. C. *Facing the Enemy: The Life and Military Career of Gen. William Tecumseh Sherman.* Boston: Lee and Shepard, 1865.

Hedley, F. Y. *Marching Through Georgia.* Chicago: M. A. Donohue & Co., 1884.

Hoehling, A. A. *Last Train from Atlanta.* New York: Bonanza Books, 1958.

Home Letters of General Sherman. Edited by M. A. DeWolfe Howe. New York: Charles Scribner's Sons, 1909.

Johnson, Rossiter. *Campfires and Battlefields.* New York: The Civil War Press, 1967. First published in 1894.

Johnson, W. Fletcher. *Life of Wm. Tecumseh Sherman.* Edgewood Publishing Company, 1891.

Johnston, Joseph E. *Narrative of Military Operations.* New York: D. Appleton and Company, 1874.

Jones, Charles C. *Address Delivered Before the Confederate Survivors' Association . . . on the Occasion of Its Twelfth Annual Reunion.* Augusta, Ga.: Chronicle Publishing Company, 1890.

———. *Address Delivered Before the Confederate Survivors' Association . . . on the Occasion of Its Fifteenth Annual Reunion.* Augusta, Ga.: Chronicle Job Printing Company, 1893.

Jones, Katharine M. *When Sherman Came: Southern Women and the "Great March."* Indianapolis, Kansas City, New York: The Bobbs-Merrill Company, 1964.

Keim, DeB. Randolph. *Sherman: A Memorial in Art, Oratory, and Literature by the Society of the Army of the Tennessee, with the aid of the Congress of the United States of America.* Washington, D.C.: Government Printing Office, 1904.

King, W. C., and Derby, W. P. *Campfire Sketches and Battlefield Echoes of the Rebellion.* Springfield, Mass.: W. C. King & Co., 1887.

Lewis, Lloyd. *Sherman: Fighting Prophet.* New York: Harcourt, Brace and Company, 1932.

Long, E. B. (with Barbara Long). *The Civil War Day by Day.* Garden City, N.Y.: Doubleday & Company, 1971.

Lossing, Benson J. *Pictorial Field Book of the Civil War.* 3 vols. New York: T. Belknap & Company, 1868.

Lucas, Marion Brunson. *Sherman and the Burning of Columbia.* Foreword by Bell I. Wiley. Texas A & M University Press, 1976.

Lunt, Dolly Sumner. *A Woman's Wartime Journal.* Macon, Ga.: The J. W. Burke Co., 1927.

McClure, Alexander K. *Abraham Lincoln and Men of War Times.* Philadelphia: The Times Publishing Company, 1892.

Merrill, James M. *William Tecumseh Sherman.* Chicago, New York, San Francisco: Rand McNally & Company, 1971.

Miers, Earl Schenck. *The General Who Marched to Hell.* New York: Alfred A. Knopf, 1951.

Moore, Frank (ed.). *The Civil War in Song and Story.* New York: P. F. Collier, 1889.

———. *The Rebellion Record.* 12 vols. New York: G. P. Putnam, 1861–1871.

Nichols, George Ward. *The Story of the Great March.* New York: Harper & Brothers, 1865.

Northrop, Henry Davenport. *Life and Deeds of General Sherman.* Waukesha, Wis.: World Publishing Company, 1891.

Our Women in the War: The Lives They Lived: The Deaths They Died. Charleston, S.C.: The News and Courier Book Presses, 1885.

Piatt, Donn. *Memories of the Men Who Saved the Union.* New York and Chicago: Belford, Clarke & Company, 1887.

Pollard, Edward A. *Early Life, Campaigns, and Public Services of Robert E. Lee; with a Record of the Campaigns and Heroic Deeds of His Companions in Arms.* New York: E. B. Treat & Co., 1871.

Porter, David D. *Incidents and Anecdotes of the Civil War.* New York: D. Appleton and Company, 1886.

Porter, Horace. *Campaigning with Grant.* New York: The Century Company, 1897.

Reed, Wallace P. *History of Atlanta, Georgia.* Syracuse, N.Y.: D. Mason & Co., 1889.

Robins, Edward. *William T. Sherman.* Philadelphia: George W. Jacobs & Company, 1905.

Senour, F. *Major General William T. Sherman and His Campaigns.* Chicago: Henry M. Sherwood, 1865.

Sherman, John. *Recollections of Forty Years in the House, Senate and Cabinet.* 2 vols. Chicago, New York, London and Berlin: The Werner Company, 1895.

Sherman, William T. *Memoirs.* 2 vols. New York: D. Appleton and Company, 1875.

Stowe, Harriet Beecher. *Men of Our Times.* Hartford: Hartford Publishing Co., 1868.

Tarbell, Ida M. *The Life of Abraham Lincoln.* 2 vols. New York: McClure, Phillips & Co., 1902.

Taylor, Richard. *Destruction and Reconstruction.* New York: D. Appleton and Company, 1879.

Tenney, W. J. *The Military and Naval History of the Rebellion.* New York: D. Appleton and Company, 1865.

The Soldier in Our Civil War. Edited by Paul F. Mottelay and T. Campbell-Copeland. 2 vols. New York: G. W. Carleton & Company, 1886.

Tomes, Robert, and Smith, Benjamin G. *The Great Civil War.* 3 vols. New York: Virtue and Yorston, 1862.

Trezevant, D. H. *The Burning of Columbia, S.C.: A Review of Northern Assertions and Southern Facts.* Columbia, S.C.: South Carolina Power Press, 1866.

Under Both Flags: A Panorama of the Great Civil War. Chicago: W. S. Reeve Publishing Co., 1896.

Upson, Theodore F. *With Sherman to the Sea.* New York: Kraus Reprint Co., 1969.

War of the Rebellion: A Compilation of the Official Records of the Union and Confederate Armies. Series I, vol. 44, and Series I, vol. 47, in three parts. Washington, D.C.: Government Printing Office, 1893, 1895.

Williams, Noble C. *Echoes from the Battlefield; or, Southern Life During the War.* Atlanta, Ga.: The Franklin Printing and Publishing Company, 1902.

Williams, T. Harry. *Lincoln and His Generals.* New York: Alfred A. Knopf, 1952.

Wright, Mrs. D. Giraud. *A Southern Girl in '61: The War-Time Memories of a Confederate Senator's Daughter.* New York: Doubleday, Page & Company, 1905.

INDEX